Oxford Essays in Jurisprudence

Oxford Essays in Jurisprudence

A COLLABORATIVE WORK

EDITED BY

A. G. Guest

Fellow of University College, Oxford

OXFORD UNIVERSITY PRESS

1961

Oxford University Press, Amen House, London E.C.4

GLASGOW   NEW YORK   TORONTO   MELBOURNE   WELLINGTON

BOMBAY   CALCUTTA   MADRAS   KARACHI   KUALA LUMPUR

CAPE TOWN   IBADAN   NAIROBI   ACCRA

Printed and bound in England by **Hazell Watson & Viney** *Ltd*

Aylesbury and Slough

Preface

In one of his lighter moods, the jurist Rudolf von Ihering depicted the existence of a *Begriffshimmel*—a Heaven of Juristic Concepts—in whose rarefied atmosphere the classic concepts of the law existed in 'their complete, flawless purity and beauty'. The air of Oxford is thought by some unkind persons to nurture similar abstractions. To these, it may come as something of a disappointment to find that, in this collection of essays on jurisprudential topics, particular emphasis has been laid on the empirical and common-sense approach of the law to the problems which are discussed. The contributors have attempted to look at some of the traditional exercises of jurisprudence with a new and practical eye. It is therefore hoped that this volume will commend itself, not only to lawyers, but also to students of philosophy and politics, as a starting point for discussion and further examination of the ideas and methods of the law.

In editing this work, I have myself been merely concerned with the modest task of arranging production. The critical aspect has most kindly been undertaken by Professor H. L. A. Hart, who read most of the essays in manuscript and made many helpful and illuminating suggestions to their authors. Contributors will, I feel sure, wish me to acknowledge their gratitude to him. Acknowledgement is also due to Messrs. Stevens & Sons, Ltd., for permission to reproduce Mr. R. F. V. Heuston's essay on 'Sovereignty', which will form part of a larger work by him entitled *Essays in Constitutional Law*.

A. G. G.

Oxford, September 1, 1960.

Contents

Table of Cases

Table of Statutes

CHAPTER I

Voluntary and Involuntary Acts

by P. J. Fitzgerald

THE problem of defining an act owes its importance partly to the constant recurrence throughout the common law of a certain theme, namely the requirement of an act. This is exemplified in the Law of Contract by the proposition that acceptance must be something more than a mere mental assent; it must be by words or conduct.[1] In the Law of Torts we find that a man who has been carried bodily and against his will onto the land of another has been held not liable in trespass because there was no act on his part;[2] and in fact it has been suggested that in general a tort consists in some act done by the defendant whereby he has without just cause or excuse caused some form of harm to the plaintiff.[3] But nowhere is this requirement so clearly seen as in the Criminal Law, where it manifests itself in the rule that *mens rea* by itself is not enough to constitute a crime: there must be an *actus reus*. Even in the case of attempts to commit crimes where the criminal intent is the dominant factor, the prosecution must prove the commission of an *actus reus* sufficient to amount to an attempt.

This problem of defining an act gains further significance from the recognition by the Common Law that certain conduct, involuntary conduct, does not involve the actor in any responsibility because it is said there is in reality no act on his part. For this reason it becomes necessary to define the term 'act' to provide the test by which we can decide whether a man's conduct should involve him in any responsibility.

Difficulties arise, however, when jurists try to produce a satis-

---

[1] Anson, *Law of Contract* (21st ed.), p. 41.   [2] *Smith* v. *Stone* (1647), Sty. 65.
[3] Salmond, *Law of Torts* (12th ed.), p. 14.

factory definition, and these difficulties are generated by the confusion of two separate questions: (1) what is an act?; and (2) when is conduct involuntary? The answer to (1) will not provide a complete solution to (2), if for no other reason than that it takes no account of the problems of involuntary omission. Nor will the answer to (2) give us the whole answer to (1), since this question includes such problems as the place and time of an act. To answer (1), we must consider the use lawyers make of the word, and examine how far this use diverges from the ordinary usage of the word.

THE NEED FOR AN ACT

This notion of the need for an act is a complex thread and at the outset we should do well to try and disentangle some of the various strands.

(1) *Physical and mental acts.*

One such strand is the distinction between physical acts on the one hand, and thoughts, intentions, etc. on the other. This is the distinction that is being made when it is said that acceptance in the Law of Contract must be more than just a mere mental assent. Here what one might call mental acts are being excluded as not sufficient for the purpose of the law. The same is true to some extent of the need in Criminal Law for an *actus reus*, which also rules out as insufficient mere thoughts and intentions. One reason advanced for this requirement of an act is the difficulty of proof of such thoughts; as Bryan C.J. remarked, 'The intention (*l'entent*) of a man cannot be tried.' But this could hardly be a conclusive reason, for the Courts frequently decide what the accused thought and intended, and they could infer this from what he did and said. Every jury that convicts a person of larceny must be satisfied that he intended, at the time of taking, to deprive the owner permanently of the property. Another reason that is put forward is the need for objectivity. Unless there were some external, observable conduct on the part of the offeree, no-one (and especially the offeror) could tell whether the offer had been accepted or not. For, as

Bryan C.J. continued, 'The devil himself knows not the intention of a man'. So until disputes and litigation arise on the matter, no-one can know (save the offeree) whether there is a contract or not.

But so far as Criminal Law is concerned, the reason why there must be an *actus reus* is partly something more important, namely, the idea that to punish mere intention, and make offences of 'thought crime', is too great an intrusion into individual liberty and privacy. Although the law seeks to protect society from harmful conduct, and intentions to commit crimes are potentially harmful in that they may lead to the commission of crimes, yet the interests of the individual must be weighed and a balance must be struck between the freedom of the citizen and the safety of the community. There is, however, a further difficulty that even if it were thought desirable to have such control over men's thoughts, the enforcement of such control might well be impossible.

(2) *Acts and omissions.*

Another strand in this notion is the distinction between acts and omissions. Only rarely does the law impose a positive duty to act. For instance a bystander has no legal duty to save a small child from drowning. The finder of a lost article has no duty to restore it to its owner, even though he knows who the owner is. The duty not to misrepresent in the Law of Contract does not normally amount to a positive duty to disclose all the information you have. In general, the law is content to say 'Thou shalt not kill, steal or deceive'. It will not take the further step and say 'Thou shalt preserve life, restore goods to the owner, disclose all the information you have'. Before this further step is taken there must usually be shown to exist some special relationship between the parties, which gives rise to this extra positive duty. For example, the bystander must be in charge of the child. The contract must be *uberrimae fidei*. The basis of this attitude seems again to be this same reluctance of the law to encroach too much on individual liberty. While ready to penalize conduct that harms a man's neighbours, the

Courts feel that to ordain the performance of conduct that will benefit one's neighbours would restrict freedom unduly and place too great a burden on the individual. So the rule that you are to love your neighbour (a positive command) is narrowed in law to the prohibition, you must not injure your neighbour.

(3) *Control.*

The most difficult distinction, however, is that between acts over which a man has control, and happenings over which he has no control. There is a general principle that a man should not be punished, or have to pay damages, for occurrences over which he could exercise no control. To penalize him in this way would seem not only unfair, because he had no choice in the matter, but also inefficacious, because it would not prevent similar occurrences in the future.

Accordingly the law does not generally hold someone responsible for the operations of nature or the acts of third parties, since both these are outside his control. To hold *A* responsible for whatever harm befalls *B*, either because of the act of *C* or because of some natural event such as the falling of a tree, would be wholly unreasonable, in the absence of special circumstances, since it would be to constitute *A* an insurer of *B*'s safety. Even where *A* has himself been negligent in the first place, he may escape liability on the ground that *C*'s act, or the falling of the tree, amounted to a *novus actus interveniens*. On the other hand, there are exceptions. On some occasions, despite *C*'s act or the natural event, *A* may still be held responsible:

(i)   Perhaps he should have foreseen that *C* might have done what he did, and have taken precautions to guard against this, *e.g.*, a man who leaves a horse unattended in a street should foresee that mischievous children might play with it.[1] A person who leaves the door of a house open should foresee that thieves might enter and steal things from the house.[2]

(ii)   Or it may be that the situation created by *A* is so

---

[1] *Lynch* v. *Nurdin* (1841), 1 Q.B. 29.   [2] *Stansbie* v. *Troman*, [1948] 2 K.B. 48.

fraught with danger that he must become the insurer of *B*. If *A* chooses to keep a lion and *C* wrongfully lets it loose so that it mauls *B*, *A* will still have to compensate *B* for his injuries.[1]

(iii) Or the third party may in fact be someone over whom *A* has control. *A* may for instance be already liable in negligence for failing to keep under control his small child, if that child subsequently injures *B*. Or the third party may be the servant of *A*, acting in the course of his employment.

Nor is the law in general concerned with what a man is, but only with what he does, since he may choose what he does, but not what he is. As Holmes observed, 'It is felt to be impolitic and unjust to make a man answerable for harm unless he might have chosen otherwise'.[2] Here again the law is refusing to hold a man liable for something outside his control. Being found by night in a building with intention to commit a felony therein, and kindred offences against Section 28 of the Larceny Act, 1916, are not complete exceptions to this principle, since even here there is this much choice, that the prisoner need not have gone to or have been in that building with that intention. This is why so much dissatisfaction was aroused by the case of *Larsonneur*,[3] who was convicted of being found in the United Kingdom contrary to orders made under the Aliens Restriction Act, when in fact she had been brought to England under police custody and was found in a police cell, since she indeed had no choice at all in the matter.

The third and most difficult species of event over which the defendant has no control is the class of involuntary acts: the bodily movements outside his control such as reflex actions, heart beats, etc. It is chiefly this type of involuntary act that has given rise to the problem and led to the various attempts

---

[1] *Baker* v. *Snell*, [1908] 2 K.B. 352; *Behrens* v. *Bertram Mills Circus, Ltd.*, [1957] 2 Q.B. 1.

[2] Holmes, *The Common Law*, p. 45.

[3] 24 Cr. App. Rep. 74. This dissatisfaction was not felt, however, in Northern Ireland, where the case was followed in the unreported case of *Kasriel* v. *Neumann* (1947): *vid.*, (1956), 12 N.I.L.Q., p. 61.

to formulate a satisfactory definition of an act in order to exclude these involuntary occurrences from liability on the ground that they are less than acts. Whereas in the first type of case where *B*'s injury results from *C*'s act, we say of *A* that it is not *his* act; in this type of case, if *B*'s injury results from a reflex action on *A*'s part, we say that it is not his *act*. So instead of asking what makes conduct involuntary, jurists have asked what exactly is an act.

THE DEFINITION OF AN ACT

Holmes' celebrated definition of an act as a willed muscular contraction, in which he followed Austin, contains two noteworthy features. The first of these seems at first sight, if perhaps unhelpful, at least innocuous: namely, the requirement that the muscular contraction should be willed. For a spasm, he argues, is not an act.[1] The other curious feature is the way Holmes restricts the term 'act' to cover only the movement of the actor's muscles or limbs, and excludes from his definition everything that follows. If *A* shoots and kills *B*, according to Holmes, *A*'s act is the willed contraction of his finger on the trigger of the gun. The firing of the gun, the bullet leaving the barrel and hitting *B*, and *B*'s falling dead, these are all consequences of *A*'s act, but not actually part of it. The reason for this oddly narrow interpretation of the term 'act', is perhaps the search for something for which to hold the actor absolutely responsible, something over which he has absolute power of control, and so complete choice. Over the firing of the gun, the bullet's hitting *B*, and *B*'s falling dead, he clearly lacks this complete control, for the gun may jam; the bullet may be deflected by a sudden gust of wind; and *B* may be saved by the bullet lodging in the bible given to him by his great-grandmother. What Holmes calls consequences are not so entirely dependent on *A*, it seems, as the original act of pulling the trigger.

But if we want something completely dependent on the will of the actor, may we not be forced logically to take a further step and claim that the only thing over which *A* has complete

[1] Holmes, *op. cit.*, p. 54.

control is his process of willing? He lacks this control over the firing of the gun. It is something that usually ensues, but may on occasion fail, for the gun may jam. But the same could be said, surely, of A's muscular contraction when he pulls the trigger. This 'motion of the body consequent on the determination of the will', as Austin termed it, usually succeeds the act of willing (whatever that may be), but in one case in a million perhaps it might not do so, and we should recognize the onset of paralysis. Though such failure to follow may be exceedingly rare, the important fact is not the rarity, but the possibility of failure, since this suggests that the difference between A's control over the firing of the gun and his control over the contraction of his finger is only one of degree. A can be much more sure that the finger will contract than he can that the gun will fire; but he cannot be absolutely certain of either. Indeed Holmes marvelled at the 'mysterious accuracy with which the adult, who is master of himself, foresees the outward adjustment which would follow his inward effort',[1] but his view of what an act is seems to lead to the result that no adult is really master of himself at all, and that since he only *foresees* but is not certain that his muscles will obey his will, his only control is over what goes on inside his mind. But if it is only with regard to these mental acts that A is in real control, should we not then have to conclude (if we still demand that A should only be punished for actions over which he has control) that he should only be punished for his mental acts; and that it is these mental occurrences with which the law is really concerned. It is as though it were not the man we see in the dock in whom we are really interested, but rather some inner figure who pulls the strings that cause (usually) the prisoner's muscles to contract. So that we should inquire not whether A shot and killed B, nor even whether A's finger contracted and pulled the trigger due to an exercise of will on A's part, but rather whether there was a determination of the will that took place in A's mind. Yet clearly this is not the investigation that we make in the Courts. Nor does common sense dictate that it should be. Jurists have

---

[1] Holmes, *op. cit.*, p. 54.

examined the notion of an act in order to illuminate the investigation we should make when faced with the problem of involuntary behaviour. The procedure should be reversed. Closer attention to the investigation we do make in cases of involuntary acts will help in effect to illuminate the notion of an act.

It might be objected that Holmes never meant to put forward a complete theory which would be thoroughly satisfactory from a philosophical point of view. All he aimed at providing us with was a rough test of what an act was; and this suffices for practical purposes. But it is for practical purposes precisely that this definition is unhelpful, because it conflicts with the general notion of what an act is. Whatever an act is, both in and out of court, we use the term in a way quite different from Holmes' way. 'Caught in the act', for example, conjures up a picture of the burglar creeping away with the swag over his shoulder; of the murderer standing over his victim, bloody knife in hand: not of a criminal contracting various muscles. So we speak of the act of stealing, and the act of shooting, and of a thousand other kinds of act. The 'act of contracting the finger' describes only the rare case when the accused tried to pull the trigger, but failed, and even here the normal description is "the act of attempting to shoot". This is why we demur at Holmes' conclusion that all acts are indifferent *per se* legally. Of course in his sense they must be (unless there were a statute prohibiting a certain willed muscular contraction) until we take into account the surrounding circumstances and the consequences of the contraction. But in the way we normally talk of acts it is quite untrue to say that they are legally indifferent *per se*. The reason why the act of stealing, the act of murdering, or the act of dangerous driving, are not so legally indifferent is precisely because the act in each of these cases includes all the surrounding circumstances and consequences which attract the condemnation of the law.

This restricted definition of an act is also liable to create difficulties in connection with the question of the locality of an act. Suppose A, standing in state X, shoots at and kills B, standing in state Y, to decide whether the courts of either state have jurisdiction to try A, it may be necessary to decide where the murder took place. The restricted definition might lead to the conclusion that it took place in state X, because it was there that A pulled the trigger. Whereas the ordinary use of the term 'act', may allow us to say that the act was begun in state X and completed in state Y, and therefore the courts of state Y should have jurisdiction in such a case. And it has been held that murder is committed in the place where the death occurs.[1] This can be reconciled with Holmes' theory only by distinguishing between the crime of murder and the act (pulling the trigger) which is only part of the crime. Yet the courts do not seem to distinguish in this way, as may be seen perhaps from the case of *R.* v. *Jarmain*.[2] Here the argument was that since the accused's gun fired without his consciously pulling the trigger, there was no act on his part and therefore he was not guilty of murder. The Court of Criminal Appeal, however, held that there was an act on his part, namely the act of robbery with violence and that as death resulted the accused was guilty.

Hence Salmond asserted that 'an act has no *natural* boundaries, any more than an event or a place has. Its limits must be artificially defined for the purpose in hand for the time being. It is for the law to determine, in each particular case, what circumstances and what consequences shall be counted within the compass of the act with which it is concerned. To ask what act a man has done is like asking in what place he lives.'[3] He also argued that the distinction between an act and its consequences is merely a verbal one; a matter of convenience of speech. But the fact that the question may be verbal does not entail that it is trivial. If the word 'act' were used in such a way that without a willed muscular contraction there is no act, Jarmain might not have been hanged. Indeed, it is true to say that many of the problems facing the courts are verbal problems. Once the facts have been found, *e.g.* that A stabbed B and Dr. C failed to treat B adequately, and B died, then the

[1] *R.* v. *Coombes* (1786), 1 Leach 388; Salmond, *Jurisprudence* (11th ed.), p. 406.
[2] [1946] K.B. 74. [3] Salmond, *Jurisprudence* (11th ed.), pp. 401–2.

Court has to decide whether on these facts it would be right to say that *A* caused *B*'s death. Similarly, if *A*, intending to burn *B*'s haystack, takes out of his pocket a box of matches and runs over to the stack and then does no more, the court must decide whether, if these facts are proved, they amount to attempted arson. In all these cases, after the factual dispute has been settled, there then arises what may be called the verbal dispute, the problem of classifying the defendant's conduct—is what he did to count as murder, attempted arson, etc.? But none of these disputes are any the less difficult, or important, for being verbal.

The difficulty of such verbal disputes stems from the fact that the general meaning of the terms, *e.g.* 'attempt', 'murder', 'cause', has been set and, though it may be hard to draw the line in a given case, it is easy to find cases well to one side or other of the line. What the courts have to decide is whether the features of the border-line case are more akin to the cases on the one side or to those on the other. And remembering the important consequences that will follow from their decision, they must be guided by various principles in deciding with which group of cases to classify the border-line case. What the court is not free to do is to define the word (attempt, murder, cause) as it pleases. With regard to the problem of defining an act, it has been said that a person is free to define a word as he pleases.[1] One is free to do so, provided one remembers (and one never does) that this arbitrary way of using the word is different from the usual way of using it, and that when lawyers ask what is an act, they are concerned with the way the term is used in legal argument, and not with any special use that some writer might decide to make of the term.

One reason for the unhelpfulness of trying to elucidate criteria of responsibility by demanding an act on the defendant's part, and then by defining what an act is, is that it reverses to some extent the procedure of ordinary language, because in ordinary speech the word 'act', together with such allied expressions as '*A* did it', is used not so much to describe what

[1] Dias & Hughes, *Jurisprudence*, p. 202.

has happened, as to ascribe responsibility.[1] In so far as the word 'act' is not being used to mark such distinctions as those referred to above, *e.g.* the distinction between acts and omissions; between acts and words (actions speak louder than words); or between acts, words and thoughts (we sin in thought, word and deed) the word is used to impute responsibility. '*A*'s act caused *B*'s death' is less a way of describing what has happened, than another way of saying that it was *A*'s fault. 'It was not *A*'s act at all' (*e.g.* because he was having an epileptic fit) is another way of saying that we should not blame *A* in this case because of some special feature in the situation.

Holmes suggested that the special feature was the lack of volition. One drawback of this approach is that it suggests that what we investigate in each case is whether the bodily movement was preceded or accompanied by some interior process. In certain cases it may be that before a man does something he goes through some such process of setting himself to do it, *e.g.* if it is something very difficult to do, but the vast majority of cases where a man does something do not contain any such feature, nor do we look for one when we consider his conduct, whether in court or out of court.

A further difficulty arises with regard to omissions. In those cases where a man is held criminally or civilly liable for an omission, it is quite clear that he may be held liable even though he never applied his mind to the matter at all. In fact he may be held liable just for not having applied his mind. There may be, of course, the rare case where he might deliberately refuse to apply his mind, or where he might deliberately refrain from doing what the law enjoins; but the usual case of omission is that of the man who just fails to act without thinking about it at all. And here it is quite untrue to say that there has been any process of willing. Any test of responsibility must surely take into account the case of omissions, and just as there are cases where a man may not be held responsible for what he has done, *e.g.* while asleep, so there are cases where he

[1] H. L. A. Hart, *The Ascription of Responsibility and Rights* (1948–9), Proc. Arist. Soc. 179.

may not be held responsible for what he has omitted to do; and the principle seems to be the same in both types of case. The real problem here is to see what is the minimum requirement of the law before a man can be held responsible, either for his act or for his omission.

VOLUNTARY AND INVOLUNTARY ACTS

The common method of stating this minimum requirement is to assert that there must be a voluntary act on the defendant's part.[1] This attempt to solve the problem, however, is no more helpful with regard to omissions, than is the definition of an act put forward by Holmes. It is a curious description of a thoughtless omission, to say that it is something voluntary on the part of the defendant. In any such cases of omission, there has been nothing on his part at all: so that it is difficult to see how one can sensibly talk here of a voluntary nothing.[2] The demand that the act should be voluntary confuses two different distinctions.

There is, it is true, a very important distinction between what a man does voluntarily and what he does under compulsion, duress, necessity, etc. Before admitting a confession in evidence, for example, the Judge may have to determine whether it was voluntary, or whether it was obtained by some threat or inducement. Or again, we may excuse someone of a crime on the ground that the accused was not acting voluntarily, but under duress. A woman's husband may have coerced her into acting as she did. In these cases the accused did have a choice; there was no need to make the confession, or to do what was done. But the choice was so difficult that we feel that the confession should be not admitted. For the inducement of bail, for example, may have led the accused to make a false confession. Or

---

[1] Cross & Jones, *Criminal Law* (3rd ed.), p. 32; Kenny, *Outlines of Criminal Law* (17th ed.), pp. 26–7; American Law Institute's *Model Penal Code, Tentative Draft No. 4*, Art. 2, s. 2.0 (1); *cf.*, Queensland Code, s. 23; Tasmanian Code, s. 13 (1); Stephen, *History of the Criminal Law of England*, Vol. II, p. 97; Barry, Paton & Sawer, *Criminal Law in Australia* (1948), p. 48.

[2] *Cf.*, Perkins (1939), 52 Harv. L.R. 912; Glanville Williams, *Criminal Law*, p. 15. Nevertheless it is not true to say that the idea of a voluntary omission makes no sense—one can be compelled to omit to do something, and equally one can omit to do it voluntarily.

the husband's coercion may have made it difficult for the wife to choose to act otherwise than as she did.

But there is a totally different distinction: the distinction between normal conduct and involuntary movements of the body, such as the beating of one's heart, spasms, what one does in sleep, etc. In these cases there is no question of choice at all. Now the voluntary act theory blurs this important difference[1] and obscures the real question, namely, why it is that the courts refuse to hold a person liable in certain cases on the ground that his act or omission was involuntary. What is the test by which we distinguish these acts and omissions from the normal acts and omissions?

The search for the answer to these questions may best be conducted by first considering the types of behaviour that have been recognized as involuntary by the courts in different branches of the law. Then we may inquire whether there is any common criterion for determining whether in general behaviour is involuntary. Thirdly, there will arise the question why different branches of the law do, and should, treat these types of involuntary behaviour differently from normal behaviour.

TYPES OF INVOLUNTARY ACTION RECOGNIZED BY LAW

These fall into two main categories.

(a) Where the defendant is compelled to do what he does by some external force; and

(b) Where he is compelled by some internal force, or where at least the compulsion is not due to any external cause.

Where the defendant is physically compelled by some external force, either by some other person or by some force of nature to act as he does, courts have recognized this type of

---

[1] 'Voluntary' and 'Involuntary' are not opposites, as was pointed out by J. L. Austin in '*A Plea for Excuses*' (1956–7), Proc. Arist. Soc. *Cf*., Bentham, *Principles of Morals and Legislation*, p. 82; see also Jerome Hall, *Principles of Criminal Law*, p. 522. Stephen opposed 'voluntary' to 'involuntary', however, and not to 'compelled', *op. cit.*, pp. 101–2.

case as exonerating the defendant from liability. So in the Criminal Law 'If *A* takes *B*'s arm and the weapon in his hand and stabs *C*, *B* would be not guilty because there was no voluntary act on his part'.[1] Such a defence would also be raised in the case of an omission, where, for example, *A*, a parent, under a legal duty to rescue *B*, his child, from drowning, is forcibly prevented by *C* from so doing. In tort the same rule has been applied: where for instance a defendant was carried by a gang of armed men on to the plaintiff's premises, he was held not liable in trespass.[2] It is important to distinguish this case of physical compulsion, as it is sometimes called, from the case of duress. If the defence is duress, then the defendant is pleading that, though he had a choice, the alternative to doing what he did was so hard that it is too much to ask of any man that he should choose the alternative. The accused has no say in how his arm moves: it is moved for him. This is the difference between the case suggested by Hale and the case of *R*. v. *Bourne*,[3] the decision in which is only explicable on the basis that the wife herself had committed a crime. Similarly, in *Gilbert* v. *Stone*[4] a defendant compelled by threat of injury to enter the plaintiff's premises was held liable in trespass.

That people's acts may be involuntary without the compulsion of any external force is a fact that has become increasingly clearer with the growth of medical science. As Paton observed,[5] 'medicine, psychoanalysis and psychiatry are opening new doors and the law will gradually be forced to reconsider the theories on which its analysis of an act is based'. The best known of these internally motivated involuntary acts are those of epileptics undergoing fits of convulsions, and it is no accident that the word 'epileptic' was coined by the Greeks to

---

[1] 1 Hale. P.C. 434, 472; Blackstone, *Commentaries on the Laws of England*, Vol. IV, p. 27; *cp.*, 1 Hawk. P.C., ch. 29, s. 3.

[2] *Smith* v. *Stone* (1647), Sty. 65.

[3] (1952), 36 Cr. App. Rep. 125. See Cross in (1953), 69 L.Q.R., p. 354, but Lord Goddard stresses at p. 128 that '(the plea of duress) means that she admits that she has committed the crime', and at p. 129 that 'the offence of buggery . . . does not depend on consent: it depends on the act, and if an act of buggery is committed, the felony is committed'.

[4] (1647), Sty. 72; Aleyn 35.   [5] Paton, *Jurisprudence* (2nd ed.), p. 243.

signify something that might fall on a man, something that seized him from within himself.[1] These involuntary acts may be roughly divided into (a) movements over which nobody has control; and (b) movements over which people normally do have control, but over which a particular defendant lacks control because of some abnormality.[2]

There is little authority in law on the first class of involuntary acts, partly because it is unlikely that such uncontrollable movements should result in any harm, and even if they did, it is so clear that a person would not be held liable for such harm that prosecution would hardly be launched. Since the tort of trespass to the person now would seem to require intention or negligence on the part of the defendant,[3] it is unlikely that a defendant in such circumstances would be sued in tort either. Writers such as Austin, Bentham and Stephen, agree in classifying all these movements as involuntary and not deserving of punishment.[4] The American Law Institute's Model Penal Code defines certain types of acts as not voluntary, among which are reflexes or convulsions, and the Code contains a final omnibus class excluding as not voluntary any bodily movements that otherwise are not products of the effort or determination of the actor, either conscious or habitual.[5]

With regard to the type of movements over which people do normally have control, but over which a particular defendant lacked control because of some abnormality, the abnor-

---

[1] For a useful medical account of such conditions see Penfield and Jasper, *Epilepsy and the Functional Anatomy of the Human Brain* (1954). See also Gowers, *Diseases of the Nervous System*, II (1893), pp. 746–9; Henderson and Gillespie, *A Textbook of Psychiatry* (8th ed.).

[2] The first sub-class may be sub-divided into:

  (i) the movement of his body of which a man knows nothing without observation, *e.g.* heart beats, the peristaltic movement of the gut;

  (ii) movements which he does know about without observation, *e.g.* twitches, ticks, jerks etc. (where the cause itself, however, is known only by observation and reflex actions, such as the jerking of one's knee when it is tapped by a doctor, or a sudden leaping back when attacked by a wild animal).

See G. E. Anscombe, *Intention*, pp. 13 ff.

[3] *Fowler* v. *Lanning*, [1959] 1 Q.B. 426.

[4] Austin, *Jurisprudence*, I. 360, 415, 419, 498; Bentham, *op. cit.*, p. 164, 171, 174–5; Stephen, *op. cit.*, p. 99.

[5] Model Penal Code, Art. 2, s. 2.0 (2) (d).

mality may be his unconsciousness, *e.g.* he may be merely asleep, and in sleep, it is said, there is no sin. 'Acts done by a person asleep cannot be criminal, there being no consciousness.'[1] Similarly, it is unlikely for instance, in the law of tort that a man would be held liable for slander, for defamatory words spoken in his sleep.[2] Likewise, the acts of a man under somnambulism will not render him guilty of any crime.[3] But the abnormality may be that the defendant's behaviour is due to disease or injury. In *R.* v. *Charlson*[4] a father who in a fit of automatism seriously injured his small son was found not guilty of any crime since the jury was not satisfied that he might not have been acting as he did on account of a brain tumour; and so they were not satisfied that he had any choice as to his actions. Similarly, a man who killed his mother when his cosciousness was clouded as a result of hypoglycaemia, was found not guilty of murder.[5] In these cases the lack of control arises because of lack of consciousness, as in cases of sleep-walking where the defendant does no know what he is doing. It may be, however, that he knows what he is doing and is yet quite incapable of exercising any control. Sufferers from fits of ictal or post-ictal conditions arising from epilepsy or injury have been known to describe their experiences by saying that though they knew in a sort of way what they were doing, yet they felt that all their actions were being controlled by some external force, as though by some remote control station.[6]

A very difficult problem is posed where the abnormal lack of control is due not to disease or injury, but to drunkenness or drugs. Involuntary drunkenness, *i.e.* where *A* secretly and against *B*'s will administers intoxicating liquor to *B*, is always said to be a defence.[7] Where, however, the accused himself was res-

---

[1] MacDonald, *The Criminal Law of Scotland* (5th ed.), p. 11.
[2] Pollock on Torts (15th ed.), p. 47.
[3] Wharton, *Criminal Law* (12th ed.), I, s. 84; Russell on Crime (11th ed.), p. 40; Glanville Williams, *op. cit.*, p. 14. See *R.* v. *Minor* (1955), 112 Can.C.C. 29.
[4] [1955] 1 All E.R. 859.
[5] *Lancet* (1943), Vol. I, pp. 526–7.
[6] *Cf.*, defendant's account in *Buckley & T.T.C.* v. *Smith Transport*, [1946] 4 D.L.R. 721.
[7] *R.* v. *Pearson* (1835), 2 Lew. C.C. 144; 1 Hale 32.

ponsible for getting drunk, he will only be excused either if he is so drunk as to be insane within the McNaghten rules, or if he is incapable of forming a specific intent required by the courts. It is no defence that his intoxication made him more easily lose control of himself.[1] As to acts done under hypnotism or post-hypnotic suggestion, there is little authority.[2] The American Law Institute classifies 'conduct during hypnosis, or resulting from hypnotic suggestion' as involuntary. But the difficulty is that it is not clear how far a hypnotized person can be tricked into doing something dishonest or felonious.[3] On the other hand, such a subject might well be tricked into doing some dangerous act by being persuaded that he was in fact doing an act of quite a different kind, *e.g.* the hypnotist might tell him to shoot someone with a water pistol while placing in his hand a real loaded pistol. But here the defence would not be so much that the defendant had no ability to control his movements, as that he did not fully appreciate the nature of his act.

What emerges from a survey of these different types of case is that the common minimal requirement of the law seems to be that the accused should have had the ability to control his movements.

CRIMINAL LAW

The most important field of law where problems arise with regard to involuntary acts is the Criminal Law. The attraction of stating the defence of involuntariness in terms of there being no act on the part of the accused is that this will be a defence even in cases of strict liability. To group this minimal requirement of power of control with the *actus reus* instead of with *mens rea*, means that a person who fails to conform to a halt sign because of a fit of automatism is not guilty of an offence,

---

[1] *D.P.P.* v. *Beard*, [1920] A.C. 479; *R.* v. *McCarthy*, [1954] 2 Q.B. 105.
[2] Glanville Williams, *op. cit.*, p. 12.
[3] See Taylor, *Principles and Practice of Medical Jurisprudence* (11th ed.). Experiments were carried out on 50 subjects, all of whom awoke rather than perform some repugnant act: J. R. Rees, *Modern Practice in Psychiatric Medicine* (1949), p. 391.

whereas one who fails because his brakes failed, or because he could not see the sign, would be guilty.[1]

The reason for the Criminal Law's insistence on this minimal requirement of ability of control is that the way in which the Criminal Law seeks to protect society from harmful conduct is in general by imposing penalties to deter would-be criminals. The imposition of penalties for involuntary acts cannot, of course, serve to prevent people from committing such involuntary acts. Furthermore, in the case of involuntary acts there arises no question of what Bentham termed the secondary mischief, *i.e.* the general effect on the community of the wrongful act, since in general if the accused acted involuntarily, there is no reason for the public to be apprehensive as to his future conduct in the same way as if he had behaved freely and willingly. Consequently, to use Bentham's phraseology, punishment would be both inefficacious and groundless. Inefficacious in that it could not prevent the primary mischief (since we cannot help our involuntary acts), and groundless because there is no secondary mischief to prevent.[2]

But not only is it therefore impolitic to punish such conduct, it is also unjust. Without inquiring too deeply into the moral justification for punishment, we may recognize the existence of a moral principle that we should not blame or punish one who could not help doing what he did. That this is a separate matter from that of deterrence can be seen from the following consideration. One can imagine that the punishment of involuntary conduct might possibly serve to deter would-be criminals in this way: While not preventing future involuntary

---

[1] *Hill* v. *Baxter*, [1958] 1 Q.B. 277; Edwards (1958), 21 M.L.R. 375; there are also repercussions from this grouping in the law of evidence, as was shown by *R.* v. *Harrison-Owen*, [1951] 2 All E.R. 726; see Cowen & Carter, *Essays on the Law of Evidence*, pp. 111–4; Cross, *Evidence*, 287–8; Glanville Williams, *op. cit.*, p. 14. The latter suggests that there are few offences of strict liability where the defence of involuntariness could apply, but road traffic offences are an exception to this contention.

[2] Bentham, *op. cit.*, pp. 164, 171, 174–5, 315. It could be argued that punishment would be equally inefficacious in the case of the motorist whose brakes failed or who failed to observe the halt sign, but surely here the justification could be that punishment might cause him to test his brakes regularly and keep a keener look-out in future.

conduct, it might prevent conduct that is not involuntary, if potential criminals said to themselves: 'See, this Draconian code even punishes those who cannot help stealing—the kleptomaniacs too. We, therefore, who can help stealing would be shown no mercy, so we had better refrain from committing crimes altogether'. Yet nobody would deny that, even if crimes could be prevented in this way, it would be unjust to punish those who cannot help what they do; and this it seems is the flaw in any theory of punishment based wholly on deterrence.

On the other hand there are cases where although the accused lacks the ability to control what he does, secondary mischief will arise and the community will be apprehensive about his future behaviour. Such cases are those where the accused's condition resulted from earlier conduct of his, over which he did have control. Stephen made this point clearly when he urged that the law ought to be that no act is a crime if the person who does it is at the time when it is done prevented, either by defective mental power or by disease affecting his mind, from controlling his own conduct, unless the absence of power of control is brought about by his own fault.[1] For this reason the courts have always leaned against allowing drunkenness as a defence when the accused allowed himself to get into a state of intoxication. Here it is felt that if he did this once he might well do it again, and men must be deterred from allowing themselves to get into such a condition. It is precisely because there was an earlier stage when the accused could have helped what he did, that punishment will serve some purpose. Likewise, if fumes suddenly overcome the driver of a motor car and the car swerves across the road into another vehicle, the driver will not be guilty of dangerous driving. But if he falls asleep at the wheel without any such external cause, then we could say that there was an earlier stage when he was driving dangerously, in that he continued to drive although he felt himself becoming drowsy. At this point he could have taken action either to ensure that he kept awake, or he could

---

[1] Stephen, *op. cit.*, p. 168. *Cp.*, Wharton, *Criminal Law* (12th ed.), I, s. 84; *Lewis v. State* (1943), 196 Ga. 755.

have stopped driving and waited until his somnolence had passed. This technique of moving back to a stage at which the defendant had a choice will sometimes enable lawyers to differentiate between cases where no blame should attach to the defendant because he could not help doing what he did, and cases where he is culpable because he could have avoided getting into the state where he was unable to help acting as he did. So we can say in a case such as *Hill* v. *Baxter*[1] that if the defendant was to blame for not forcing himself to stay awake, or for not stopping until he felt fit to drive, it was at this earlier stage that he was committing the crime of dangerous driving, rather than at the later stage when he actually was asleep. But this technique runs into difficulties with regard to omissions. For if the defendant argues that he is not guilty of failing to conform to a traffic sign because he was unconscious, we can hardly differentiate between the case where fumes suddenly bereft him of consciousness, and the case where he just fell asleep, by saying that in the latter case there was an earlier point of time where he was failing to conform. It is not yet clear how the courts will distinguish between these two types of case, but perhaps it can be suggested that where fumes overcome the driver he should be acquitted, not on the ground that there was no act on his part, but on the ground that he was unable to prevent himself from falling asleep, and at the same time there was no warning of what was going to happen, so that both his dangerous driving and his failure to conform to the traffic sign were involuntary. Where, however, he realizes he is falling asleep, has some warning, and yet takes no precautions, then this defence should not be open to him. The term 'involuntary' can then be reserved for those cases where no ability to control his actions arises at any stage;[2] and this defence of involuntariness should be excluded in cases where the accused either brought about his own lack of power of control, or fore-

---

[1] [1958] 1 Q.B. 277.

[2] *i.e.*, once he has commenced a course of conduct, for otherwise the suggested test would exclude even the case of the motorist overcome by fumes, since he could have always abstained from driving, and so the test would become vacuous.

saw that he might lack control and took no precautions. Here culpability and deterrence go hand-in-hand, for we feel that where there was the power of choice at an earlier stage, and the defendant could have helped it, he is culpable; and we also feel that punishment will serve to deter people from similar behaviour in the future. This, to some extent, supports the decision in *Jarmain's case*.[1] Even if he had no choice as to whether the gun went off or not, nevertheless he did have some say in the question whether or not to commit armed robbery, so that he was to some extent responsible, and his punishment would deter others from committing this crime.

There are, however, cases where there is no choice at all on the defendant's part, but his condition is such that he is liable to cause harm to others. Epileptics, for example, cannot help the fits they have. But if they know that they are likely to injure others in the course of these fits, it may not be wholly unreasonable to demand that they refrain from engaging in activities where the onset of a fit might lead to disastrous injury to other people. Such harm could clearly ensue if a fit overtook an epileptic in the course of driving a car, and for this reason the Motor Vehicle (Driving Licence) Regulations, 1950, prohibit epileptics from obtaining a driving licence.[2] Similarly a diabetic who fails to take sufficient food and suffers from an insulin reaction may not unreasonably be convicted of driving under the influence of drugs, even though this was not perhaps the type of case originally envisaged by the Road Traffic Acts.[3] In these cases the defendant could not help the onset of the fits, or the insulin reaction. Nor is it true to say that his lack of control of his action is in any way due to anything he has done. But since he knows of the possible dangers, he should refrain from certain types of activity: and here choice does come into play, for he can choose, for instance, whether or not to drive a motor-car in the first place. He is not, therefore, absolutely justified in saying, 'I could not help what happened'. Here too, therefore,

---

[1] *Supra*, p. 9.   [2] Regulation 5.
[3] See *The New Scientist*, 4th June, 1959, p. 1244.

there is a stage at which we can say that he had some choice as
to what has occurred.

There may, however, even be cases where there is no choice
at all on the part of the accused. So far we have discussed two
cases where a man cannot help acting as he does:

(*a*) where his inability arose from previous behaviour which
he could have helped; and

(*b*) where his inability is no fault of his but, knowing that
he is unable to help behaving as he does, he should avoid
putting himself in a position where his involuntary behaviour may injure others; and he could so avoid putting
himself into this position.

There is, however, the third case: that of the man who cannot
help his involuntary behaviour, and cannot avoid putting himself in the position where his involuntary behaviour may injure
others; and whose involuntary actions may be so dangerous to
the community that deterrence gives place to prevention. The
fits of an epileptic may be so dangerous that we no longer merely
feel that he ought to refrain from certain activities requiring
special care and skill, such as driving. It may even be necessary
to confine him in order to prevent him altogether from mixing
with other people. At this stage we begin to leave the question
of punishment and turn to the question of what we should do
to protect society from possible danger. Deterrents and cor-
rection no longer have any effect, and prevention is the only
remedy.[1]

---

[1] Prevention can often be seen as the basis of punishment, *e.g.*, in preventive
detention, imposed when a court concludes from the prisoner's record that he is
beyond reform and the only course is to lock him up so that he can no longer get
at other people's property; in the incarceration of the guilty but insane; in the
death penalty, and in the older penalties of transportation and mutilation; and in
the more modern penalty of disqualification from driving. On the ground that the
community must be protected, it may not be unreasonable that a man suffering
so frequently from epileptic fits as to be dangerous should, if he raises a defence of
automatism, run the risk of the prosecution contending that his condition brings
him within the McNaghten Rules, as in *R. v. Kemp*, [1957] 1 Q.B. 399. *Cf.*,
Henderson & Gillespie, *op. cit.*, p. 683, where it is contended that it is not justifiable
to certify a man in the course of an epileptic fit. Contrast the South African
decision *R. v. Mkize*, 1959 (2) S.A. 260 (N).

CIVIL LIABILITY

The way that the courts deal with involuntary acts with regard to civil liability is not necessarily the same as the way of the Criminal Law. How far lack of ability to control one's movements exempts a defendant from liability in tort is bound up with the question whether liability in tort is based on fault or not. In so far as liability depends on fault, clearly involuntary acts or omissions on the part of the defendant should not render him liable, for a person is not at fault for doing what he cannot help doing. Accordingly, nobody should be held liable in negligence for an act or omission which he could not help, unless his inability to avoid the act or omission is due to some previous act or omission over which he does have control. A lunatic, therefore, could plead as a defence to negligence that he was not guilty of a breach of duty of care owing to the plaintiff, since the act or omission complained of was involuntary, and therefore could not constitute such a breach.[1] (It is submitted that this is a more satisfactory approach to the problem than to contend that the lunatic does not owe the same duty of care as the reasonable man). An intoxicated man could not put forward such an argument because, if his breach of duty of care was involuntary, it resulted from his previous negligence in allowing himself to get into a state of intoxication.[2]

How far, however, is the fact that the defendant's behaviour was involuntary, a defence to torts of strict liability? Since the courts appear inclined to restrict trespass to the person to intentional or negligent acts,[3] and since inevitable accident is accepted as a defence to trespass to goods,[4] clearly an invol-

---

[1] Clerk & Lindsell on Torts (11th ed.), pp. 92–3; Salmond, *Law of Torts* (12th ed.), 76; Street, *Law of Torts*, p. 500; Pollock, *Law of Torts* (15th ed.), p. 47; Winfield, *Law of Tort* (6th ed.), p. 130; *Morriss* v. *Marsden*, [1952] 1 All E.R. 925; Todd (1952), 15 M.L.R. 486. *Cf.*, *White* v. *White*, [1950] P. 39, at p. 52.

[2] Even in Negligence, however, liability is not wholly dependent on fault, as can be seen from the objective standard, whereby an abnormally stupid or abnormally clumsy man cannot be heard to say that, being unable to help being stupid or clumsy, he should not be held liable. See Holmes, *op. cit.*, 107 ff., Prosser, *Torts* (2nd ed.), 118, 29, and American Restatement of the Law of Torts, I, 2.

[3] *Fowler* v. *Lanning, supra*, p. 15.

[4] *N.C.B.* v. *Evans*, [1951] 2 K.B. 861.

untary trespass would be a defence to either of these actions:
though the courts may well have to distinguish between the
case where this was due to no fault of the defendant, and the
case where the defendant brought about his own inability to
control his movements. With regard to trespass to land, it has
been held that involuntary trespass, where the defendant could
not help what he was doing, is a defence.[1] Even in those cases
of strict liability, therefore, the lack of ability to control one's
movements seems to operate as a defence. For liability may be
so strict as not to allow a defendant to plead that he was mistaken, *e.g.* that he did not know that the land was not his own,
but it does not force the courts to award damages against a
man who had no choice at all as to what he did. This gives
point to the above quoted defence of tort, that it is in general
an act, for as Holmes remarked, an act implies choice.[2]

Even where the law of tort appears to be based purely on the
need to compensate the plaintiff for the injury he has suffered,
as in the ruling on *Rylands* v. *Fletcher* (though even here, the
defence of act of God, or act of a third party, will avail), or in
the Scienter action (where the wrongful act of a third party
will not avail the defendant as a defence), nevertheless it seems
that there must be some power of control exercisable at some
stage by the defendant. The principle is, in these cases, that
the defendant has created the dangerous situation and should
therefore compensate a plaintiff who suffers harm as a result.
The defendant need not have brought in and accumulated the
water on his land. He need not have kept a ferocious animal.
But where the bringing in of the water, or the keeping of the
animal was not done by the defendant, it would be contrary
to common sense to hold him responsible. Otherwise, 'Why
need the defendant have acted at all, and why is it not enough
that his existence has been at the expense of the plaintiff?'[3]

Involuntary conduct also raises problems with regard to
causation. A conscious act on the part of the plaintiff will in
general snap the chain of causation, whereas if the act is in-

---

[1] *Smith* v. *Stone* (*supra*); *cf.*, *Beckwith* v. *Shordike* (1767), 4 Burr. 2092.
[2] Holmes, *op. cit.*, p. 54; *cf.*, Pollock, *op. cit.*, p. 47.   [3] *Ibid.*, p. 95.

voluntary, the resulting harm may still be laid at the door of the defendant. So if *A* injures *B* who, as a result of the injury, commits suicide, *A* may be liable to *B*'s dependants under the Fatal Accidents Act, provided the deceased's condition was such that his act is regarded as involuntary.[1] Similarly, if *A* puts *B* in such a position of peril that he acts involuntarily, and so makes matters worse, *A* will be both civilly and criminally liable for the harm resulting to *B*.[2] This same principle is found at work in the rescue cases.

EVIDENCE

In the law of evidence, however, different questions arise with regard to involuntary acts which, in this context, comprise involuntary statements. The question is no longer whether the defendant should be held responsible for his involuntary behaviour, but whether any admission made involuntarily should be allowed in evidence against a party. The generally accepted reason for excluding statements made out of court as evidence to prove the truth of what they assert, is twofold:[3] (*a*) because such statements were not made on oath, and therefore may not be trustworthy; and (*b*) because there is no possibility of their veracity or correctness being decided by cross-examination. Admissions are, however, allowed as evidence against a party because (i) though not on oath, they are likely to be true since they were against the interest of the man who made them; and (ii) because the party who made them will have an opportunity by his own evidence to explain the circumstances, and show how much reliance is to be placed on them; and this will serve the purpose normally served by cross-examination. Admissions made in sleep, therefore, or in delirium, or under hypnosis, could it seems be admissible on this reasoning. Suppose, for example, the prisoner is charged with burgling premises, and denies ever having visited these premises; if he talks in his sleep and describes these premises, should this admission necessarily

---

[1] *Pigney* v. *Pointer's Transport Services*, [1957] 2 All E.R. 807.

[2] *R.* v. *Pitts* (1842), Car. & M. 284; Hart & Honoré (1956), 72 L.Q.R. 272; Salmond, *Law of Torts*, p. 735, and cases there noted.

[3] Cross, *Evidence*, p. 350; Wigmore on Evidence, s. 1048.

be excluded? The prisoner will be able to explain the statement and these circumstances (so that the objection of lack of cross-examination is met), and there is no reason to suppose that the statement (if against interest) is untrue. Such admissions have been received.[1] On the other hand, when the prisoner is arrested he must be cautioned that he need not say anything; consequently if he is in a state of delirium and cannot help saying what he does, perhaps it is only fair that anything he says in custody in such conditions should not be received in evidence against him. Otherwise he would be denied the choice offered to him by the law, the right not to say anything.[2]

Confessions, on the other hand, raise a different problem. Here the law of evidence lays down that a confession must be voluntary, *i.e.* it must not be obtained by force, threats, or inducement, since in such cases there is always the danger that such confessions may be false. That this is the principle seems to emerge from the fact that where the confession is obtained by fraud (as opposed to threats or inducement) it is not thereby excluded, because it is not thereby any the more likely to be untrue.[3] A confession that is involuntary, however, in that it is obtained by means of hypnosis or truth drugs cannot be excluded on this ground, for so far from the prisoners being induced to speak falsely, it may be that he is being forced to speak the truth. At present, however, medical experts are not agreed as to the success of hypnosis or the truth drug.[4] The former, it is suggested, involves the danger that the accused may agree to anything that is suggested to him. A confession made while drunk has been received in evidence,[5] but in an American case

---

[1] Wigmore, *op. cit.*, s. 500. *Cp.*, Gardiner & Lansdown, *South African Criminal Law and Procedure* (6th ed.), I, pp. 597, 603, 605; in S. Africa confessions to be admissible, must be made by the accused in sound and sober senses. But *cf. R. v. Lincoln*, 1950 P.H., H. 68 (A.D.) Contrast Indian Evidence Act, 1872, s. 29—a confession is not irrelevant because the accused is drunk or has been deceived.

[2] Wigmore, *op. cit.*, s. 841; Indian Evidence Act, 1872, s. 29.

[3] See Inbau, *Journal of Criminal Law and Criminology* (1934), XXIV, 1153; Mosier & Hames, *ibid.* (1935), XXVI, 431.

[4] In *R. v. Booher*, [1928] 4 D.L.R. 795 a confession following an alleged hypnotic suggestion was excluded.

[5] *Vaughan's Trial* (1696), 13 How. St. Tr. 507; *R. v. Spilsbury* (1835), 7 C. & P. 187.

where the Sheriff deliberately made a prisoner drunk in order to obtain the confession, it was excluded.[1] This suggests the existence of another principle, that confessions obtained by removing from the defendant any choice as to what he says, should be excluded, not because they are any the less likely to be true, but because of the interference with personal liberty. To allow in evidence confessions obtained in such a manner would not only be serving to facilitate just the sort of police activity which the courts are astute to prevent, but would be inconsistent with the general principle of our legal system, which gives the prisoner the choice of whether to give evidence in court or not. It would be inconsistent with this principle to force the prisoner to make a confession and give evidence against himself outside the court, when you cannot force him to give evidence in the witness box. Indeed, in England, the Judges' rules require that a prisoner should first be cautioned that he need not say anything.[2] To get a confession from him against his will (even though the confession were clearly true) would contravene this principle of giving the prisoner the option of silence.

CONCLUSION

In conclusion, it may be said:

(1) that the correct definition of the word 'act' is to be found by looking at the use made of the word by lawyers. It is used partly to mark certain distinctions and partly to ascribe responsibility.

(2) that this question should be kept separate from the other question, namely, in what circumstances does an act or omission fail to attract liability (criminal or civil) on the ground that it is involuntary. The answer to this may be found by examining the types of behaviour recognized as involuntary, by searching for a connecting quality, and by considering how far different branches of the law treat such involuntary behaviour

---

[1] *McNutt* v. *State* (1903), 68 Nebr. 207.
[2] Archbold, *Criminal Pleading, Evidence and Practice* (33rd ed.), p. 414, Rules 4 & 5. See Silving (1956), 69 Harv. L.R. 693.

differently from normal behaviour. The common quality connecting all these types of behaviour would seem to be inability to control one's bodily movements, *i.e.* in the case of an act, inability to avoid doing it; in the case of an omission, inability to do the act prescribed by law, provided that this inability is not the result of previous behaviour which was under the actor's control. How far the law treats, or ought to treat, such behaviour differently depends upon the purposes and principles of different branches of the law. It must be remembered that the considerations to be born in mind in criminal cases are not necessarily the same as in actions in tort or in divorce, or yet again in the cases referred to above raised by the law of evidence.

CHAPTER II

Negligence, *Mens Rea* and Criminal Responsibility

by H. L. A. Hart

'I DIDN'T *mean* to do it: I just didn't think.' 'But you should have thought.' Such an exchange, perhaps over the fragments of a broken vase destroyed by some careless action, is not uncommon; and most people would think that, in ordinary circumstances, such a rejection of 'I didn't think' as an excuse is quite justified. No doubt many of us have our moments of scepticism about both the justice and the efficacy of the whole business of blaming and punishment; but, if we are going in for the business at all, it does not appear unduly harsh, or a sign of archaic or unenlightened conceptions of responsibility, to include gross, unthinking carelessness among the things for which we blame and punish. This does not seem like the 'strict liability' which has acquired such odium among Anglo-American lawyers. There seems a world of difference between punishing people for the harm they unintentionally but carelessly cause, and punishing them for the harm which no exercise of reasonable care on their part could have avoided.

So 'I just didn't think' is not in ordinary life, in ordinary circumstances, an excuse; nonetheless it has its place in the rough assessments which we make, outside the law, of the gravity of different offences which cause the same harm. To break your Ming china, deliberately or intentionally, is worse than to knock it over while waltzing wildly round the room and not thinking of what might get knocked over. Hence, shewing that the damage was not intentional, but the upshot of thoughtlessness or carelessness, has its relevance as a mitigating factor affecting the quantum of blame or punishment.

THE CRIMINAL LAW

These rough discriminations of ordinary life are worked out with more precision in the criminal law, and most modern writers would agree with the following distinctions and terminology. 'Inadvertent negligence' is to be discriminated not only from deliberately and intentionally doing harm but also from 'recklessness', that is, wittingly flying in the face of a substantial, unjustified risk, or the conscious creation of such a risk. The force of the word 'inadvertent' is to emphasize the exclusion both of the intention to do harm and the appreciation of the risk; most writers, after stressing this point, then use 'negligence' simply for inadvertent negligence.[1] Further, within the sphere of inadvertent negligence, different degrees are discriminated: 'gross negligence' is usually said to be required for criminal liability in contrast with something less ('ordinary' or 'civil' negligence) which is enough for civil liability.

In Anglo-American law there are a number of statutory offences in which negligence, in the sense of a failure to take reasonable precautions against harm, unaccompanied either by intention to do harm or an appreciation of the risk of harm, is made punishable. In England, the Road Traffic Act, 1930, affords the best known illustration: under section 12 driving without due care and attention is a summary offence even though no harm ensues. In other jurisdictions, criminal codes often contain quite general provisions penalizing those who 'negligently hurt' or cause bodily harm by negligence.[2] *Pace* one English authority, Dr. Turner (whose views are examined in detail below), the Common Law as distinct from statute also

---

[1] This terminology is used by Glanville Williams, *Criminal Law*, ch. 3, p. 82 *et seq.*, and also by the American Law Institute Draft Model Penal Code s. 2.0.2 (Tentative Draft, p. 12 and Comment *ibid.*, pp. 126–127). So, too, Cross and Jones who also use 'criminal negligence' to include both 'recklessness' and gross inadvertent negligence (*Introduction to Criminal Law* (4th ed.), pp. 47, 48).

[2] See for these and other cases Glanville Williams, *op. cit.*, pp. 97–98, n. 13.

admits a few crimes,[1] including manslaughter, which can be committed by inadvertent negligence if the negligence is sufficiently 'gross'.[2] It is, however, the case that a number of English and American writers on criminal law feel uneasy about different aspects of negligence. Dr. Glanville Williams[3] thinks that its punishment cannot be justified either on a retributive or a deterrent basis. Professor Jerome Hall[4] who thinks that moral culpability is the basis of criminal responsibility and punishment should be confined to 'intentional or reckless doing of a morally wrong act', disputes both the efficacy and justice of the punishment of negligence.

In this essay I shall consider a far more thorough-going form of scepticism. It is to be found in Dr. Turner's famous essay *The Mental Element in Crimes at Common Law*.[5] There he makes three claims: first, that negligence has no place in the Common Law as a basis of criminal responsibility, and so none in the law of manslaughter; secondly, that the idea of degrees of negligence and so of gross negligence is nonsensical; thirdly (and

---

[1] Other common law crimes commonly cited are non-repair of a highway and public nuisance. Besides these there are more important controversial cases including certain forms of murder (*R. v. Ward*, [1956] 1 Q.B. 351) Cross and Jones, *op. cit.*, 48–52.

[2] See Cross and Jones, *op. cit.*, pp. 145–149. The American Law Institute accepts this view of the English law of manslaughter (Tentative Draft 9, p. 50) but advocates treatment of negligent homicide as an offence of lower degree than manslaughter. Glanville Williams, *op. cit.*, p. 88 (s. 29) after stating that manslaughter 'can be committed by inadvertent negligence for the accused need not have foreseen the likelihood of *death*' says that the 'ordinary formulations' leave in doubt the question whether foresight of some bodily harm (not necessarily serious injury or death) is required for manslaughter. He describes as 'not altogether satisfactory' the cases usually taken to establish that no such foresight is required viz. *Burdee* (1916), 86 L.J. K.B. 871, 12 Cr. App. Rep. 153; *Pittwood* (1902), 19 T.L.R. 37; *Benge* (1865), 4 F. & F. 504; *John Jones* (1874), 12 Cox 628. Of *Bateman* (1925), 28 Cox 33; 19 Cr. App. Rep. 8 he says 'it may be questioned whether [this] does not extend the law of manslaughter too widely' and thinks in spite of *Andrews* v. *D.P.P.*, [1937] A.C. 583 that the issue is still open for the House of Lords.

[3] *Op. cit.*, pp. 98–99.

[4] *Principles of Criminal Law*, pp. 149, 166, 167, 245. Professor Herbert Wechsler (Reporter in the A.L.I. Draft Model Penal Code) rejects this criticism and holds that punishment for conduct which inadvertently creates improper risks 'supplies men with additional motives to take care before acting to use their faculties and to draw on their experience in gauging the potentialities of contemplated conduct'. Tentative Draft 4, p. 126.

[5] *The Modern Approach to Criminal Law* (1945), p. 195.

most important), that to detach criminal responsibility from what he terms 'foresight of consequences', in order to admit negligence as a sufficient basis of such responsibility is necessarily to revert to a system of 'absolute' or strict liability in which no 'subjective element' is required.

Dr. Turner's essay has of course been very influential: he has reaffirmed the substance of its doctrines in his editions both of Kenny[1] and Russell.[2] This, however, is not my reason for submitting his essay to a fresh scrutiny so long after its publication. My reason is that his arguments have a general interest and importance quite independent of his conclusions about the place of negligence in the Common Law. I shall argue that they rest on a mistaken conception both of the way in which mental or 'subjective' elements are involved in human action, and of the reasons why we attach the great importance which we do to the principle that liability to criminal punishment should be conditional on the presence of a mental element. These misconceptions have not been sufficiently examined: yet they are I think widely shared and much encouraged by our traditional legal ways of talking about the relevance of the mind to responsibility. Dr. Turner's arguments are singularly clear and uncompromising; even if I am right in thinking them mistaken his mistakes are illuminating ones. So much cannot always be said for the truths uttered by other men.

Before we reach the substance of the matter one tiresome question of nomenclature must be got out of the way. This concerns the meaning of the phrase *'mens rea'*. Dr. Turner, as we shall see, confines this expression to a combination of two elements, one of which is the element required if the accused's conduct is to be 'voluntary', the other is 'foresight' of the consequences of conduct. Dr. Glanville Williams, although he deprecates the imposition of criminal punishment for negligence, does not describe it or (apparently) think of it, as Dr. Turner does, as a form of 'strict' or 'absolute' liability; nonetheless, though not including it under the expression 'strict liabil-

---

[1] Kenny's *Outlines of Criminal Law* (17th ed.), pp. 33–35, 172–174.
[2] Russell on Crime (11th ed.), pp. 46–47, 53–56, 60–66.

ity', he excludes it from the scope of the term '*mens rea*', which he confines to intention and recklessness. Judicial pronouncements, though no very careful ones, can be cited on either side.[1]

There is, I think, much to be said in mid-twentieth century in favour of extending the notion of '*mens*' beyond the 'cognitive' element of knowledge or foresight, so as to include the capacities and powers of normal persons to think about and control their conduct: I would therefore certainly follow Stephen and others and include negligence in '*mens rea*' because, as I argue later, it is essentially a culpable failure to exercise such capacities. But this question of nomenclature is not important so long as it is seen for what it is, and not allowed either to obscure or prejudge the issue of substance. For the substantial issue is not whether negligence should be *called* '*mens rea*'; the issue is whether it is true that to admit negligence as a basis of criminal responsibility is *eo ipso* to eliminate from the conditions of criminal responsibility the subjective element which, according to modern conceptions of justice, the law should require. Is its admission tantamount to that 'strict' liability which we now generally hold odious and tolerate with reluctance?

VOLUNTARY CONDUCT AND FORESIGHT OF CONSEQUENCES

According to Dr. Turner, the subjective element required for responsibility for common law crimes consists of two distinct items specified in the second and third of three general rules which he formulates.

'Rule I—It must be proved that the conduct of the accused person caused the *actus reus*.

Rule II—It must be proved that this conduct was *voluntary*.

Rule III—It must be proved that the accused person *realised*. *at the time* that his conduct would, or might *produce results of a*

---

[1] See Glanville Williams, *op. cit.*, p. 87, n. 12. Examples on each side are Shearman J. in *Allard* v. *Selfridge*, [1925] 1 K.B. 129, at p. 137. ('The true translation of that phrase is criminal intention or an intention to do the act which is made penal by statute or common law') and Fry L.J. in *Lee* v. *Dangar, Grant & Co.*, [1892] 2 Q.B. 337, at p. 350. 'A criminal mind or that negligence which is itself criminal' See also for a more discursive statement *R.* v. *Bateman* (1925), 19 Cr. App. Rep. 8 or 133 L.T. 730 *per* Hewart, L.C.J.

certain kind, in other words that he must have foreseen that certain consequences were likely to follow on his acts or omissions. The extent to which this foresight of consequences must have extended is fixed by law and differs in the case of each specific crime. . . .'[1]

We shall be mainly concerned with Rule III—as is Dr. Turner's essay. But something must be said about the stipulation in Rule II that the accused's 'conduct' must be 'voluntary'. Dr. Turner himself considers that the truth contained in his Rule III has been obscured because the mental element required to make conduct voluntary has not been discriminated as a separate item in *mens rea*. I, on the other hand, harbour the suspicion that a failure on Dr. Turner's part to explore properly what is involved in the notion of 'voluntary conduct' is responsible for much that seems to me mistaken in his further argument.

Certainly it is not easy to extract either from this essay or from Dr. Turner's editions of Kenny or Russell what is meant by 'conduct', and what the mental element is which makes conduct 'voluntary'. At first sight Dr. Turner's doctrine on this matter looks very like the old simple Austinian[2] theory that what we normally speak of and think of as actions (killing, hitting, etc.) must be divided into two parts (*a*) the 'act' or initiating movement of the actor's body or (in more extreme versions) a muscular contraction, (*b*) the consequences of the 'act'; so that an 'act' is voluntary when and only when it is caused by a 'volition' which is a desire for the movement (or muscular contraction). But such an identification of Dr. Turner's 'conduct' with the Austinian 'act' (or movement of the body), and the mental element which makes it voluntary with the Austinian volition or desire for movement, is precluded by two things. First, Dr. Turner says conduct includes not only physical acts but omissions. Secondly, though 'conduct' is always something less than the *actus reus* which is its 'result' (*e.g.* killing in murder) it is by no means confined by him as

---

[1] *The Modern Approach to Criminal Law* (1945), p. 199.
[2] Austin, *Lectures on Jurisprudence* (5th ed.), Lecture XVIII.

'act' is by Austin to the mere initiating movement of the actor's body. Dr. Turner tells us that 'by definition *conduct*, as such, cannot be criminal'.[1] He also explains that 'conduct is of course itself a series of deeds, each of which is the result of those which have come before it; but at some stage in this series a position of affairs may be brought into existence which the governing power in the state regards as so harmful as to call for repression by the crinimal law. It is this point of selection by the law, this designation of an event as an *actus reus*, which for the purposes of our jurisprudence marks the distinction between *conduct* and *deed.*'[2]

About the mental element required to make conduct voluntary, Dr. Turner tells us[3] only that it is a 'mental attitude to [his] conduct' (as distinct from the consequences of conduct) and that if conduct is to be voluntary 'it is essential that the conduct should have been the result of the exercise of the will'. He does however give us examples of involuntary conduct in a list not meant to be exhaustive 'for example, if *B* holds a weapon and *A*, against *B*'s will, seizes his hand, and the weapon and therewith stabs *C*; and possibly an act done under hypnotic suggestion or when sleep-walking or by pure accident. In certain cases of insanity, infancy and drunkenness the same defence may be successfully raised.'[4]

This account of voluntary conduct presents many difficulties. What is it for conduct to be 'the result of the exercise of the will'? Must the actor desire or will only the initiating movement of his body or the whole course of 'conduct' short of the point when it becomes an *actus reus*? And how does this account apply to omissions, as Dr. Turner asserts it does? How can we draw in the case of omissions the distinction between the course of conduct and the *actus reus* which is said to be its 'result'? The examples given suggest that Dr. Turner is here grossly hampered by traces of the old psychology of 'act' and 'volition', and no satisfactory account of what it is which makes 'conduct'

---

[1] *Op. cit.*, p. 240.   [2] *Op. cit.*, p. 239.   [3] Kenny (17th ed.), p. 27.
[4] *The Modern Approach to Criminal Law* (1945), p. 204. See the further examples suggested in Kenny (17th ed.), p. 26–27: *viz.*, when harm 'results from a man's movements in an epileptic seizure or while suffering from St. Vitus's Dance'.

voluntary or involuntary, capable of covering both acts and omissions can be given in his terminology of 'states of mind', or 'mental attitude'. What is required (as a minimum) is the notion of a general *ability* or *capacity* to control bodily movements, which is usually present but may be absent or impaired.

But even if we waive these difficulties, Dr. Turner's twofold account of *mens rea* in terms of 'voluntary conduct' and 'foresight of consequences' is at points plainly inadequate. It does not fit certain quite straightforward, familiar cases where criminal responsibility is excluded because of the lack of the appropriate subjective element. Thus it does not, as it stands, accommodate the case of mistake; for a mistaken belief sufficient to exclude liability need not necessarily relate to *consequences*; it may relate to *circumstances* in which the action is done, or to the character or identity of the thing or person affected. Of course, Dr. Turner in his edition of Kenny under the title of 'Mistake as a Defence at Common Law' discusses well-known cases of mistake such as *Levett's case*,[1] where the innocent victim was killed in mistake for a burglar, and says (in a footnote) that the subjective element in such cases relates to the agent's 'knowledge of the facts upon which he takes action'.[2] He does not think this calls for a modification in his two-limbed general theory of *mens rea*; instead he adopts the view that such mistakes, since they do not relate to consequences, negative an element in the *actus reus* but do not negative *mens rea*. Besides this curious treatment of mistake, there is also the group of defences which Dr. Turner discusses in the same work under the heading of Compulsion,[3] which include marital coercion and duress *per minas*. Here, as the author rightly says, English law is 'both meagre and vague'; nonetheless, confidence in his general definition as an exhaustive account of *mens rea*, has led him into a curious explanation of the theoretical basis of the relevance to responsibility of such matters as coercion or duress. He cites first as a simple example of compulsion the case of 'a powerful man who, seizing the hand of one much weaker

[1] (1638), Cro. Car. 538. [2] *Op. cit.* (17th ed.), p. 53. [3] *Ibid.*, p. 61.

than himself and overcoming his resistance by sheer strength, forces the hand to strike someone else'.[1] Of this case he says, 'the defence . . . must be that the mental element of 'volition' is absent. The accused, in other words, pleads that his conduct was not voluntary'[2] and to explain this he refers back to the earlier account of voluntary conduct which we have discussed. The author then says that compulsion can take other forms than physical force,[3] and he proceeds to discuss under this head obedience to orders, marital coercion, duress, and necessity. It is, however, clear that such defences as coercion or duress (where they are admitted) lie quite outside the ambit of the definition of voluntary *conduct* given by Dr. Turner: they are not just different instances of *movement* which is not voluntary because, like the case of physical compulsion or that of epilepsy cited earlier, the agent has no control over his bodily movements. Defences like duress or coercion refer not to involuntary *movements*, but, as Austin[4] himself emphasized, to other, quite different ways in which an *action* may fail to be voluntary; here the *action* may not be the outcome of the agent's free choice, though the *movements* of the body are not in any way involuntary.

So far, my objection is that Dr. Turner's formulation of the subjective element in terms of the two elements of voluntary conduct and foresight of consequences leads to a mis-assimilation of different cases; as if the difference between an action under duress and involuntary *conduct* lay merely in the kind of compulsion used. But in fact the definition of *mens rea* in terms of voluntary conduct *plus* foresight of consequences, leads Dr. Turner to great incoherence in the division of the ingredients of a crime between *mens rea* and *actus reus*. Thus in discussing the well-known case of *R. v. Prince*[5] (where the accused was found guilty of the statutory offence of taking a girl under 16 out of the possession of her father notwithstanding that he believed on reasonable grounds that she was over 16) Dr.

---

[1] *Ibid.*   [2] *Ibid.*   [3] *Ibid.*

[4] *Op. cit.*, p. 417. Notes to Lecture, XVIII, 'Voluntary—Double Meaning of the word Voluntary'.

[5] (1875), L.R. 2 C.C.R. 154.

Turner examines[1] the argument that the word 'knowingly' might have been read into the section creating the offence (in which case the offence would not have been committed by the prisoner) and says 'this change would not affect the *mens rea* of the accused person, but it would merely add another necessary fact to the *actus reus*, namely the offender's knowledge of the girl's age'. But there is nothing to support[2] this startling view that where knowledge is required as an ingredient of an offence this may be part of the *actus reus*, not of the *mens rea*, except the author's definition of *mens rea* exclusively in terms of the two elements of 'voluntary conduct' and 'foresight of consequences'. If knowledge (the constituent *par excellence* of *mens rea*) may be counted as part of the *actus reus*, it seems quite senseless to insist on any distinction at all between the *actus reus* and the *mens rea*, or to develop a doctrine of criminal responsibility in terms of this distinction.

NEGLIGENCE AND INADVERTENCE

So far it is plain that, quite apart from its exclusion of negligence, the account of the subjective element required for criminal responsibility in terms of the two elements 'voluntary conduct' and 'foresight of consequences' is, at certain points, inadequate. Dr. Turner's arguments against the inclusion of negligence must now be examined. They are most clearly presented by him in connexion with manslaughter. Of this, Dr. Turner says[3] 'a man, to be guilty of manslaughter, must have had in his mind the idea of bodily harm to someone'. On this view, what is known to English law as 'manslaughter by negligence' is misdescribed by the words; and Dr. Turner expressly says that judges in trying cases of manslaughter should avoid all reference to 'negligence' and so far as *mens rea* is concerned should direct the jury to two questions:

---

[1] In 'The Mental Element in Crimes at Common Law': *The Modern Approach to Criminal Law* (1945), p. 219.

[2] There is plain authority against it: see *R.* v. *Tolson* (1889), 23 Q.B.D.168 *per* Stephen J. 'The mental element of most crimes is marked by one of the words "maliciously", "fraudulently", "negligently", or "knowingly".'

[3] *The Modern Approach to Criminal Law* (1945), p. 228.

(1) Whether the accused's conduct was voluntary;

(2) Whether at the time he either intended to inflict on someone physical harm, or foresaw the possibility of inflicting
a physical harm and took the risk of it.[1]

To treat these cases otherwise would, it is suggested, be to
eliminate the element of *mens rea* as an element in criminal
liability and to return to the old rule of strict or absolute liability.

In developing his argument Dr. Turner roundly asserts that
negligence is a state of mind. It is 'the state of mind of a man
who pursues a course of conduct without adverting at all to the
consequences'.[2] Dr. Turner admits that this state of mind may
be 'blameworthy'[3] and ground *civil* liability. Here it is important to pause and note that if anything is 'blameworthy', it is not
the 'state of mind' but the agent's failure to inform himself of
the facts and so *getting into* this 'state of mind'. But, says Dr.
Turner, 'Negligence in its proper meaning of inadvertence
cannot at Common Law amount to *mens rea*',[4] for 'no one
could reasonably contend that a man, in a fit of inadvertence,
could make himself guilty of the following crimes, arson,
burglary, rape, robbery . . . '[5] This of course is quite true; but
proves nothing at all, until it is independently shown that to act
negligently is the same as to act in 'a fit of inadvertence'.
Precisely the same comment applies to the use made by Dr.
Turner of many cases[6] where the judges have insisted that for
criminal responsibility 'mere inadvertence' is not enough.

It is of course most important at this point to realize that the
issue here is *not* merely a verbal one which the dictionary might
settle. Much more is at stake; for Dr. Turner is really attempting by the use of his definitions to establish his general doctrine
that if a man is to be held criminally responsible he must 'have
in his mind the idea of bodily harm to someone', by suggesting
that the only alternative to this is the quite repugnant doctrine
that a man may be criminally liable for mere inadvertence

---

[1] *Ibid.*, p. 231.   [2] *Ibid.*, p. 207.   [3] *Ibid.*, p. 208.   [4] *Ibid.*, p. 209.   [5] *Ibid.*
[6] *E.g.*, *R.* v. *Finney* (1874), 12 Cox 625. See also *R.* v. *Bateman, Andrews* v. *D.P.P.*,
and others discussed *op. cit.*, pp. 216–217.

when, through no failure of his to which the criminal law could attach importance, his mind is a mere blank. This alternative indeed would threaten to eliminate the doctrine of *mens rea*. But we must not be stampeded into the belief that we are faced with this dilemma. For there are not just two alternatives; we can perfectly well both deny that a man may be criminally responsible for 'mere inadvertence' and also deny that he is only responsible if 'he has an idea of harm in his mind to someone'. Thus, to take the familiar example, a workman who is mending a roof in a busy town starts to throw down into the street building materials without first bothering to take the elementary precaution of looking to see that no one is passing at the time. We are surely not forced to choose, as Dr. Turner's argument suggests, between two alternatives: (1) Did he have the idea of harm in his mind? (2) Did he merely act in a fit of inadvertence? Why should we not say that he has been grossly negligent because he has failed, though not deliberately, to take the most elementary of the precautions that the law requires him to take in order to avoid harm to others?

At this point, a careful consideration is needed of the differences between the meaning of expressions like 'inadvertently' and 'while his mind was a blank' on the one hand, and 'negligently' on the other. In ordinary English, and also in lawyers' English, when harm has resulted from someone's negligence, if we say of that person that he has acted negligently we are not thereby *merely* describing the frame of mind in which he acted. 'He negligently broke a saucer' is not the same *kind* of expression as 'He inadvertently broke the saucer'. The point of the adverb 'inadvertently' *is* merely to inform us of the agent's psychological state, whereas if we say 'He broke it negligently' we are not merely adding to this an element of blame or reproach, but something quite specific, *viz.* we are referring to the fact that the agent failed to comply with a standard of conduct with which any ordinary reasonable man *could* and *would* have complied: a standard requiring him to take precautions against harm. The word 'negligently', both in legal and in non-legal contexts, makes an essential reference to an omission to do what is thus required: it is not a flatly descriptive psychological expression like 'his mind was a blank'.

By contrast, if we say of an agent 'He acted inadvertently', this contains no implications that the agent fell below any standard of conduct. Indeed it is most often proffered as an excuse. '*X* hit Smith inadvertently' means that *X*, in the course of doing some other action, (*e.g.* sweeping the floor) through failing to attend to his bodily movements (*e.g.* his attention being distracted) and *a fortiori* not foreseeing the consequences, hit Smith.

There is of course a *connexion*, and an important one, between inadvertence and negligence, and it is this. Very often if we are to comply with a rule or standard requiring us to take precautions against harm we must, before we act, acquire certain information: we must examine or *advert* to the situation and its possible dangers (*e.g.* see if the gun we are playing with is loaded) and watch our bodily movements (handle the gun carefully if it is loaded). But this connexion far from identifying the concepts of negligence and inadvertence shows them to be different. *Through* our negligence in not examining the situation before acting or in attending to it as we act, we may fail to realise the possibly harmful consequences of what we are doing and as to these our mind is in a sense a 'blank'; but the negligence does not, of course, consist in this blank state of mind but in our failure to take precautions against harm by examining the situation. Crudely put, 'negligence' is not the name of 'a state of mind' while 'inadvertence' is.

We must now confront the claim made by Dr. Turner that there is an absurdity in stipulating that a special (gross) degree of negligence is required. 'There can be no different degrees of inadvertence as indicating a state of mind. The man's mind is a blank as to the consequences; his realization of their possibility is nothing and there are no different degrees of nothing,'[1] This *reductio ad absurdum* of the notion of gross negligence depends entirely on the view that negligence is merely a name for a state of mind consisting in the absence of foresight of consequences.

[1] *Op. cit.*, p. 211.

Surely we should require something more to persuade us to drop notions so firmly embedded, not only in the law, but in common speech, as 'very negligent', 'gross carelessness', a 'minor form of negligence'. Negligence is gross if the precautions to be taken against harm are very simple, such as persons who are but poorly endowed with physical and mental capacities can easily take.[1] So, in the workman's case, it was gross negligence not to look and see before throwing off the slates; perhaps it was somewhat less gross (because it required more exertion and thought) to have failed to shout a warning for those not yet in view; it was less gross still to have failed to have put up some warning notice in the street below.

NEGLIGENCE AND NORMAL CAPACITIES

At the root of Dr. Turner's arguments there lie, I think, certain unexamined assumptions as to what the mind is and why its 'states' are relevant to responsibility. Dr. Turner obviously thinks that unless a man 'has in his mind the idea of harm to someone' it is not only bad law, but morally objectionable as a recourse to strict or absolute liability, to punish him. But here we should ask why, in or out of law courts, we should attach this crucial importance to foresight of consequences, to the 'having of an idea in the mind of harm to someone'. On what theory of responsibility is it that the presence of this particular item of mental furniture is taken to be something which makes it perfectly satisfactory to hold that the agent is responsible for what he did? And why should we necessarily conclude that in its absence an agent cannot be decently held responsible? I suspect, in Dr. Turner's doctrine, a form of the ancient belief that possession of knowledge of consequences is a necessary and sufficient condition of the capacity for self-control, so that if the agent knows the consequences of his action we are bound to say 'he could have helped it'; and, by parity of reasoning, if he does not know the consequences of his action, even though he failed to examine

---

[1] 'It is such a degree of negligence as excludes the loosest degree of care' *per* Hewart C.J. in *R. v. Bateman* (1925), 133 L.T. 730.

or think about the situation before acting, we are bound to say that he could not have helped it.

Neither of these views are acceptable. The first is not only incompatible with what large numbers of scientists and lawyers and plain men now believe about the capacity of human beings for self-control. But it is also true that there is nothing to compel us to say 'He could not have helped it' in *all* cases where a man omits to think about or examine the situation in which he acts and harm results which he has not foreseen. Sometimes we do say this and should say it; this is so when we have evidence, from the personal history of the agent or other sources, that his memory or other faculties were defective, or that he could not distinguish a dangerous situation from a harmless one, or where we know that repeated instructions and punishment have been of no avail. From such evidence we may conclude that he was unable to attend to, or examine the situation, or to assess its risks; often we find this so in the case of a child or a lunatic. We should wish to distinguish from such cases the case of a signalman whose duty it is to signal a train if the evidence clearly shows that he has the normal capacities of memory and observation and intelligence. He may say after the disaster, 'Yes, I went off to play a game of cards. I just didn't stop to think about the 10.15 when I was asked to play.' Why, in such a case, should we say 'He could not help it—because his mind was a blank as to the consequences'? The kind of evidence we have to go upon in distinguishing those omissions to attend to, or examine, or think about the situation and assess its risks before acting which we treat as culpable, from those omissions (*e.g.* on the part of infants or mentally deficient persons) for which we do not hold the agent responsible, is not different from the evidence we have to use whenever we say of anybody who has failed to do something 'He could not have done it' or 'He could have done it'. The evidence in such cases relates to the general capacities of the agent; it is drawn, not only from the facts of the instant case, but from many sources, such as his previous behaviour, the known effect upon him of instruction or punishment, etc. Only a theory that mental operations like attending to, or thinking about, or examining a situation are somehow 'either there or not there', and so utterly outside our control, can lead to the theory that we are *never* responsible if, like the signalman who forgets to pull the signal, we fail to think or remember. And this theory of the uncontrollable character of mental operations would, of course, be fatal to responsibility for even the most cold-blooded, deliberate action performed by an agent with the maximum 'foresight'. For just as the signalman, inspired by Dr. Turner's argument, might say 'My mind was a blank' or 'I just forgot' or 'I just didn't think, I could not help not thinking' so the cold-blooded murderer might say 'I just decided to kill; I couldn't help deciding'. In the latter case we do not normally allow this plea because we know from the general history of the agent, and others like him, that he could have acted differently. This general evidence is what is relevant to the question of responsibility, not the mere presence or absence of foresight. We should have doubts, which now find legal expression in the category of diminished responsibility, even in the case of deliberate murder, if it were shown that in spite of every warning and every danger and without a comprehensible motive the agent had deliberately and repeatedly planned and committed murder. After all, a hundred times a day persons are blamed outside the law courts for not being more careful, for being inattentive and not stopping to think; in particular cases, their history or mental or physical examination may show that they could not have done what they omitted to do. In such cases they are not responsible; but if anyone is ever responsible for anything, there is no general reason why men should not be responsible for such omissions to think, or to consider the situation and its dangers before acting.

SUBJECTIVE AND OBJECTIVE

Excessive distrust of negligence and excessive confidence in the respectability of 'foresight of harm' or 'having the thought of harm on the mind' as a ground of responsibility have their roots in a common misunderstanding. Both oversimplify the character of the subjective element required in those whom we punish if it is to be morally tolerable according to common notions of justice to punish them. The reason why, according to modern ideas, strict liability is odious, and appears as a sacrifice of a valued principle which we should make, if at all, only for some over-riding social good, is not merely because it amounts, as it does, to punishing those who did not at the time of acting 'have in their minds' the elements of foresight or desire for muscular movement. These psychological elements are not *in themselves* crucial though they are important as aspects of responsibility. What is crucial is that those whom we punish should have, when they acted, the normal capacities, physical and mental, for doing what the law requires and abstaining from what it forbids, and a fair opportunity to exercise these capacities. Where these are absent as they are in different ways in the varied cases of accident, mistake, paralysis, reflex action, coercion, insanity, etc., the moral protest is that it is morally wrong to punish because 'he could not have helped it' or 'he could not have done otherwise' or 'he had no real choice'. But, as we have seen, there is no reason (unless we are to reject the whole business of responsibility and punishment) *always* to make this protest when someone who 'just didn't think' is punished for carelessness. For in some cases at least we may say 'he could have thought about what he was doing' with just as much rational confidence as one can say of any intentional wrongdoing 'he could have done otherwise'.

Of course, the law compromises with competing values over this matter of the subjective element in responsibility as it does over other matters. All legal systems temper their respect for the principle that persons should not be punished if they could not have done otherwise *i.e.*, had neither the capacity nor a fair opportunity to act otherwise. Sometimes this is done in deference to genuine practical difficulties of proof; sometimes it represents an obstinate refusal to recognise that human beings may not be able to control their conduct though they know what they are doing. Difficulties of proof may lead one system to limit consideration of the subjective element to the question whether a person acted intentionally and had volitional control of his muscular movements; other systems may let the inquiry go further and, in relation to some offences, consider whether the accused had, owing to some external cause, lost the power of such control, or whether his capacity to control was 'diminished' by mental abnormality or disease. In these last cases, exemplified in 'provocation' and 'diminished responsibility', if we punish at all we punish *less*, on the footing that, though the accused's capacity to self-control was not absent, its exercise was a matter of abnormal difficulty. He is punished in effect for a *culpable* loss of control; and this too is involved when punishment for negligence is morally justifiable.

The most important compromise which legal systems make over the subjective element consists in its adoption of what has been unhappily termed the 'objective standard'. This may lead to an individual being treated for the purposes of conviction and punishment as if he possessed capacities for control of his conduct which he did not possess, but which an ordinary or reasonable man possesses and would have exercised. The expression 'objective' and its partner 'subjective' are unhappy because, as far as negligence is concerned, they obscure the real issue. We may be tempted to say with Dr. Turner that just because the negligent man does not have 'the thought of harm in his mind', to hold him responsible for negligence is necessarily to adopt an objective standard and to abandon the 'subjective' element in responsibility. It then becomes vital to distinguish this (mistaken) thesis from the position brought about by the use of objective standards in the application of laws which make negligence criminally punishable. For, when negligence is made criminally punishable, this itself leaves open the question: whether, before we punish, both or only the first of the following two questions must be answered affirmatively:

(i)   Did the accused fail to take those precautions which any reasonable man with normal capacities would in the circumstances have taken?

(ii) Could the accused, given his mental and physical capacities, have taken those precautions?

One use of the dangerous expressions 'objective' and 'subjective' is to make the distinction between these two questions; given the ambiguities of those expressions, this distinction would have been more happily expressed by the expressions 'invariant' standard of care, and 'individuated conditions of liability'. It may well be that, even if the 'standard of care' is pitched very low so that individuals are held liable only if they fail to take very elementary precautions against harm, there will still be some unfortunate individuals who, through lack of intelligence, powers of concentration, memory, or clumsiness, could not attain even this low standard. If our conditions of liability are invariant and not flexible, *i.e.* if they are not adjusted to the capacities of the accused, then some individuals will be held liable for negligence though they could not have helped their failure to comply with the standard. In *such* cases, indeed, criminal responsibility will be made independent of any 'subjective element': since the accused could not have conformed to the required standard. But this result is nothing to do with negligence being taken as a basis of criminal liability; precisely the same result will be reached if, in considering whether a person acted intentionally, we were to attribute to him foresight of consequences which a reasonable man would have foreseen but he did not. 'Absolute liability' results not from the admission of the principle that one who has been grossly negligent is criminally responsible for the harm that results even if 'he had no idea in his mind of harm to anyone', but from the refusal in the application of this principle to consider the capacities of an individual who has fallen below the standard of care.

It is of course quite arguable that no legal system could afford to individuate the conditions of liability so far as to discover and excuse all those who could not attain the average or reasonable man's standard. It may, in practice, be impossible to do more than excuse those who suffer from gross forms of incapacity, *viz.* infants, or the insane, or those afflicted with recognizably inadequate powers of control over their movements, or who are clearly unable to detect or extricate themselves from situations in which their disability may work harm. Some confusion is, however, engendered by certain inappropriate ways of describing these excusable cases which we are tempted to use in a system which, like our own, defines negligence in terms of what the reasonable man would do. We may find ourselves asking whether the infant, the insane, or those suffering from paralysis did all that a reasonable man would *in the circumstances* do, taking 'circumstances' (most queerly) to include personal qualities like being an infant, insane or paralysed. This paradoxical approach leads to many difficulties. To avoid them we need to hold apart the primary question (1) What *would* the reasonable man with ordinary capacities have done in these circumstances? from the second question (2), *Could* the accused with *his* capacities have done that? Reference to such factors as lunacy or disease should be made in answering only the second of these questions. This simple, and surely realistic, approach avoids difficulties which the notion of individualizing the standard of care has presented for certain writers; for these difficulties are usually created by the mistaken assumption that the only way of allowing for individual incapacities is to treat them as part of the 'circumstances' in which the reasonable man is supposed to be acting. Thus Dr. Glanville Williams says that if 'regard must be had to the make-up and circumstances of the particular offender, one would seem on a determinist view of conduct to be pushed to the conclusion that there is no standard of conduct at all. For if every characteristic of the individual is taken into account, including his heredity the conclusion is that he could not help doing what he did.'[1]

But 'determinism' presents no special difficulty here. The question is whether the individual had the capacity (inherited or not) to act otherwise than he did, and 'determinism' has no relevance to the case of one who is accused of negligence which it does not have to one accused of intentionally killing. Dr. Williams supports his arguments by discussion of the case of a motorist whom a blow or illness has rendered incapable of driving properly. His conclusion, tentatively expressed, is that if the blow or illness occurred long ago or in infancy he should not be

[1] *Op. cit.*, p. 82.

excused, but if it occurred shortly before the driving in respect of which he is charged he should. Only thus, it seems to him, can any standard of conduct be preserved. But there seems no need to make this extraordinary distinction. Again, the first question which we should ask is: What *would* a reasonable driver with normal capacities have done? The second question is whether or not the accused driver had at the time he drove the normal capacity of control (either in the actual conduct of the vehicle in driving or in the decision to engage in driving). If he was incapable, the date recent or otherwise of the causal origin of the incapacity is surely beside the point, except that if it was of long standing, this would suggest that he knew of it and was neglectful in driving with at knowledge.

Equally obscure to me are the reasons given by Dr. Williams for doubting the efficacy of punishment for negligence. He asks, 'Even if a person admits that he occasionally makes a negligent mistake, how, in the nature of things, can punishment for inadvertence serve to deter?'.[1] But if this question is meant as an argument, it rests on the old, mistaken identification of the 'subjective element' involved in negligence with 'a blank mind', whereas it is in fact a failure to exercise the capacity to advert to, and to think about and control, conduct and its risks. Surely we have plenty of empirical evidence to show, as Professor Wechsler has said, that 'punishment may stimulate persons to make a better use of the faculties which they have in the past failed to exercise'. Again there is no difficulty here peculiar to negligence, though of course we can doubt the efficacy of any punishment to deter any kind of offence.

I should add (out of abundant caution) that I have not been concerned here to advocate punishing negligence, though, perhaps, better acquaintance with motoring offences would convert me into a passionate advocate. My concern has been to show only that the belief that criminal responsibility for negligence is a form of strict or absolute liability, rests on a confused conception of the 'subjective element' and its relation to responsibility.

[1] *Op. cit.*, p. 92.

CHAPTER III

Means, Motives, and Interests in the Law of Torts

by J. F. Lever

THIS ESSAY is concerned with the principles which govern tortious liability where one man has done some act knowing that it would inflict loss or harm on another in circumstances in which mere negligence would not be sufficient to raise liability. A common element in many, though not all, the situations which will be discussed is the fact that the loss to the plaintiff is due to the actor's having in some way caused third parties to behave in a manner detrimental to the plaintiff.

In all cases of the knowing infliction of loss four considerations have to be borne in mind, depending on the particular circumstances to a greater or less extent, in determining whether or not legal liability exists. First, it is necessary to consider the means the actor employed to attain his object—whether, for example, these be the peaceful persuasion of third parties to exercise their rights, or, on the other hand, the commission of torts against those third parties. The second consideration is the interest of the actor, if any, in furtherance of which the act was done, and this we can only discover by inquiring into the motive of the actor. Thirdly, the requirements of public policy, using that expression in a narrow sense, will have to be considered. And finally, the interest of the plaintiff, which the actor has infringed, will be relevant: thus a different degree of protection is given to bodily security from that afforded to mere economic interest; or, to take another example, a plaintiff's interest in existing contractual relations is more strictly safe-

guarded than that in the prospective advantage which he is
likely to gain from contracts not yet in existence.

I. THE MEANS EMPLOYED

The classification of rights into those which are absolute and
those which are qualified is relevant to a consideration of the
means employed by an actor when he knowingly inflicts harm
upon another. When we say that a person has a right to do
something, we generally mean, in relation to the law of tort, that
if, in doing it, he causes harm to another, he will not be liable
to that other. But one can seldom, if ever, state categorically
that a person has a right to do any particular act, such as to
sink shafts on his land, for his right to do so may be qualified in
one or both of two different ways. First, the right may be qualified by a consideration of the *motive* with which it was exercised.
Thus one's right to prosecute another without reasonable
cause is qualified by the fact that one's motive must have been
the bringing of a believed criminal to book. Secondly, the right
to do something may be qualified by a consideration of *what
sort of harm* is caused to another by the doing of the act. For
example, in English law one has apparently a right to build on
one's land without qualification as to motive, but one's right
is subject to the qualification that one does not thereby infringe
a neighbour's easement of light. But it is not every sort of loss
from which one's neighbour is protected by the possession of an
easement or natural right; as we shall see, one's building operations may, with impunity, deprive him of his view.

Where the qualification of the right is of the second sort only,
we sometimes say that the right is absolute, meaning thereby
only that it is not qualified by any considerations of the motive
with which the act was done. We shall consider the motives
and interests which qualify rights in parts II and IV of this
essay.

But in certain cases the means employed knowingly to inflict
loss upon another are such that they cannot constitute the
exercise of a right, whether absolute or qualified. In these cases
the means are, without qualification, unlawful, and no matter

why the actor chose to act as he did, nor what interest was infringed, the act is a tort.[1]

If the means employed to attain an object at the expense of another, or simply to harm him, are in themselves wrongful towards a third party, *e.g.* a tort against him, then the infliction of the harm amounts to a tort against the party aimed at. And coercion by force[2] or fraudulent deception of third parties in order to strike at another fall into this category of unlawful acts. The origin of this doctrine is to be found in the old cases of *Garret* v. *Taylor*[3] and *Tarleton* v. *M'Gawley*,[4] together with dicta of Holt C. J. in *Keeble* v. *Hickeringill*.[5] In these cases it was held to be a tort to attempt to advance one's own trade interests at the expense of a competitor by frightening his customers away, in the one case by threats to mayhem them and vex them with suits, and in the other by firing a cannon at them and killing one of their number.

A more recent example is provided by *J. Lyons and Sons* v. *Wilkins*[6] where the Court of Appeal held, both before and after the House of Lords decision in *Allen* v. *Flood*,[7] that the picketing of *S*'s house by the defendants, to prevent *S* from continuing to make goods for the plaintiffs, was a wrong against the plaintiffs since the method adopted by the defendants amounted to a criminal offence, or alternatively to a Common Law nuisance, that is to say a tort, against *S*.[8]

---

[1] But even where the means used are referred to as 'unlawful without qualification' the exception must be recognized that, to the extent that necessity is a defence, (see *infra*, p. 58, n. 3) the unlawfulness of the means could be qualified thereby.

[2] See *Allen* v. *Flood*, [1898] A.C. 1, at p. 18.   [3] (1620), Cro. Jac. 567.

[4] (1793), 1 Peake 270.   [5] (1705), 11 East 574 n., at p. 576.

[6] [1896] 1 Ch. 811 (C.A.), interim injunction granted; [1899] 1 Ch. 255 (C.A.), injunction made perpetual.

[7] [1898] A.C. 1.

[8] And see *Conway* v. *Wade*, [1909] A.C. 506, where the plaintiff relied on the defendant's threats against third parties. (But Lord Collins' contention, at p. 519, that the House was not there concerned with the question of whether a cause of action existed at all, may be correct). See also *Ajello* v. *Worsley*, [1898] 1 Ch. 274, for an example on the other side of the line. The defendant there knowingly harmed the plaintiff's business by misleading the public. The action only failed because the cause of the plaintiff's loss could not be said to be the defendant's deception of members of the public, since the loss would have occurred equally whether the statement had been true or false. Stirling J.'s reliance on this argu-

In these cases, because of the means employed, the defendant's desire to further his own trade interests was no defence. Another leading case which illustrates this principle is *G. W. K., Ltd.* v. *Dunlop Rubber Co., Ltd.*[1] In that case the first plaintiffs, manufacturers of motor-cars, had agreed with the second plaintiffs, tyre manufacturers, that all G. W. K. motor cars should be fitted with the latters' tyres whenever the cars were exhibited. The first plaintiffs sent two of their cars to an exhibition, and the defendants, the night before the exhibition opened, by a trespass against the first plaintiffs, removed the tyres, which were of the second plaintiffs' manufacture, and replaced them with their own. The issue was whether the second plaintiffs had a cause of action. Lord Hewart C. J. held that they had. Jenkins L. J. in *Thomson (D. C.) and Co., Ltd.* v. *Deakin*[2] regarded *G. W. K.* v. *Dunlop* as turning not upon the use of unlawful means, but upon the defendants' violation of contractual relations between others, closely analogous to inducement of breach of contract.[3]

With respect, it is submitted that such an analysis is unsatisfactory, because it ignores the importance of the means employed and over-emphasizes that of the interest of the victim which is affected. To illustrate this, let us suppose that a photographer, *A*, contracts with a newspaper proprietor, *X*, that he will supply the latter with the first aerial photograph of Luneville, for publication in *X*'s journal. *X* thereupon incurs certain

ment clearly shows that had there been the necessary causal *nexus* the action would have lain.

[1] (1926), 42 T.L.R. 376, 593.

[2] [1952] Ch. 646, at p. 694 (unreserved judgments in interlocutory proceedings). 'Again, so far from persuading or inducing or procuring one of the parties to the contract to break it, the third party may commit an actionable interference with the contract, against the will of both and without the knowledge of either, if with knowledge of the contract he does an act which, if done by one of the parties to it would have been a breach, *G.W.K.* v. *Dunlop*.'

[3] This emphasis of the element of interference with contractual relations, as opposed to the use of unlawful means, was contained in *obiter dicta*, since the decision depends on the failure of the plaintiffs to establish a causal connexion between the defendant's acts and their loss; and since the case concerned an interference with contractual relations, the use of unlawful means not having been proved, it would be wrong to place too great reliance upon *obiter dicta* on the question of what is the position where unlawful means are present but there are not necessarily any contractual relations with which the defendant can interfere.

preparatory expenses. *Y*, knowing of the contract, succeeds in securing, before *A* does so, an aerial photograph of Luneville, which he presents to a rival of *X*'s for publication. It is quite clear from *Thomson* v. *Deakin* itself that *Y* would not here be liable in tort to *X*. Yet he has 'procured' a breach of contract by *A* to as great an extent as Dunlop procured a breach of contract by G. W. K. in *G. W. K.* v. *Dunlop*. The element which is missing in our example is the use of unlawful means. This will be clearly seen if we alter the facts of the illustration by supposing that *A* succeeds in taking the first aerial photograph of Luneville, but that he is deliberately prevented from delivering it to *X*, owing to its theft by *Y* who then gives it to *X*'s rival. Harm having been deliberately inflicted on *X*, there can be no doubt that the addition of the use of unlawful means by *Y* against the photographer, *A*, gives *X* a good cause of action against *Y*.

It is curious that *Allen* v. *Flood*,[1] in which the House of Lords laid down the law about unlawful means in the manner outlined above, should apparently have been so wholly misunderstood by subsequent writers. The House of Lords was not there concerned with establishing the truism that one cannot commit a tort against another, however bad one's motive, unless one commits a tort against that other. The question before the House in that case was whether a person, who deliberately inflicts loss on another for a morally bad purpose or simply for the sake of inflicting that harm, is always liable to the person whom he harms. The decision conclusively lays down that, in English law, there is no such general rule. But the majority who so decided made it clear that the actor will be liable if he uses unlawful means to accomplish his ends, by which their language and the authorities they cited[2] clearly show them to mean

---

[1] [1898] A.C. 1.

[2] *E.g.*, see [1898] A.C. at pp. 97–98, 101, 105 *per* Lord Watson; at pp. 135, 137 *per* Lord Herschell. Lord Morris and Lord Halsbury, two of the dissenting minority, who believed that the defendant was liable, relied on the defendant's misrepresentations to and coercion of the plaintiffs' employers. Lord Shand, one of the majority, specifically answered these arguments by denying, as a matter of fact, that unlawful means were here present, but agreeing that had they been, the plaintiffs would have succeeded (at pp. 162, 165, 167).

methods which constitute torts against third parties, or which are similarly wrongful towards third parties.[1]

II. MOTIVES AND INTERESTS

We now come to consider whether a man's motives for acting in a certain way are relevant to the tortious or non-tortious nature of his act.

Motives

The question why a man has acted in this manner or that may be answered in a number of different ways, of which a 'motive answer' is but one. Thus to the question why *A* went to Brighton we might answer that it was because he had been told that it was a pleasant resort, or because he was tired, or because he was forced to, or because he had got on to the wrong train, or because he wanted to see his mother, or we might even answer briefly that it was because he was angry. By no means all these answers are concerned with motives—for example, one clearly could not say that *A*'s motive for going to Brighton was because he got on to the wrong train.

Motive answers, like other answers to why questions, may be specific or general. Thus, a specific motive answer to a *why* question is '*A* broke open the box because he wanted to see what was inside.' A general answer would be to say that he did it out of curiosity. Answers of the second sort describe fairly common permanent or temporary mental states which, because of their commonness, have a single word to describe them. Answers of the first sort are specific and give us more detailed information about the particular situation in point.

The particular characteristic of the motive answer is that it is forward looking: that is to say, it does not tell us about past or pre-existing facts outside *A*'s mind, in the light of which it is significant to view *A*'s act, but instead about some state of

---

[1] Injurious Falsehood is merely one instance of the knowing infliction of economic loss by unlawful means—that is, by deceitful misrepresentations about the plaintiff to a third party. And the cases of injurious falsehood provide yet further evidence that the existence of a contract between the plantiff and the third party is not essential.

affairs which *A* had in mind at the time of his act and towards which he hoped that it would carry him. Thus, anger, as such, is not usually given as a motive, because a man who is actuated solely by anger is not influenced by a desire to achieve anything; in other words, to say that someone is angry provides a backward looking answer only.

Malice provides a general motive answer in every day speech of two slightly different kinds: it may mean that an act was done in order to hurt another for *no* particular reason at all, or in order to do so for a *morally insufficient* reason. A difficulty appears to arise when we say that *A*'s motive for *hurting B* was malice; but all we are really saying here is that on a forward looking analysis *A* regarded the hurt to *B* as a desirable end in itself, for no reason at all or for a morally insufficient reason.

The law of tort is not concerned with the emotions of one who knowingly inflicts harm on another, but it is concerned with the weighing of the actor's interest against the interest of the person harmed by his act. Motive is therefore only relevant in so far as it provides a forward looking explanation of the actor's behaviour which shows that his act was or was not done in pursuance of some interest of the actor's. Such an interest can then be weighed against the interest of the other which has been infringed.

Interests

This brings us to a consideration of what is an interest. The notions of advantage and detriment are essential to the concept of an interest. We are said to have an interest in something when changes in its state could affect us advantageously or disadvantageously. Thus a man has an interest in his trade relations with his customers since any change in those relations may redound to his advantage or otherwise. The advantage need not be pecuniary; one has an interest in the quiet of one's house because one will suffer if it is shattered by noise or vibration; and one has another interest in holding musical parties at one's house because of the pleasure derived therefrom. For convenience, we classify interests according to common characteristics:

so, for example, we group together those concerning bodily security where the disadvantages envisaged involve physical harm to the person, and those concerning bodily comfort where the harm does not entail actual damage to the body although discomfort is involved.   Motive is therefore only important to the law of tort when it looks forward to a state of affairs in which the actor's interest is important. The motive is as important as the weight which can be given to the interest.

The Effect of Improper Motive

We can now pass on to a brief consideration of how the branch of the law with which we are here concerned in fact takes motives and interests into account. We discussed in Part I, cases in which the means adopted by the actor were unqualifiedly wrong, so that the actor was liable no matter what his motive was. We now come to those cases in which the means he adopts are not unqualifiedly wrong, but are only wrong if the actor behaves with an improper motive. The actor's motive cannot be considered in isolation and without reference to the means employed and the interest of the other which is infringed. This is illustrated by the fact that the actor's pursuit of his trading advantage is a proper motive in, and a good defence to, an action for conspiracy in which he is alleged merely to have combined with others to injure a rival trader;[1] but it is an improper motive and no defence where he has induced another to break his contract with that trader.[2] 'Propriety' of motives is therefore, in law, entirely relative to the means adopted by the actor and the interest he infringes, and has no moral connotation.[3]

The interests in pursuance of which a man may properly act fall into two classes; first there are certain private interests of

---

[1] *Mogul S.S. Co., Ltd.* v. *McGregor Gow and Co.*, [1892] A.C. 25.

[2] *South Wales Miners' Federation* v. *Glamorgan Coal Co., Ltd.*, [1905] A.C. 239; but see Trade Disputes Act, 1906, s. 3.

[3] This makes it clear why it is undesirable to define malice as meaning 'legally improper motive', as to do so either prevents one from saying that absolute rights can be exercised maliciously, or it deprives the notion of propriety of motive of all legal significance.

the actor's which, in some contexts, the law regards with favour; and secondly there are certain such public interests.

(1) RIGHTS OF LANDOWNERS

We discuss first some of the private interests in pursuit of which the law sometimes allows us to inconvenience or harm our neighbours. One example is our interest in living our every-day lives in our own homes and on our own property. Thus if my musical evenings displease my neighbour, that is his misfortune, provided that the volume of sound is not itself unreasonable. But if, not in the course of every-day life, but in order to inconvenience my neighbour, I make the same volume of noise as before, I commit an actionable nuisance.[1] But certain of my neighbour's interests carry greater weight than his comfort, so that if I cause physical damage to his property it is no excuse for me to say that I was merely going about my every-day business.[2] Thus activity on my land, directly causing physical damage to person or property, falls into the same class of nuisance as sounds or smells which are themselves excessive, and which therefore give rise to tortious liability despite even the best of motives.[3]

The precise application of these principles has not yet been fully worked out. One difficulty which arises is exemplified in *Bradford Corporation* v. *Pickles*,[4] although it was not relevant to

---

[1] *Christie* v. *Davey*, [1893] 1 Ch. 316; *Hollywood Silver Fox Farm, Ltd.* v. *Emmett.* [1936] 2 K.B. 468. To give another example, the cries of an ordinary baby in a flat would surely not amount to a nuisance in law; but that does not mean that one is entitled to make a recording of such cries and play them at the same volume in order to annoy the people next door.

[2] *St. Helen's Smelting Co.* v. *Tipping* (1865), 11 H.L.C. 642.

[3] But even where a nuisance does cause damage to property it will be a defence to show that the damage was caused in order to safeguard human lives; 'The safety of human lives belongs to a different scale of values from the safety of property. The two are beyond comparison and the necessity of saving life has at all times been considered a proper ground for inflicting such damage as may be necessary upon another's property.' *per* Devlin J. in *Esso Petroleum Co., Ltd.* v. *Southport Corporation*, [1956] A.C. 218, at p. 228; on the other hand, Devlin J. was 'not prepared to hold without further consideration that a man is entitled to damage the property of another without compensating him merely because the infliction of such damage is necessary in order to save his own property', *ibid.* at p. 227; *Cf., Cope* v. *Sharpe*, [1912] 1 K.B. 496.

[4] [1895] A.C. 587.

the decision there. In that case the defendant's motive in sinking a shaft on his land seems to have been to compel the plaintiffs, whose scheme for a reservoir was thereby interfered with, to buy his land at a generous figure. Could it be said that in such a case the defendant was acting, not in order to cause harm to the plantiffs, but in order to advance his own economic interests, and was therefore in just the same position as someone carrying out drainage works on his land to improve it, but knowing that his neighbour would be damaged thereby? A possible distinction might be drawn between those cases in which a man seeks to advance his own interests *by causing harm to another* and those in which he does so merely in the knowledge that this will incidentally cause harm to another. The distinction depends not on foresight which is present in both cases; rather, it depends on the fact that in the first case the actor would not have acted as he did but for the harm to another which he was thereby trying to cause, (and as a result of causing it, to gain some advantage for himself); while in the second case the actor would have acted as he did even if no harm to another had been likely to ensue.

In *Bradford Corporation* v. *Pickles*[1] it was not necessary to draw the distinction since it was held that, whatever the defendant's motives, the means he employed were the exercise of a right absolute as far as motive was concerned. An alternative way of putting this is to say that one has *under no circumstances* a natural right in water percolating under the land of another. This is a better way of putting it since, if by sinking the shaft, Pickles had disturbed a right of support of the Corporation's, he would certainly have been liable in Nuisance. Thus, it would seem that in English law if a landowner's activities cause no 'escape' from his land onto another's he will be liable, if at all, not on account of the motives with which the acts were done, but only on account of the interest of the plaintiff which is infringed.

Another example of this is provided by one's right to erect a spite fence. A spite fence is a fence erected, not for an ordinary, useful purpose, but solely in order to obscure another's view.

---

[1] [1895] A.C. 587.

In England, unless an easement, such as a right to light, is infringed, one's neighbour has no redress, for one can have no right to a view.[1]

In the United States the right to alter the physical state of one's property has not been so fully protected and is sometimes qualified by considerations of motive, even in the absence of an 'escape'. *Bradford Corporation* v. *Pickles* has not gained universal acceptance and its application by some jurisdictions has been described by one text-book writer as 'a rather stiff-necked adherence to a doctrine which had little to commend it when first announced'.[2] As to the erection of spite fences, the position in the United States is that the motive for the erection of the fence is immaterial when the structure serves a useful purpose,[3] but, although the authorities are conflicting, the trend of recent decisions seems to favour the view that a spite fence which serves no useful or beneficial purpose is unlawful and the aggrieved party can bring an action for nuisance for damages and abatement.[4]

(2) COMPETITION AND CONSPIRACY

To turn now to another field, competition in trade provides an important motive which may justify acts which cause loss to others. So it is a good defence to an action against a group of traders for conspiracy by mere combination if they show that they combined in furtherance of their trade interests.[5] Such a motive makes the combination justifiable in a way in which it would not be were the conspirators acting without having in mind any further object at all other than harm to the plaintiff,[6] or in order to further an interest which the courts were to deem insufficient, such as a mere demonstration of power.[7]

---

[1] 9 Co. Rep., p. 58b; 'That for prospect, which is a matter only of delight, and not of necessity, no action lies for stopping thereof . . . the Law don't give an action for such things of delight'. But this consideration may not apply in the case of easements created *ab homine*: *Re Ellenborough Park*, [1956] Ch. 131.

[2] Powell, *Real Property* (1956), pp. 725, 726.

[3] *Musemeci* v. *Leonardo* (1950), 77 R.I. 255.

[4] Powell, *Real Property* (1956), p. 696.   [5] *The Mogul Case*, [1892] A.C. 25.

[6] *E.g., Huntley* v. *Thornton*, [1957] 1 All E.R. 234.

[7] *Crofter Hand Woven Harris Tweed Co., Ltd.* v. *Veitch*, [1942] A.C. 435.

But, in order to be sufficient justification in an action for conspiracy, the interest in pursuance of which the defendants acted need not necessarily be a material interest, in the sense of being an interest which could be exchanged for cash. The interest, to afford a justification, must be a 'lawful' interest, and its lawfulness is necessarily to be judged in the light of the courts' unstated notions of broad public policy. Thus a combination founded on a dislike of the policy of racial discrimination is not unlawful, at any rate where the defendants include or represent persons of the race discriminated against;[1] whereas where the objects of a combination are the dislike of the race or colour of the plaintiff it is almost certainly unlawful.[2]

There is however no clear authority as to whether those who combine in opposition to a policy of racial discrimination could justify their acts if none of their members were directly affected in the sense of belonging to or being dependent upon the race discriminated against. It may be that, notwithstanding that fact, they would have a lawful interest, albeit a public one shared by the rest of the community.[3]

But is the absence of a desire to further one's own lawful interests relevant to cases where the defendant has acted by himself, without adopting unqualifiedly unlawful means? English law has given a negative answer to this question.[4] But there is no logically compelling reason nor any principle inherent in the Common Law for adopting this solution, which is really the result of a judicial 'policy decision'. Some jurisdictions in the United States have rejected the rule and have laid down that, even in the absence of unlawful means, the knowing infliction of economic loss on another must be justified to the same extent as if done in combination.

So, in *Tuttle* v. *Buck*[5] the plaintiff was a barber and the defendant a banker. The plaintiff pleaded that the defendant had set up and run a barber's shop close to the plaintiff's solely

---

[1] *Scala Ballroom (Wolverhampton), Ltd.* v. *Ratcliffe*, [1958] 3 All E.R. 220.
[2] *The Crofter Case*, [1942] A.C. 435, *per* Viscount Maugham at p. 451.
[3] See *Brimelow* v. *Casson*, [1924] 1 Ch. 302 (*infra*, pp. 64-65).
[4] *Allen* v. *Flood*, [1898] A.C. 1 (*supra*, p. 54).
[5] (1909), 107 Minn. 145 (Sup. Ct. of Minnesota).

in order to destroy the plaintiff's business. The court carefully considered the English decisions and, in particular *Allen* v. *Flood*,[1] but concluded that, although competition is justifiable, '. . . when a man starts an opposition place of business, not for the sake of profit to himself but regardless of loss to himself, and for the sole purpose of driving his competitor out of business, and with the intention of himself retiring upon the accomplishment of his malevolent purpose, he is guilty of a wanton wrong and an actionable tort.'

(3) LIBEL

But it is perhaps in the law of libel that the importance of propriety of motive is most obvious. The existence of qualified privilege depends on the need to protect public or private interests: providing that the speaker's motive for saying what he did was not inappropriate to the protection of the interest on account of which the privilege of the occasion arises, no tort is committed. This being so 'Any indirect motive, other than a sense of duty, is what the law calls malice' for the purpose of defeating a plea of qualified privilege. Malice in this context is therefore the absence of a proper motive, and hence, although malice in the sense of a desire to inflict harm as an end in itself or for a morally wrong purpose is usually sufficient to destroy qualified privilege, it is not necessary for that purpose. Thus in *Hooper* v. *Truscott*[2] it was held that where the defendant, having some cause for suspicion, went to the plaintiff's relatives and charged him with theft, any privilege of the occasion was destroyed by the defendant's motive, which was rather to compromise the felony for £50 than to enable the relations to redeem the plaintiff's character.

(4) ABUSE OF LEGAL PROCESS

The mental element which is requisite to found liability for malicious prosecution is similar to that which is sufficient to destroy qualified privilege in libel: it amounts to an abuse of the right to prosecute which is based on the public interest in

---

[1] [1898] A.C. 1.   [2] (1836), 2 Bing, N.C. 457.

bringing criminals to book. The abuse here arises from the fact that the prosecution is animated by a desire to use the criminal law for some purpose for which it is not intended. It is particularly unfortunate that the word 'malice' was ever used in this context since it is quite possible for a prosecutor to have been inspired by personal dislike of the plaintiff and by a desire for vengeance against him and yet not be liable for malicious prosecution; and this may happen even where the proceedings were instituted without reasonable and probable cause, if the prosecutor honestly believed that he had a good case and that he could therefore satisfy his animosity against the plaintiff by obtaining his conviction.

It is interesting to note that Prosser discusses another tort, similar to malicious prosecution, which he calls 'abuse of process'.[1] This tort depends solely on the impropriety of the motive with which any legal process, criminal or civil, is used. Prosser cites *Grainger* v. *Hill*[2] as one authority; but in English law it would seem that it is necessary that the plaintiff should have been *arrested* through abuse of the process of the court and duress have been applied through such arrest,[3] or that the proceedings are in some other respect closely analogous to criminal proceedings, in that *by their very institution* they injure a man's 'fair fame' or otherwise cause him special damage.[4] Thus, malicious bankruptcy proceedings[5] and the malicious presentation of a petition to wind up a company[6] have been held to be actionable. Because of these limitations, therefore, the law of England permits one not only to sue a man at an

[1] Prosser, *Torts* (2nd ed.), para. 100.

[2] (1838), 4 Bing. N.C. 212; in this case the plaintiff had borrowed £80 from the defendants on the security of a ship which he owned. The defendants in order to obtain, as further security, the ship's register, without which the plaintiff could not go to sea, threatened to arrest the plaintiff for the debt unless he gave them the register. The plaintiff then did so. As the defendants knew, the debt was not yet due.

[3] Salmond, *Law of Torts* (12th ed.), p. 297, takes this view of the decision in *Grainger* v. *Hill*.

[4] *Whiffen* v. *Bailey and Romford Urban District Council*, [1915] 1 K.B. 600, at p. 606.

[5] *Quartz Hill Gold Mining Co.* v. *Eyre* (1883), 11 Q.B.D. 674, *per* Bowen L.J. at p. 691.

[6] *Johnson* v. *Emerson* (1871), L.R. 6 Ex. 329.

inopportune time for a debt which he owes one and so to gratify a malicious spite, but also to bring an action in order to obtain some extraneous benefit. Thus, in *Fitzroy* v. *Cave*[1] the plaintiff was allowed to enforce debts which he had had assigned to him for the very purpose of bankrupting the defendant and so forcing him off the directorate of a company. Even where the original civil suit was brought in the knowledge that it was unfounded it will generally be impossible for the original defendant to prove that, owing to the institution of those proceedings, he has suffered that special damage which is necessary to support a cause of action; for the original defendant is sufficiently compensated in the eyes of the law for his costs of defending the original suit by the order for costs made in his favour at its termination.[2]

(5) INDUCEMENT OF BREACH OF CONTRACT

We remarked earlier that inducing a breach of contract could not be justified on the ground that one's motive was to advance one's trade interests. But inducement of breach of contract is not unqualifiedly unlawful and certain motives will justify it. The interests in pursuance of which the inducer acts must be a great deal more important than those which suffice to justify a conspiracy by mere combination. An example of a sufficient private interest is provided by that which the inducer has in an earlier contract with the person induced, the performance of which will necessitate a breach of the later contract between the person induced and the plaintiff.[3] Another striking and well known example of a justification for inducement of contract is provided by *Brimelow* v. *Casson*[4] where it was held that the fact that a chorus girl was led to lead an immoral life because her wages were insufficient to live on was adequate justification for procuring her to break her contract of employ-

---

[1] [1905] 2 K.B. 364; Collins M.R. at p. 370 regarded *Bradford Corporation* v. *Pickles*, [1895] A.C. 587 as governing the question of malice here.

[2] *Cotterell* v. *Jones* (1851), 11 C.B. 713. The old authorities on this question are conveniently collected in the argument in this case. And see *Corbett* v. *Burge, Warren and Ridgley, Ltd.* (1932), 48 T.L.R. 626.

[3] Salmond, *Law of Torts* (12th ed.), p. 636.   [4] [1924] 1 Ch. 302.

ment. It is not clear whether the judgment depends upon the fact that the defendants were representatives of the theatrical profession whose interests were at stake, or whether the result would have been the same had they been an independent philanthropic body in no way connected with the oppressed girls other than by the general ties of humanity.[1]

But proper motive is very narrowly circumscribed in this tort which, in this respect, stands midway between the deliberate causing of harm by unlawful means, which can hardly ever be justified, and conspiracy by mere combination which can be justified very easily.

III. PUBLIC POLICY

Public policy in the broadest sense is the yardstick against which all the considerations, which we have so far discussed and have yet to discuss, are to be measured. But there is a narrower sense in which public policy may be relevant in these cases of deliberate infliction of harm on others. It is sometimes necessary to the performance of some function of government, whether it be the enforcement of the law or the work of the legislature, to permit certain acts to be done without fear of legal liability. These cases differ from those, which we have discussed above, of persons who are protected from liability in tort because they have acted to protect some public interest; the difference lies in the fact that the motive with which the act is done is in these cases irrelevant, whereas in the case of privilege arising from the existence of a public interest, the existence of the privilege actually depends upon the motive. Thus, where a speaker enjoys absolute privilege in defamation, he may have spoken with a motive no matter how evil, and yet he will escape liability. Public policy, in all such cases, makes it imperative that it should be impossible to have any prospect whatsoever

---

[1] [1924] 1 Ch. at p. 313, *per* Russell J.; 'These defendants, as it seems to me, owed a duty to their calling and to its members, *and, I am tempted to add, to the public*, to take all necessary peaceful steps to terminate the payment of this insufficient wage'. In this case conspiracy was alleged as well as inducement of breach of contract, and Russell J., in considering justification in the circumstances of this case, drew no distinction between the two.

of success in litigating against those who enjoy such privilege, as, for example, those who speak in Parliament or the law courts.

IV. THE INTEREST INFRINGED

We come finally to a consideration of the importance of the interest of the plaintiff which the defendant has infringed—in other words, the sort of detriment which the plaintiff has suffered. Bodily security and a man's reputation are the interests most carefully safeguarded against intentional harm. There are very few defences to deliberately causing bodily harm to another, and even fewer authorities in tort, since Trespass and Negligence give such broad protection even in the absence of proof of intention to harm or deliberateness. But it may sometimes be necessary to prove that intent; for example, it surely cannot be doubted that if I sold a house to another, ensuring that a bed-room gas-fitting was faulty, with the intent that the purchaser's wife should suffer grave injury, she could sue me even though there is strictly no trespass, and no action for negligence could succeed.[1] *Wilkinson* v. *Downton*[2] is an example of the courts giving redress for the knowing infliction of nervous shock, which is to be regarded, for this purpose,[3] as indistinguishable from bodily injury. The motives which do justify the deliberate infliction of bodily harm upon another are self-defence, the protection of certain private rights, *e.g.* the ejection of a trespasser from one's land, and the protection of certain public rights, *e.g.* the obstruction and arrest of a felon. These justifications all clearly depend on the social value of the public or private interest which the actor seeks to protect, and will be destroyed if he goes beyond what is necessary to protect those interests. And a reference to what has been said in part II about privilege in defamation shows that similar considerations are applied to limit the otherwise almost absolute protection afforded to a man's reputation.

In the case of bodily security, reputation and also injury to

---

[1] *Davis* v. *Foots*, [1940] 1 K.B. 116.   [2] [1897] 2 Q.B. 57.
[3] *Cf.*, *Behrens* v. *Bertram Mills Circus, Ltd.*, [1957] 2 Q.B. 1, at pp. 27–28 which illustrates the different rule where the infringement was negligent.

chattels the existence of strict liability or liability for negligence makes a consideration of motives of comparatively minor significance. But when we come to consider a man's more refined interests, such as those which he has in his physical comfort or in his trade relations with others or in his general economic position, where there has been no injury to body, reputation or property, means and motives are more important. Thus, we noted that one who was responsible for a noxious escape which damaged another's property could not plead propriety of motive in the same way as one who, by making a smell or, in American law, blocking a view, was responsible for a mere disturbance of his neighbour's comfort. Again, a man's interest in his existing contractual relations with others is better protected than the interest which he has in making future contracts.

It is not altogether settled in English law whether a man's interest in his trade relations is more generously protected than that in his general welfare. When we discussed unlawful means, in part I, we drew no distinction between the two: indeed a dictum of Lord Herschell in *Allen* v. *Flood*[1] specifically denies that such a distinction can be drawn. On the other hand, in all the decided cases of liability for the use of unlawful means, the plaintiff's interest has in fact been in his trade relations with others. We cannot therefore at the moment be sure whether in English law a good cause of action would be disclosed by, for example, the following facts: *B* accepts an offer by *A* of a lift to London in *A*'s car. *C*, wishing to harm *B*, then deceitfully tells *A* that *B* has not waited for him, but has left by train. The doubt arises because although *B* has a financial interest in his lift from *A* (i.e. the train fare to London), he has no trade relations with *A*—his relations are of a social nature only. In the United States the use of unlawful means, like deceit, would seem to entail tortious liability, even where there has been no interference with trade relations. Thus, in one case, the New York Court of Appeals stated that a good cause of action would be disclosed if the plaintiff could show that he had been deported by the immigration authorities because they had

[1] [1898] A.C. 1, at pp. 137–138.

been deliberately supplied with false information by the defendant.[1]

V. CONCLUSION

The law of torts is as infinitely complex as life itself and any attempt to analyse even a branch of it and show that a pattern emerges is liable to be criticized for over-simplification. It may well be that the analysis which we have suggested above can be refined and broken down further. But we have tried to break away from the search for a magically simple formula, which seems to have been in some writers' minds—a formula with which to sum up the law of torts in so far as it concerns the knowing infliction of harm upon others. Our contention has been that no such simple formula is possible, for the solution of any particular case depends upon a consideration of the four principles which we have discussed above. If the means adopted by the actor are unqualifiedly unlawful, whether in relation to the plaintiff *or to third parties*, then the actor is liable without more. If on the other hand they are not unqualifiedly unlawful, then the actor's interest, in pursuance of which he inflicted loss upon the plaintiff, may have to be weighed against the nature of the plaintiff's loss. Finally, and occasionally, the requirements of public policy in a narrow sense may have to be considered. The law is here, as much as, if not more than, in any other branch, concerned with the weighing of one interest against another. For this reason, no truisms like 'All harm knowingly inflicted without justification is actionable.' or 'It is a tort to cause loss to another maliciously or with an improper motive.' can help one to set about finding the solution of fresh questions as they arise.

[1] *Al Raschid* v. *News Syndicate Co., Inc.* (1934), 265 N.Y. 1.

CHAPTER IV

The Concept of Possession in English Law

by D. R. Harris

THE concept of Possession has always had a strange fascination for lawyers. Many writers have attempted to analyse the concept whether in Roman law, in a modern system, such as German law, or in English law. It is not the intention of the present writer to review in detail any previous theories of possession, but rather to suggest a new approach to the concept so far as English law is concerned. English judges have been rightly suspicious of a uniform rigid 'theory' of possession in the common law: for instance, Earl Jowitt has said[1] '—in truth, the English law has never worked out a completely logical and exhaustive definition of "possession".'

It is the thesis of this essay that the English decisions preclude us from laying down any conditions, such as physical control or a certain kind of intention, as absolutely essential for a judicial ruling that a man possesses something. A theory which postulates physical control and intention of one kind or another as the basic ingredients of possession must include artificial glosses or fictions to cover the actual English decisions; we find the ideas of 'constructive' physical control or of 'constructive' intention to act as owner, propounded to make the theories fit the cases. The writer has attempted to read the cases with an open mind in order to discover those factors which have weighed with English judges in reaching a conclusion that a man is entitled to the benefit of a rule of law expressed in terms of possession, *e.g.* 'Because *A* was in possession of this ring when *B* took it, *A* can recover £50 damages from *B* for trespass.'

Professor Hart[2] has shown us that it is impossible to *define* a

---

[1] *U.S.A.* v. *Dollfus Mieg*, [1952] A.C. 582, at p. 605.   [2] Hart (1954), 70 L.Q.R. 37.

legal concept, and that the task of legal writers should be rather to *describe* the use of a word like 'possession, in the particular legal rules in which it occurs. 'Possession' in the legal sense has no meaning at all apart from the rules of law in which it is used as a tool of legal thought. In the imaginary judgment just quoted, 'Because *A* was in possession . . .', the word 'possession' is really a piece of legal shorthand, which, in an abbreviated form, states a legal conclusion based on the application of law to particular facts.[1]

We should therefore study the way in which the word 'possession' is used in English rules of law; we cannot study the legal concept of possession in the abstract, for the word has no legal meaning apart from the context of these particular rules. We should look at such rules as the following, which are merely a selection of 'possessory' rules in English law:

(1)   The plaintiff in an action of trespass to goods must, have been in *possession* at the time of the interference alleged against the defendant.

(2)   The plaintiff in an action for conversion of goods must, at the time of the conversion, have either been in *actual possession* of them, or been *entitled to the immediate possession* of them.

(3)   As soon as the vendor of land has let the purchaser into *possession* under an oral contract, there is an act of part performance which renders it too late for either party to repudiate the contract on the ground that there is no memorandum or note in writing as required by section 40 (1) of the Law of Property Act, 1925.

(4)   Where an owner of land is entitled to possession, the twelve-year period of limitation under the Limitation Act, 1939, runs against him from the moment *adverse possession* is taken by another.

---

[1] Compare the position in a negligence case, where the Court first finds the 'primary facts' (observable by the senses) and then applies to these facts the legal standard of the reasonable man in order to draw the legal conclusion that the defendant was 'negligent'. See *Benmax* v. *Austin Motor Co., Ltd.*, [1955] A.C. 370; and *Qualcast (Wolverhampton), Ltd.* v. *Haynes*, [1959] A.C. 743.

(5) ' "Delivery" means voluntary transfer of *possession* from one person to another.' (Section 62 of the Sale of Goods Act, 1893).[1]

(6) 'Where a mercantile agent is, with the consent of the owner, in *possession* of goods, any sale, pledge or other disposition of the goods, made by him when acting in the ordinary course of business of a mercantile agent, shall . . . be . . . valid . . .' (Section 2(1) of the Factors Act, 1889.)[2]

(7) 'A bailee . . . receives *possession* of a thing from another . . . upon an undertaking with the other person . . . to keep and return . . . to him the specific thing . . .'[3]

(8) 'The expression "owner" [in the statutory definition of larceny] includes any part owner, or person having *possession* or control of, or a special property in, anything capable of being stolen.' (Section 1(2) (iii) of the Larceny Act, 1916).

(9) A taking, for the purposes of larceny, 'consists in acquisition of *possession* without the consent of the previous possessor to part with the *possession*'.[4]

These rules, all employing the word 'possession', deal with such different situations that it is not in the least surprising that English judges have not adopted any consistent approach to the meaning of possession. They have used 'possession' in the various rules of law as a functional and relative concept, which gives them some discretion in applying an abstract rule to a concrete set of facts. When a plaintiff has claimed the benefit of a rule expressly based on possession of a chattel at a certain time, the judge has tended subconsciously to ask himself a question like this: 'Do the facts show that before or at the relevant time the plaintiff had entered into a sufficiently close

---

[1] The words 'delivery', 'deliver', 'possess', and 'possession' occur in many sections of this Act, which makes no attempt to define 'possession'.

[2] Seven other sections in the same Act contain rules based on 'possession'.

[3] Pollock and Wright, *Possession in the Common Law*, p. 163.

[4] Pollock and Wright, *op. cit.*, p. 215. (This common law meaning of 'taking' is widened for larceny cases by Section 1 (2) (i) of the Larceny Act, 1916.)

relationship with the chattel that he ought to be given the benefit of this particular rule against this particular defendant?'

In marginal cases, the judge clearly has a discretion to decide the issue of possession one way or the other, according to his own appraisal of the relative merits of the parties' cases, and of the social purpose of the rule in question. But this is not to say that the judge's decision depends on his own whim, for the courts are evolving a list of factors which must be considered when deciding whether the plaintiff's relationship to the chattel amounts to possession.

The following list of factors which may be relevant to a conclusion that a man 'possesses' a chattel is based on a reading of many cases. No single factor in the list will necessarily be decisive on the issue of 'possession', for that is a legal conclusion based on the cumulative effect of those factors which the court holds operative in the circumstances. The judge will weigh up the relevant factors in order to decide whether on balance they come down in favour of the plaintiff or against him. This approach should not be unfamiliar to English lawyers: other concepts, such as what is 'a judicial or quasi-judicial decision' as distinguished from 'a purely administrative decision' in administrative law, or the concept of what is 'reasonable in all the circumstances' in the law of torts, are in frequent use in our courts, though they are not based on any rigid criteria.

Nor is the following list of factors exhaustive. There is no reason why the judges should not in the future be faced with additional factors which ought to be considered on the issue of 'possession'; the judicial view of justice or of the policy behind a particular 'possessory' rule may well change, and demand that weight should be given to new factors in certain circumstances. This essay, following the list of factors, will attempt to examine some decisions by using this approach.

I. FACTORS RELEVANT TO POSSESSION

The following is a list of factors which have been held relevant to a conclusion that the plaintiff has acquired 'possession' of a chattel for the purposes of a particular rule of law.

Three preliminary observations on this introductory sentence are necessary. First, the 'the plaintiff' is merely illustrative of the person invoking, or subject to, a possessory rule; according to the circumstances, of course, he may be the defendant, the accused or a third party, such as a mercantile agent. Secondly, this essay deals mainly with possession of chattels, though it is submitted that possession of land in English law may be approached in the same way with a similar list of factors. Thirdly, this sentence, in using the words 'acquired possession' adopts the view of Holmes[1] and Kocourek[2] that the law is concerned only with the acquisition and loss of possession, and not its retention. There is no need to ask what is necessary to 'retain' possession, since once the plaintiff is held to have acquired possession, he continues to be entitled in law to the benefit of the possessory rule, until he 'loses' possession, *e.g.* when he abandons the chattel, or a stranger acquires possession of it.[3] There is no need to think of possession as a continuing physical relationship between a man and an object, or as depending on a continuing, conscious intention. Once the facts which justify the application of the possessory rule arise in the first place, they need not necessarily continue to exist in the same form, degree or intensity. The court will continue to apply the word 'possession' to the plaintiff's relationship with the object until the law recognizes that changed facts operate to divest the plaintiff of his possessory right.

It is true that judges often speak as if the facts necessary for possession must continue; they ask, for instance in trespass cases, 'Was the plaintiff in possession at the time of the defendant's interference?' rather than 'Had the plaintiff acquired possession before the defendant's interference and had nothing

---

[1] *The Common Law*, pp. 235–238.

[2] *Jural Relations* (2nd ed.), pp. 361–423 (*passim*).

[3] Pollock and Wright, *op. cit.*, pp. 21–22: (Rule 4: 'Possession is acquired and lost in certain specific ways. An existing possession can be determined only in one of those ways.' See also p. 119: Possession 'is defined by modes or events in which it commences or ceases, and by the legal incidents attached to it, the most important of which are those connected with trespass and theft.' The second quotation from Wright is a penetrating statement, and despite the use of the word 'defined' rather than 'described', anticipates a functional approach to the meaning of possession.)

occurred to divest that possession?' But it is submitted that the latter question is the vital one. Where it is not clear how or when the plaintiff first acquired possession, an inquiry into the facts relevant to the plaintiff's possession at the time of the defendant's interference may justify an inference of lawful acquisition.

Factors (1) and (2): Physical Control

(1)   The degree of physical control over the chattel which the plaintiff actually exercises, or is immediately able to exercise. The plaintiff's degree of physical control should not be considered in isolation, but in relation to the greatest degree of physical control which it is possible for the particular plaintiff to exercise over the particular chattel. Thus the limited physical control of a child or an epileptic may be properly recognized, as is the limited control possible over a very large chattel or a wreck at the bottom of the sea.[1] The plaintiff's physical control must also be compared with that of the defendant or anyone else. (Factor 2).

(2)   The degree of physical control over the chattel actually or potentially exercised by any other person, whether the defendant or a stranger. Obviously, factor (1) must be weighed against factor (2). A limited degree of physical control exercised by the plantiff may suffice for the acquisition of possession in the absence of opposition from others, but if other persons are at the same moment attempting to seize or hold the chattel, the plaintiff's control over it must be greater and more exclusive, unless a further factor is applicable, *e.g.* the lawfulness of the plaintiff's attempt to gain control. For if the parties were each asserting a similar degree of control over the object, the courts will award possession to whichever of the contending parties had a relatively better right to possess than the other.[2] A high degree of physical control is necessary for the original acquisition of possession and ownership

---

[1] *The Tubantia*, [1924] P. 78.

[2] Pollock and Wright, *op. cit.*, pp. 24–25, and p. 79. ('Possession in law follows the right to possess where physical possession is in dispute.') See also *Ramsay v. Margrett*, [1894] 2 Q.B. 18.

of something not possessed or owned by anyone: *occupatio* of a *res nullius* in Roman law. Decisions on the capture of fish and of wild animals show that possession is acquired only when the thing cannot escape of its own power; the net must have closed completely around the fish;[1] close pursuit, short of actual capture, of a wild animal is likewise insufficient.[2]

Factors (3)—(6): Knowledge and Intention

(3) The plaintiff's knowledge of (*a*) the existence of the chattel, and (*b*) its major attributes or qualities, and (*c*) its location at the relevant time.

(4) The plantiff's intention in regard to the chattel. Such intention, of course, must be based on his knowledge (Factor (3)).

It is impossible to draw the conclusion from the reported cases that English judges have regarded only one kind of intention as relevant to possession. Sometimes they have referred to the plaintiff's intention to act as owner of the chattel, at other times to his intention to exclude other persons from it.[3] The weight to be given to the plaintiff's knowledge and intention depends on whether the defendant or any stranger also had such knowledge and intention. (Factors (5) and (6)). If the plaintiff is the only person who knows of the chattel and its location, and the only one who intends to exercise control over it, his claim to be in a unique relationship with it will be greatly strengthened.

(5) The knowledge of the defendant, or of any stranger to the dispute, of the existence of the chattel, its attributes and location (as in Factor (3)).

(6) The intention of the defendant, or of any stranger, in regard to the chattel (as in Factor 4)). Under this head, the court may also consider the intention of a previous

---

[1] *Young* v. *Hichens* (1844), 6 Q.B. 606.
[2] Pollock and Wright, *op. cit.*, pp. 37, 125–6.
[3] Salmond, *Jurisprudence* (11th ed.), p. 322.

possessor of the chattel to deliver possession or exclusive control over it to the plaintiff, by way of sale, gift, bailment or otherwise.

Factors (5) and (6) are important in order to assess the weight to be given to factors (3) and (4). If both the parties to the dispute knew of the existence and location of the chattel, the crucial factor may be the intent of only one of them to exercise control over it or to exclude others from it; if both parties had knowledge and also a similar intention in regard to it (or if neither party had knowledge or intention) other factors will decide the issue, *e.g.* the relative degrees of physical control exercised by the parties, or the fact that one was the occupier of the premises where the chattel lay.

In civil cases, especially those concerning delivery or bailment of chattels, the intention of the parties is often decisive in the acquisition of possession. Where a possessor deliberately intends to transfer possession to another person there is sometimes no transfer of physical control over the chattel, sometimes a very limited transfer of control. There is some authority that goods under lock and key may be delivered to another person by delivering the key, partly as a 'symbol' of possession, and partly, as Pollock argues, as 'such a transfer of control in fact as the nature of the case admits'.[1] The delivery of a key, considered in the abstract, is neutral in regard to the possession of what is locked up; it is the intention of the parties to the transaction which determines whether possession of the premises or goods locked up is to pass to the recipient of the key.

In *Ashby* v. *Tolhurst*,[2] the intention of the parties was all-important. The question was whether there had been a bailment (involving delivery of possession to the bailee) when the plaintiff left his car in the defendant's car park for a nominal fee. The Court of Appeal decided that there was no intention to deliver possession to the defendants. It was merely a licence whereby the defendant granted the plaintiff permission to leave

---

[1] *Ancona* v. *Rogers* (1876), 1 Ex. D. 285. See Pollock and Wright, *op. cit.*, p. 61.

[2] [1937] 2 K.B. 242. See also *Tinsley* v. *Dudley*, [1951] 2 K.B. 18.

his car on the defendant's land; the plaintiff therefore still possessed it even while it stood on another's land.

Factor (7): *The Possession of Premises*

The legal relationship of the plaintiff (compared with that of the defendant) to the premises where the chattel is lying at the relevant time: the plaintiff may be the occupier, or the owner and occupier; or he may be merely a licensee or trespasser. Similarly, the defendant may fall into any one of these categories. This factor may be vital when the preceding factors give no clear answer to the issue of possession. For instance, in order to protect occupiers against trespassers, the courts are likely to hold that an occupier possesses chattels lying thereon despite his ignorance of them. If the occupier of premises claims possession of chattels lying thereon, the courts have sometimes considered relevant the intention of the occupier to exclude other persons from his premises and so from any chattels which may happen to be there. In many cases, of course, this factor is not relevant *e.g.* because no one occupies the place where the chattel lies, or because the occupier is not a party to the dispute and makes no claim to the chattel; the other factors in the list will then govern the question of possession.

A factor similar to the occupation of land is the possession of a vehicle or other container, such as a bureau, in which a chattel is lying. The possessor of the vehicle or container may be held to possess the chattel even when he does not know of it.[1]

Factor (8): *Other legal relationships or special rules of law applicable to the facts*

The facts may bring into operation an overall legal relationship between the parties to the dispute, or between one of them and a third party, which governs the question of possession by virtue of a special rule as to which person in that relationship enjoys possession. The most notable instance is the

---

[1] *E.g.*, *Williams* v. *Phillips* (1957), 41 Cr. App. Rep. 5 (refuse placed in dust cart).

rule that, at least as against his master, a servant, who in the course of his service receives chattels from his master, has mere custody of them and not possession, for the master still enjoys possession through his servant. Such a rule generally awards possession to one person in the relationship irrespective of the preceding factors of physical control, knowledge, intention or occupation of premises. The law directs peremptorily that persons in a certain category may or may not enjoy the benefit of possessory rules.

The law governing the relationships of bailor and bailee, principal and mercantile agent under the Factors Act, 1889, and buyer and seller, are other cases where special rules covering possession and its legal consequences have been developed. Similarly there is a special rule that a guest using the chattels of his host, such as his furniture and cutlery, has custody not possession; the host continues to possess his chattels though his guest may have complete physical control over them at the moment. Likewise a shopkeeper retains possession of goods which he permits a customer to handle and inspect.

These special rules have resulted from particular historical or economic conditions, and reflect a particular policy of the law in the given circumstances, which can only be implemented by superimposing a precise rule on the usual factors determining possession.

Factor (9) : *The Policy behind the Rule*

The last factor is the judge's concept of the social purpose of the particular rule of law relied on by the plaintiff. Especially in cases where the judge is left undecided by the preceding factors, he will, whether consciously or unconsciously, ask himself a question to this effect: 'Will a conclusion that the plaintiff was in possession of the chattel at the relevant time tend to carry out the social purpose of this rule of law in the particular circumstances of the case?' The determining factor, when the other factors appear to be evenly balanced, may often be the assumed purpose of the rule in question; the judge can hardly attempt to examine the physical or psychological facts apart from the legal rule, and apart from his foreknowledge of the result in the case before him if he decides for the plaintiff on the issue of possession.

The reported decisions on larceny provide an outstanding illustration of the importance of this factor, and these will be considered in some detail later in this essay.

A cursory examination of the selected possessory rules quoted above will reveal the quite different topics they cover; naturally the policies behind the different rules must vary, and this justifies the courts in giving varying weight to the different factors relevant to possession according to the particular rule in question. The lack of consistency in the English decisions on possession is quite defensible on this ground. Emphasis on a particular factor may assist the court in carrying out the purpose of one possessory rule, whereas a similar emphasis on the same factor would hinder the achievement of the purpose of another rule.

It is not suggested that any English judge has yet, in a reported decision, consciously worked through a list of factors such as the one just tabulated. This list is an attempt to elucidate a process of judicial reasoning which has apparently been mainly subconscious in the past. This process of weighing various factors has been kept in bounds by another subconscious approach to possession problems through an 'ideal' concept of possession. The judges seem to have had at the back of their minds a perfect pattern in which the possessor has complete, exclusive and unchallenged physical control over the object, full knowledge of its existence, attributes and location, and a manifest intention to 'act as its owner' and to exclude all other persons from it. But in the practical world, however, the judges realize that justice and expediency compel constant modification of the ideal pattern, as is cogently illustrated by the authorities to be analysed in this essay. The plaintiff may have a very limited degree of physical control over the object;[1] or he may have no intention in regard to an object of whose existence he is unaware, though he does exercise control over the place where

---

[1] *E.g., The Tubantia,* [1924] P. 78.

the object is lying;[1] or he may have a clear intention to exclude other people from the object, though he has no physical control at the moment.[2]

The judges seem sub-consciously to be asking themselves whether the facts before them are sufficiently analogous to the perfect pattern of possession for the plaintiff to be given the particular remedy he desires. It is during this process that the various factors outlined in the list above are weighed against each other. The approach of the judges appears to be essentially functional and empirical, since they are prepared to allow further departures from this ideal concept of possession for the purposes of some rules of law than for others. The fact that a particular rule of law is based on 'possession' permits a judge to exercise some discretion to achieve justice on the merits of the actual case before him, when he decides whether or not to accord 'possession' to the facts.

We shall now examine some cases illustrating this judicial process whereby the conclusion is reached that a person has possession.

II. THE LOSS AND FINDING OF CHATTELS

The topic of loss and finding of chattels has provided some of the most difficult problems on possession in English law. Though there are few reported decisions, a careful classification of the different situations leads to clarity. The following headings adopt the classification suggested by Riesman[3] according to the two parties involved in the dispute; different problems arise in each kind of dispute, and it is submitted that the use of possession as a flexible concept could permit English law to develop desirable rules in the different situations.

Owner versus Finder

Possession as such has little relevance here, because the true owner can usually rely on his immediate right to possession, and maintain conversion or detinue against a finder who refuses

---

[1] E.g., *South Staffordshire Water Co.* v. *Sharman*, [1896] 2 Q.B. 44.
[2] E.g., *Ashby* v. *Tolhurst*, [1937] 2 K.B. 242.   [3] (1939), 52 Harv. L.R. 1105.

to return the chattel to him. The owner must, of course always demand the return of the chattel before he can sue the finder; and if the finder is in genuine doubt whether the claimant is the true owner, the law permits him to make a temporary and provisional refusal to return it, while he makes inquiries.[1]

The act of finding by an honest finder is not a trespass against the true owner, since the law presumes that the taking is for the true owner's benefit.[2] An honest finder will always take steps to discover the true owner and return the chattel to him, so his taking of possession is for the purpose of protecting the chattel on behalf of the true owner. Pollock termed this 'an excusable taking'.[3]

Finder versus Stranger

English law is straightforward in regard to the finder's legal relationship with anyone who is neither the true owner of the chattel nor the occupier of the premises on which it was found. The finder acquires possession of the chattel by taking it into his control, and so can bring trespass or conversion against any stranger who wrongfully interferes with his possession. The leading authority is the old case of *Armory* v. *Delamirie*[4] where Pratt C.J. at Nisi Prius laid down that 'The finder of a jewel, though he does not by such finding acquire an absolute property or ownership, yet has such a property as will enable him to keep it against all but the rightful owner, and consequently may maintain trover.' (No claim was apparently made by the occupier of the premises where the jewel was found.) This decision has led to our present rule that a plaintiff who sues for conversion may rely merely on his possession of the chattel at the relevant time, as an alternative to the more usual title of a plaintiff in conversion, namely, the immediate right to posses-

---

[1] *Clayton* v. *Le Roy*, [1911] 2 K.B. 1031.
[2] See Coke C.J. in *Isaack* v. *Clark* (1615), 2 Bulstr. 306, at p. 312.
[3] It may be noted that since English law has left all the problems of finding to be dealt with by the ordinary possessory remedies, trespass, detinue and conversion, there are serious gaps in our law, *e.g.*, an honest finder who commits no tort acquires no title to the chattel as against the true owner, no matter how long he retains it; again, except in salvage cases, a finder has no claim for his expenses.
[4] (1722), 1 Str. 505.

sion of the chattel. Neither the fact that the finder was trespassing on the land where he found the chattel, nor that he was a dishonest finder, guilty of larceny by finding, is relevant to the issue of the finder's possession *vis-à-vis* a complete stranger.[1] These facts, however, may well be relevant in a dispute between an occupier and finder.

Occupier versus Finder

In this situation, one man finds a lost chattel on land which is in the possession of another. Potentially it is a three-party problem, since there is often the possibility that the true owner might appear to claim his chattel. This possibility complicates any dispute between the occupier and the finder, because the court, in deciding whether the occupier possessed the chattel before it was found, may consider the protection of the interests of the missing owner as one of the purposes of the possessory remedies. From one point of view, the result of the case between the finder and the occupier will decide who is to be permitted to hold the chattel on behalf of the missing owner until he appears to claim it. Policy suggests that in most circumstances the owner would be more likely to recover his chattel if possession was awarded to the occupier. There is some chance that the owner might remember the place where he last had the chattel, and retrace his steps to inquire for it; and since a finder is under no obligation in English law to advertise his find, nor to register it anywhere, a rule awarding possession to the finder might make it more difficult for the missing owner to trace it. The rule, then, which would best assist owners to trace their lost property would permit the occupier of the premises where the chattel was found to hold it, at least for a reasonable period after the finding. But if the owner is not discovered within that period the situation is different, for the issue is then whether the occupier or the finder is to retain the chattel more or less permanently. As time goes on, the possibility of a claim by the true owner becomes even less likely, and in practice the question becomes: 'Which of the two, the occupier or the finder, ought

[1] *Bird* v. *Fort Francis*, [1949] 2 D.L.R. 791.

to hold the chattel for himself?' For when the owner is not discovered after a reasonable time, the possessor of the chattel will normally use it himself, or sell it and use the proceeds of the sale; he will undertake the risk that the owner might later appear, and be prepared, if that happens, to pay damages to him for conversion or detinue. When we contemplate a probably permanent possession, which the owner is unlikely to challenge, the claim of the occupier to hold the chattel is morally no stronger than that of the finder. Hence the specific rule in Roman law, and under the legislation of some American states, that the windfall is to be divided equally between the finder and the occupier.

English law has developed no rules which expressly deal with these basic problems between the occupier and finder. Since these problems have been left to the ordinary possessory remedies the English judge can give weight to these considerations only when he attempts to find an answer to the question 'Did the occupier possess the chattel immediately before it was found?' The reported decisions give no clear guidance on the judicial view of the underlying purpose of our possessory remedies in disputes between occupier and finder. It seems that judges subconsciously think more of the question 'Who ought to hold the chattel in the event of the true owner never appearing?' than of the question 'Is the true owner more likely to discover his chattel if possession is given to one rather than to the other?' The former is naturally the more important question, but even it is never openly referred to in any English law report; the judges purport to be deciding a technical issue of possession, when they are really deciding an important issue of policy about the relative merits of the conflicting claims of the occupier and finder. Factor (9), the policy behind the rule, is the crucial one, since the judge's conclusion on possession will depend mainly on his view of what the policy of the law should be in such cases. If he favours the claim of the occupier, his conclusion will be clothed in the outward form of an apparently technical decision that the occupier, despite his lack of knowledge of the existence of the chattel, was in possession of it before it was found; hence the earlier possession of the occupier will give him a better right to possess than the finder, whose possession was subsequent. If the judge favours the finder, he will hold that the occupier did not possess the chattel before it was found, that it was therefore not then possessed by anyone, so that the finder acquired a possession which was good against all the world except the missing owner.

We have few reported civil cases on the topic, and one cannot resist the impression that the judges in practice have first decided the real merits of the case in the light of their view of justice and the policy of the law, and then concealed their policy decision in a ruling that the occupier either did or did not possess the chattel before it was found. This will be true only so long as there are few precedents, and the common law on the subject is in a formative stage. When we have more precedents, the judges will discover that they have developed a set of fixed rules awarding possession to a determinate person in such situations.

(I) THE WIDE RULE IN FAVOUR OF THE FINDER

With these considerations in mind we can now look at the decided cases, beginning with the famous one of *Bridges* v. *Hawkesworth*.[1] Bridges was a travelling salesman who regularly did business with Hawkesworth, a shopkeeper. In 1847, when leaving Hawkesworth's shop, Bridges noticed a small parcel of banknotes on the floor, in a part of the shop frequented by customers. He immediately opened the parcel, in the presence of the shopman, and when he found £55 in it, he handed the notes to Hawkesworth, asking him to hold them for their owner. Though Hawkesworth advertised in newspapers for the owner, no one claimed the notes. Three years later, when the true owner still had not appeared, Bridges asked Hawkesworth to return the notes to him, and offered to pay for the advertisements. Hawkesworth refused, and was upheld by the County Court judge, on the ground that the notes had been found in his shop. But on appeal the Divisional Court reversed

---

[1] (1851), 21 L.J., Q.B. 75; 15 Jur. 1079.

this judgment, and decided in favour of the finder, Bridges. Patteson, J., in a reserved judgment cited *Armory* v. *Delamirie*[1] (a finder versus stranger case) as authority for the general right of the finder to a lost article as against all the world but the true owner, and he applied this rule to the facts before him, though they constituted a 'finder versus occupier' situation. He held that there was no legal difference between finding the notes inside or outside the shop, and that the County Court judge was wrong in thinking that the place where the notes were found was relevant. The occupier of the shop could have a right to the notes only if such a right had accrued to him *before* the finding, that is, only if it could be said that Hawkesworth possessed the notes while they lay on the floor of the shop unnoticed by anyone. But Patteson J. decided that 'The notes never were in the custody of the defendant, nor within the protection of his house, before they were found, as they would have been had they been intentionally deposited there.'[2] The court approved the ruling of the judge below that Bridges had handed the notes to Hawkesworth simply as his agent, for the purpose of advertising for the true o wner, and so Hawkesworth was held liable to repay the money to him.

Academic controversy has raged over this decision, and it is worth while reviewing some of the interpretations placed on it, since they illustrate the futility of searching for a unitary concept of possession in English law. Pollock[3] thought it was rightly decided, because the shopkeeper lacked the degree of *de facto* physical control over the notes, which in Pollock's view, was an essential element in legal possession. Hawkesworth, he pointed out, did not expect objects of that kind to be on the floor of his shop, and it was more likely that a customer would be the first to see the notes and pick them up, since they had been dropped in business hours and in the public part of the shop. The facts on which Pollock relied were undoubtedly present in the case, but the judge did not refer to them as the grounds for his decision that the notes were not in the custody or

---

[1] (1722) 1 Str. 505 (*supra*, p. 81).   [2] (1851), 21 L.J., Q.B. 75, at p. 78.
[3] Pollock and Wright, *op. cit.*, pp. 37 *et seq.*

control of anyone while they lay on the floor of the shop. The judgment simply states this conclusion, without giving any explicit reasons, beyond the negative one that there was nothing in the circumstances to take the case outside the wide *Armory* v. *Delamirie* principle in favour of the finder.

Salmond[1] followed his own analysis of possession into the two ingredients of *corpus* and *animus*, that is, physical control over the object, and the intent to exclude others from interfering with it. He approved the decision, on the basis that Hawkesworth did not have the necessary '*animus*' in regard to the banknotes, because he did not know of their existence; in other words without knowledge he could form no intention, and without intention he could not possess. It is submitted, first, that in English law neither specific knowledge of the existence and location of a chattel, nor the formation of a particular kind of intent in regard to it is always essential to a conclusion that a man possesses that chattel.[2] Secondly, the judgment of Patteson J. at no point refers to the occupier's lack of knowledge, and it is submitted that we must dismiss Salmond's interpretation of the decision as an illegitimate attempt to squeeze it into his own pre-ordained concept of possession.

Holmes[3] also upheld the actual result of the case, and relied on the shopkeeper's lack of knowledge that the notes were on the floor of his shop; the occupier could therefore not have had an intent to appropriate the notes, and, having impliedly invited the public to his shop, he could not have had an intent to exclude other people from the notes. In Holmes' analysis, both kinds of intent were necessary for possession, but his explanation of the decision must also be dismissed as *ex post facto* rationalization since the judge did not suggest that either kind of intent was essential.

Dr. Goodhart[4] submits that the case was wrongly decided,[5]

---

[1] *Jurisprudence* (11th ed.), pp. 329–330.

[2] See pp. 87–62, *infra*, for a discussion of *Elwes* v. *Brigg Gas Co.* (1886), 33 Ch. D. 562, and of *South Staffordshire Water Co.* v. *Sharman*, [1896] 2 Q.B. 44.

[3] *The Common Law*, pp. 221 *et seq.*

[4] *Essays in Jurisprudence and the Common Law*, p. 75, at p. 83 (reprinted from (1928) 3 Camb. L.J. 195).

[5] Glanville Williams in Salmond, *Jurisprudence* (11th ed.), p. 330, agrees.

since the shopkeeper did have the necessary control. He argues that a shopkeeper, though permitting the public to walk in the public part of his shop as potential customers, intends to exclude them from any chattels which may be in his shop, whether in the public part or not. Dr. Goodhart would like to see the case over-ruled, and the principle laid down that an occupier of land possesses those things on his land which are not possessed by someone else.

In the opinion of the present writer, the actual judgment in *Bridges* v. *Hawkesworth* was based on a wide principle developed from that in *Armory* v. *Delamirie*, namely, that in the absence of a claim by the true owner, the finder of a lost article has a better claim to it than anyone else, including even the occupier of the premises where it was found. This *ratio decidendi* ignores the important differences between the 'finder versus stranger' and the 'finder versus occupier' situations, and in the light of later decisions, it must now be regarded as subject to several qualifications. However, these qualifications may not affect the actual decision in favour of Bridges, the finder. We must now consider the various qualifications to a wide rule in favour of the finder which have been suggested by judges and writers.

(2) SUGGESTED QUALIFICATIONS TO THE WIDE RULE IN FAVOUR OF THE FINDER

(*a*) *Finding on private property not open to the public*

In *Bridges* v. *Hawkesworth* the notes were found on the floor of the public part of the shop. Though the judgment itself laid no emphasis on this fact, it may have had some influence on the decision. Suppose that Hawkesworth had invited Bridges to dinner in his private living quarters above the shop, and that Bridges had found the notes on the floor of the dining-room: in the absence of the owner of the notes, would the claim of the finder still prevail over that of the occupier?

First we must consider *Elwes* v. *Brigg Gas Company*.[1] In this case the plaintiff was the tenant for life in possession of some land, which he leased to the gas company for 99 years,

---

[1] (1886), 33 Ch. D. 562.

with a reservation of 'all mines and minerals'. Gas-holders and other buildings were to be erected by the lessee company according to plans to be approved by the lessor and under the supervision of the lessor's surveyor. In the course of excavating the site for a gasholder the servants of the lessee company discovered a pre-historic 'dug-out' canoe, about 45 feet long and possibly 2,000 years old, embedded in the clay six feet below the surface and within a few yards of a river. The lessee company refused to hand the boat to the plaintiff, and claimed that the boat belonged to them.

In the ensuing action in detinue, Chitty J. expressly refrained from deciding finally whether the boat was a mineral (and so within the clause in the lease expressly reserving all mines and minerals to the lessor), or was part of the soil, or still retained its character as a chattel. The judgment is therefore based on three alternative suppositions, and for this reason is rather unsatisfactory for the purpose of analysing the judge's use of the concept of possession. The lessor was clearly in possession of the land before he granted the lease, but after the lease possession of the land passed to the lessee except in respect of mines and minerals. The crucial question was whether the lessor possessed and owned the boat before the lease was granted. If the boat was regarded as a mineral or as part of the soil within the maxim *quicquid plantatur solo, solo cedit*, he did possess and own it. If it was regarded as a chattel (and the judgment implies that if the judge had been compelled to decide the question he would probably have held it to be a chattel), the question arose whether an occupier could possess a chattel without knowing of its existence. The plaintiff 'was in possession of the ground, not merely of the surface, but of everything that lay beneath the surface down to the centre of the earth, and consequently in possession of the boat . . . . For the boat was embedded in the land; a mere trespasser could not have taken possession of it, he could only have come at it by further acts of trespass. The Plaintiff then, being thus in possession of the chattel, it follows that the property in the chattel was vested in him.' (The right of the original owner, he continued, had been barred for centuries, even if ownership had not been abandoned.) 'In my opinion, it makes no difference in these circumstances, that the Plaintiff was not aware of the existence of the boat.'[1] Finally, the judge held that the lease gave the lessee merely a licence to make whatever excavations were approved by the lessor, and an implied permission to dispose of the clay or ordinary soil so excavated; but this permission did not extend to an object like the boat, whose existence was not contemplated by the parties at the time of granting the lease.

Apparently no writer has argued that *Elwes* v. *Brigg Gas Co.* was wrongly decided, and it is submitted that this judgment (among others) precludes any theory of possession in English law which is rigidly based on the necessity for some kind of specific intention directed towards the particular object in question. The judge expressly held that the plaintiff's absence of knowledge of the existence of the boat was irrelevant to his possession; *a fortiori*, therefore, the fact that the plaintiff had no intention relating to the specific chattel was also irrelevant. The plaintiff may have had some potential control over the chattel because it was embedded in his land, but the important factor in the judge's mind was the legal relationship between the plaintiff and the place where the boat lay. Before the lease, he was the tenant for life in possession of that land, and this was the vital consideration when no one had actual physical control, knowledge or specific intention in regard to the boat. The reference in the judgment to a trespasser's position suggests that it may be relevant to consider the usual intention of an occupier to exclude unauthorized persons from his land, and so from any chattels which may happen to be in or on his land. Hence although the occupation of premises is of great importance in the absence of other factors, less weight should be given to it where the occupier did not intend to exclude other persons from his land. The Court of Appeal or House of Lords could uphold the decision in *Bridges* v. *Hawkesworth* on this narrower ground.

The next authority on the 'occupier versus finder' situation is

[1] (1886), 33 Ch. D. 562, at pp. 568–569.

South Staffordshire Water Company v. *Sharman*.[1] Here the plaintiffs owned and occupied the land covered by the Minster Pool in Lichfield. Sharman was employed by them to clean out the pool, and he found two gold rings in the mud at the bottom of the pool. The police were unable to find the owner, and so the plaintiffs brought detinue against their servant, Sharman, for the return of the rings. Lord Russell of Killowen C.J., in a short judgment with which Wills J. concurred, emphasized the plaintiffs' ownership of the place in question, and their right to exclude anyone from the pool. He assented to the proposition of counsel for the defendant that 'the plaintiffs must show actual control over the *locus in quo* and the things in it', but thought that this test was satisfied in the circumstances. He then distinguished the decision in *Bridges* v. *Hawkesworth* by saying that the notes in that case were dropped in the public part of the shop and so were not within the protection of his house. Lord Russell concluded that 'the general principle' was that 'where a person has possession of house or land, with a manifest intention to exercise control over it and the things which may be upon[2] or in it, then, if something is found on that land, whether by an employee of the owner or by a stranger, the presumption is that the possession of that thing is in the owner[3] of the *locus in quo*.'[4]

Let us now approach *Sharman's Case* using the list of factors suggested above. Assuming that Sharman acquired possession when he found the rings, the vital question was whether the plaintiff company possessed them immediately before Sharman found them. No one then knew of their existence or location, and so the factors of knowledge and of any intention directed to the specific rings were absent. Nor had anyone actual physical

---

[1] [1896] 2 Q.B. 44.

[2] The words quoted earlier in the judgment from Pollock and Wright, *op. cit.*, p. 41, were 'everything which is *attached to or under* that land.'

[3] Lord Russell must mean 'the possessor', since he began his principle by speaking of 'where a person has possession . . . of land.' The plaintiffs both owned and possessed the land, and Lord Russell did not contemplate a case such as *Hannah* v. *Peel*, [1945] K.B. 509 (*infra*, p. 93) where an owner who was out of occupation claimed a chattel found on the land.

[4] [1896] 2 Q.B. 44, at p. 47.

control over the rings, but since the plaintiff company controlled the pool in which the rings were lying, it could be said that they had some potential control over them. But the crucial factor mentioned in the judgment was the legal relationship of the plaintiffs to the pool, compared with that of all other persons, including Sharman. The plaintiffs owned and possessed the pool, whereas the defendant was merely their licensee with permission to enter their land to fulfil his duties as their servant; anyone who entered without the plaintiff's permission would be a trespasser. The Court also took into account the plaintiffs' intention to exclude all others from the pool, and to exercise control over anything which, even unknown to them, might happen to be lying there. Though an intention to exclude all trespassers is not essential for a decision that the occupier possesses something lying on his land, if he has shown such an intention his claim to possess it is much stronger.

The court did not consider relevant the special relationship of master and servant existing between the parties (Factor (8)), but it could well have done so, as Salmond[1] and Riesman[2] have pointed out. The plaintiff company, being the occupier of the land, employed Sharman to clean out the pool, and it was in the course of his employment that he found the rings. It would not be unreasonable for the courts to hold that the over-all legal relationship of master and servant warranted a special rule that, as between master and servant, anything the servant found in the course of his employment passed immediately into the possession of his master. (Whether the servant might acquire possession as against strangers is a different question.) Dixon J. in an Australian case,[3] thought, that where a sailor was ordered to search a ship for stowaways and found some smuggled coins hidden in the forepeak, possesssion of the coins passed immediately to his employers, the owners of the ship.

In *Sharman's Case* the social purpose of the particular rule of law in question (Factor (9)) was highly relevant. Wills J. stated explicitly that 'a contrary decision would, as I think,

---

[1] *Jurisprudence* (7th ed.), p. 307.   [2] (1939), 52 Harv. L.R. 1105, at pp. 1116–1117.
[3] *Willey* v. *Synan* (1937), 57 C.L.R. 200, at pp. 216–217.

be a great and most unwise encouragement to dishonesty'.[1] This sentence is an open acknowledgment that the judges were consciously promoting what they considered to be a proper social purpose in the circumstances. The word 'dishonesty' suggests that Wills J. had particularly in mind the fidelity of a servant, but the *ratio decidendi* was not limited to the master-servant relationship. The purpose he had in mind must have been wider, possibly something like this: a conclusion that the plaintiff company possessed the rings before Sharman found them would discourage trespassers and licensees (including servants) from prospecting for chattels on land occupied by others; such a conclusion would also avoid an undesirable legal 'vacuum' in which some chattels lying on private land would not be possessed by either the occupier or anyone else. But whatever policy the Common Law were to adopt in this situation could be implemented only by a ruling on the possession of the chattel immediately before it was found.

The judgment in *Sharman's Case* does not distinguish between chattels lying unattached on the surface of private land, and chattels attached to or under the land. Lord Russell spoke of things 'upon' the land, and though it has been argued that in fact the rings were 'attached to or under' the land[2] it is submitted that the judge accepted the wider formulation. If this distinction is not accepted, *Bridges* v. *Hawkesworth* can stand with *Sharman's Case* only if Lord Russell's explanation of the former is upheld, namely, that the occupier does not possess something which, unknown to him, is lying on a part of his land open to the public. Lord Russell was not endeavouring to expound the *ratio decidendi* of *Bridges* v. *Hawkesworth* in terms of this 'private' or 'open to the public' distinction; he was making an important qualification to the 'finders-keepers' rule propounded in the former case, and turning that rule into the exception rather than the rule, when the occupier of private land makes a claim. This is the way in which Common Law rules have often been developed or modified from case to case.

---

[1] [1896] 2 Q.B. 44, at p. 48.
[2] Goodhart, *Essays in Jurisprudence and the Common Law*, pp. 87–88.

In the opinion of the writer, the law ought at least to award possession in civil cases to the occupier against a trespassing finder (this point is dealt with later); but a better rule would be wider, and provide that the occupier possessed all chattels in or on his land which are not possessed by anyone else. This wider rule would prevent licensees as well as trespassers from claiming possessory rights to anything found on private land. If the Common Law finally adopts this rule it might well accept Lord Russell's opinion that the occupier cannot make such a claim to possess when he has permitted the public, or a large section of the public, to come on his land. In these circumstances the place of finding could be treated as analogous to a public highway. Such special rules could be engrafted by the judges upon the ordinary possessory rules in the same way as the special rule on possession between master and servant was laid down (Factor (8)).

The case of *Hannah* v. *Peel*[1] is frequently cited on the ground that it followed *Bridges* v. *Hawkesworth*. The defendant Peel was the owner of a house but not its occupier at any relevant time. The house had been requisitioned for the army at the beginning of the war in 1939. The plaintiff, a soldier, was in a bedroom of the house adjusting the black-out curtains when he touched something in a crevice on the top of a window-frame. It dropped on to the outside window ledge, and the next morning he found that it was a brooch. He was an honest finder, and took the brooch to the police, but nearly two years later, when the police had failed to find the owner of the brooch, they gave it to the defendant, the owner of the house, who sold it for £66. The defendant had no knowledge of its existence before it was found, but he refused the plaintiff's claim for either the return of the brooch or its value.

Birkett J. deplored the uncertain state of the law, but thought that the authorities established the rule that 'a man possesses everything which is attached to or under his land.'[2] But the

---

[1] [1945] K.B. 509.
[2] [1945] K.B. 509, at p. 520. The words 'his land' must refer to possession, and not bare ownership of the land.

law had not been clearly formulated in regard to things lying unattached on the surface of a man's land. In the present case the judge emphasized that the defendant, though he was the owner of the land, was 'never physically in possession of these premises at any time'[1] and that he had no knowledge of the brooch until it was found. In the result he thought that he should follow *Bridges* v. *Hawkesworth* and hold that the finder was entitled to it as against the defendant, since he felt that the facts before him were similar to those in that case.

Presumably the Crown, following the requisitioning of the house, was in possession of the land through its servants in the Army. The Crown, however, made no claim to the brooch, so it was not a 'finder versus occupier' situation; the claimants were the finder and the non-occupying owner of the premises. As in the earlier cases, the technical issue was whether the defendant possessed the brooch before it was found; if so, his earlier possession would give him a relatively better right to possess than the plaintiff, and he could resist the plaintiff's claim in detinue. The factors of physical control over the brooch itself, of specific knowledge of it, and of intention were not present in the circumstances. The only relevant factors were the legal relationship of the litigants to the place of finding, and the social purpose of the rule in question.

As to the first, the plaintiff was a servant and licensee of the occupier of the premises where the brooch lay. (He did not, however, find it in the course of his employment which meant that the special rule suggested for servants would not apply.) The defendant had the bare legal ownership of the premises, but not possession. Earlier authorities showed that possession of premises may be relevant to the possession of chattels found thereon, but in no case had the ownership of premises been considered relevant, unless it was coupled with possession. The decision of Birkett J. suggests that ownership without possession is not relevant; but, although the judge makes the point that the defendant did not possess the premises, it cannot be said that it is part of his *ratio decidendi*, which proceeded on the

----

[1] [1945] K.B. 509, at p. 521.

assumption that the plaintiff-finder could succeed against even an occupier. But it is submitted that a higher court would explain *Hannah* v. *Peel* on the narrower ground that the defendant was not in possession of the premises.[1]

The social policy involved in the decision lay in the choice between the finder and the owner of the premises as the person to enjoy the windfall in the absence of claims by the owner of the brooch, or by the occupier. There was no authority on the point, and the judge therefore had some discretion in choosing the finder.[2]

(b) Finding by a trespasser

Would it have made any difference in *Bridges* v. *Hawkesworth* if Bridges had been a trespasser? Suppose the two men had previously quarrelled and Hawkesworth had thereupon forbidden Bridges to enter his shop again. It is submitted that in civil cases the courts should not permit a trespassing finder to acquire possession against an occupier, but there is not yet any direct authority in civil law for this view.

However, in the criminal case of *Hibbert* v. *McKiernan*[3], the appellant was trespassing on private golf links where he had gone in order to look for lost balls; he intended to take away and sell any he found. The golf club employed a policeman on special duty to warn off any trespassers, and to arrest anyone found taking balls from the course. The appellant was convicted of the larceny of some balls he had taken, although the court found that they had been 'abandoned' by their original owners; the golf club was held to have sufficient possession or control of any lost balls on its course for the 'property' in a charge of larceny against a stranger to be laid in them. We shall see later that the concept of possession in larceny has diverged from the concept employed in civil cases, but it is relevant to

---

[1] See Winfield (1945), 61 L.Q.R. 333.

[2] *In re Cohen*, [1953] Ch. 88 is a decision where *Sharman's Case* was cited for the proposition that the owner of land is the owner of chattels found thereon. The usual formulation has been based on the possession of land, as we have seen; but it was not an 'occupier versus finder' dispute, and the case does not assist a discussion of possession.

[3] [1948] 2 K.B. 142.

the present topic to note that the Divisional Court laid some emphasis on the fact that the appellant had trespassed on the course for the sole purpose of taking any lost articles he could find. Furthermore, he was a dishonest finder, in that he intended to keep for himself anything he found, without advertising his find.

The judgment did not discuss the civil aspect of the facts but we can infer that the courts will be unlikely to award possession in civil cases to a trespassing finder against the occupier. If such a finder may be punished criminally when he has a guilty intent, as in *Hibbert* v. *McKiernan*, he surely ought not to acquire in civil law any possessory remedies to the chattel against the occupier. There are *dicta* in other cases which indicate that the judges will be loath to give any such remedy to a trespassing finder.[1] The argument for giving the occupier a possessory right to recover anything found on his land by a trespasser is of course strongest when it is proved that the trespasser intended to search for lost articles; but if the policy of the law is to discourage trespassing as far as possible, the rule could be laid down that the occupier is entitled to claim even a chattel found casually by a trespasser who was not searching for lost articles.

The courts cannot make these distinctions unless they superimpose a special rule upon the ordinary factors governing possession, which would put trespassers into a special category in the same way as servants are put into a special category for rules based on possession.[2]

(c) *Failure to make inquiries for the true owner*

This matter concerns the honesty of the finder, and should be considered as a separate point from that of trespassing, though a dishonest finder may often be a trespasser as well. The honest

---

[1] *E.g., South Staffordshire Water Company* v. *Sharman*, [1896] 2 Q.B. 44.

[2] Salmond in his *Jurisprudence* (7th ed.), p. 307, suggested another ground for denying any rights to a trespasser: 'If a trespasser seeks and finds treasure in my land, he must give it up to me not because I was first in possession of it (which is not the case) but because he cannot be suffered to retain any advantage derived from his own wrong.'

finder will wish to return the article to its true owner, and will take all reasonable steps to discover him. The most obvious step will be to inform the occupier of the land where it was found, since the owner may inquire for it there; the finder in each of the civil cases considered above had done this. Even if English law does not adopt the two qualifications to *Bridges* v. *Hawkesworth* which have already been discussed, and a wide rule in favour of the finder prevails, it is submitted that if the finding occurs on land in the occupation of another, it should be a condition precedent to the finder's assertion of a possessory title against the occupier that he has informed the occupier of the find as soon as possible, and taken any other reasonable steps to publicize his find. This would be another special rule superimposed on the ordinary factors governing possession.[1]

(d) Finding by a servant of the occupier

This matter was considered in the discussion of *Sharman's Case*, where a rule was suggested that a servant-finder should not prevail against his employer, at least when his employer was also the occupier. It could even be made a wider rule, incidental to the master and servant relationship, that a master should immediately acquire possession of anything found by his servant in the course of his employment. Riesman[2] suggests that this rule would be particularly justified in the case of those servants whose task makes it likely that they will find lost articles, *e.g.* road-sweepers, railway guards, bus conductors, cleaners, laundry-workers, etc.

(e) The distinction between 'things lost' and 'things mislaid'

Many American states have accepted a distinction between a thing which is 'mislaid', where a person deliberately puts it down in a particular place, and later forgets it, and a thing which is 'lost' or dropped by accident. A Massachusetts court[3] in 1866

---

[1] The law of larceny partly covers this matter by providing that it is larceny 'where at the time of the finding, the finder believes that the owner can be discovered by taking reasonable steps.' Larceny Act, 1916, Section 1 (2) (i) (d).
[2] *Op. Cit.*, at p. 1117. [3] *M'Avoy* v. *Medina* (1866), 11 Allen 548.

held that where one bank customer voluntarily placed his wallet on a desk in the bank, and then apparently forgot about it, the wallet was 'mislaid', and possession of it passed immediately to the banker. Another customer who found it could therefore not treat it as 'lost' and assert a possessory claim to it. English law has not yet adopted this distinction, which is employed to assist the missing owner by giving possession to the occupier rather than the finder. Its justification is that the owner of a 'mislaid' article is more likely to remember where he last had it, and to return there to inquire for it.

The distinction can be based on a concept of possession only by means of the fiction that the person who mislaid an article intended to entrust it to the occupier should he forget it. It suffers from the further defect that it depends entirely upon an inference drawn from the circumstances and place of finding, and these may not permit any clear inference. It is submitted that English law would not need to adopt the distinction if the other suggested rules in favour of the occupier are laid down.

(3) CONCLUSION

In conclusion of this protracted discussion of finding problems, it is submitted that the existing Common Law is deficient in 'finder versus occupier' situations, and that the possessory remedies will be adequate for such cases only if the judges are prepared to develop a flexible approach to the concept of possession, and to lay down special rules awarding possession to the occupier in certain circumstances. The common law has in the past developed special rules on possession for particular cases, and since it is Utopian to hope for legislation on finding problems from an over-burdened Parliament, the Court of Appeal and the House of Lords should provide the solutions within the Common Law.

III. THE LAW OF LARCENY AND THE CONCEPT OF POSSESSION

Throughout the history of the Common Law, larceny has been regarded as a dishonest change of possession of a chattel. It was an offence committed (1) against the victim's possession of the stolen thing and (2) by the thief taking possession of that thing; and though legislation has made some glosses on the Common Law, this concept of larceny is still basically correct. Section 1 of the Larceny Act, 1916, now provides: 'For the purposes of this Act (1) a person steals who, without the consent of the owner, fraudulently and without a claim of right made in good faith, takes and carries away anything capable of being stolen, with intent, at the time of such taking, permanently to deprive the owner thereof . . . .'

First we must inquire into the meaning of the word 'owner' in this enactment; and secondly the meaning of 'takes', and 'at the time of such taking.'

(1) *The 'possession' of the victim in larceny*

The Act has not left the meaning of the word 'owner' entirely to the Common Law. Section 1 (2) (iii) provides that 'the expression "owner" includes any part owner or person having possession or control of, or a special property in, anything capable of being stolen.' By the use of the word 'includes', instead of 'means', this subsection does not give an exhaustive definition; the Common Law is probably extended in one way at least, by the use of the words 'or control of'. In the early Common Law the rules of larceny protected nothing beyond an actual physical holding of chattels. As civilization developed, however, owners desired the sanction of the law to protect their interests in a wider range of chattels; they were particularly concerned to secure the punishment of dishonest servants or guests for taking away chattels entrusted to them. This result was only possible within the framework of the existing rules if the judges would deny possession to servants and guests; such a ruling was finally laid down and, thereafter, a servant or guest was liable to conviction for larceny if he infringed the continuing possession of his master or host by misappropriating his goods. This is a good illustration of the influence upon the doctrine of possession of the judge's desire to further a particular social policy. The judges were prepared to make an artificial extension of the primitive notion of possession, if, apart from legislation, that was the only way to convict dishonest servants of felony.

Once the rule was laid down that a master still possessed goods in his servant's hands, it was not limited to cases of dishonest servants; the master was permitted to use the wider concept of his continuing possession so that a stranger who took a chattel from the servant's custody could be convicted of larceny against the master.[1] However, although the master's possession was extended in this way, the judges felt that it would be going too far to give the master possession of something which his servant received for him from a stranger away from his master's premises. The 'ideal' concept of possession may have acted as a check on the dictates of policy and convenience in this matter. The judges laid it down that in such cases the servant himself acquired possession, and so could not be convicted of larceny if he dealt with it dishonestly before he delivered it to his master or returned with it to his master's premises. Possession was attributed to the master only when he actually received it, or it was received into the protection of his house or premises; the servant could be guilty of larceny if he thereafter misappropriated it.

This result was plainly contrary to public policy, since it was just as dishonest for a servant to take a thing destined for his master as it was to take a thing already in his master's possession. But the distinction drawn on the basis of when the master acquired possession led to death for the servant in the latter event, and complete freedom from criminal liability in the former. It was not till 1799 that what we now call embezzlement was made a crime by statute to remedy this anomaly. Though the judges still recognized the social policy of punishing any fraudulent taking of chattels, they felt instinctively that it would remove the concept of possession too far from the primitive idea of actual physical control if they extended it further in the master's favour. No doubt the view that the penalty for larceny was too severe also discouraged the extension.

---

[1] Similarly the master could sue in trespass any stranger who interfered with his chattel in his servant's hands.

Now if the judges had been consistent they would have held that since a dishonest servant did not possess a thing belonging to his master before he misappropriated it, he could not possess it so as to lay a charge of larceny from himself against a stranger who took it from him. On a pedantic approach, the judges might have said that only the master could be the victim of such a theft, and that a charge of larceny should fail if it wrongly attributed the 'property' or 'possession' to the servant. But the judges have ignored any goal of logical consistency in their desire to punish dishonesty, and, in order to gain the maximum number of convictions, have stretched the legal concept of possession in different ways, according to whether they were considering the 'possession' of the victim or the 'possession' taken by the thief. If the servant himself is dishonest, then in order to punish his taking as larceny, the law says he did not have possession before he misappropriated it. But if a stranger took it out of the physical control of the servant, the Court of Criminal Appeal, in *R. v. Harding*[1] has permitted the 'property' to be laid in the servant instead of the master. In this case a domestic servant was alone in her master's house, while her master was in the garden. The accused was charged with robbing her of a mackintosh in the house belonging to her master. The Court, in a judgment delivered by Lord Hewart C.J., held that the maidservant had a sufficient 'special property' in the mackintosh for the charge of robbery (a form of larceny) to be correctly laid. It is clear that had the maidservant dishonestly appropriated the mackintosh she could have been convicted of larceny from her master, on the basis that she had bare custody of it before the misappropriation and had therefore taken it out of her master's possession.

It is true that *R. v. Harding* can be explained on the ground that the statutory extension of the meaning of 'owner' in the Larceny Act had freed the courts from a narrower meaning of 'possession' at Common Law, but the gradual widening of the concept of the victim's 'possession' or 'special property' in

---

[1] [1929] All E.R. Rep. 186; 21 Cr. App. Rep. 166. See also *R. v. Deakin and Smith* (1800), 2 Leach 862.

larceny cases had been in progress long before 1916. A few illustrations of this will suffice. In *Reg.* v. *Rowe*[1] some iron was found at the bottom of a canal, having apparently been dropped from a barge, and it was held by six judges that the iron was sufficiently within the possession of the canal company (who neither owned it nor knew of it) for a dishonest stranger who took it away to be guilty of larceny from the company. A similar case is *Hibbert* v. *McKiernan*,[2] where the secretary and members of a golf club were held to have a sufficient special property in lost golf balls abandoned on their land for a trespassing finder to be guilty of larceny from them. The golf club knew that there must be some lost balls on their land, though of course they did not know of the existence or exact location of any particular ball. The thief, however, knew that they had deliberately prohibited unauthorized persons from coming on their land to look for lost balls.

In *Cartwright* v. *Green*[3] Lord Chancellor Eldon held that it would be larceny for the repairer of a bureau to take money which he discovered in a secret drawer; this implies that the owner of the bureau, despite his ignorance of the secret drawer and its contents, retained sufficient 'possession' of the money to support a charge of larceny. Similarly, in *Merry* v. *Green*[4] another civil case, the Court of Exchequer Chamber ordered a new trial to determine whether the sale of a bureau had been intended to pass its unknown contents, if any. In the absence of such intention, the court assumed that the seller still retained sufficient possession of, or special property in, some money in a secret drawer, for the purchaser to be guilty of larceny when he found the money and misappropriated it. The seller neither owned the money nor knew of its existence, since he was not aware of the secret drawer. The purchaser acquired lawful possession of the bureau itself by delivery following the sale, and so the conclusion that the seller would retain a possessory interest in the money is an extreme illustration of how the concept of the victim's 'possession' has been extended

[1] (1859), Bell's C.C. 93; 8 Cox 139.   [2] [1948] 2 K.B. 142 (*supra*, p. 95).
[3] (1802), 8 Ves. 405; 2 Leach 952.   [4] (1841), 7 M. & W. 623.

to catch dishonest persons within the net of the criminal law.

In each of these four cases, a person without knowledge of the existence or location of a chattel (and therefore without any intention directed specifically towards it) was held to possess or control it for the purpose of laying a charge of larceny against another. It is true that in *R. v. Rowe* and in *Hibbert v. McKiernan*, there was some degree of physical control exercised over the place where the chattels lay; but in the bureaux cases, the victims of the alleged larcenies did not possess the bureaux containing the money in question. The vital factor in all these decisions on possession or control was the policy of the law to convict dishonest persons wherever possible.

Larceny in early Common Law was regarded not only as a fraudulent deprivation of the victim's possession, but as a taking against the King's Peace. From the point of view of the thief, he knows that he is violating someone else's special relationship to the chattel, but he does not care whether that person is owner, bailee, servant, occupier, or other kind of possessor. Often a thief does not know who has any legal claim to the chattel; he simply intends to take and keep it in defiance of any one else's rights, and it is for this that the courts wish to punish him. The injury to the King's Peace, or public order, is the same despite legal distinctions as to possession, custody, control or special property in a chattel; nor do such distinctions affect the moral blame attached to the act of taking something with knowledge that one is not entitled to it. Therefore here, as elsewhere, the courts have not followed any doctrinaire concept of possession; in particular they have on occasion disregarded the victim's lack of knowledge or intention about the stolen chattel.

But when we consider the thief's act in taking a thing, we naturally feel that he ought to be punished only when he had full knowledge of what he took and nevertheless dishonestly intended to take it; for it is only then that he is fully responsible for his act. The law of larceny is therefore justified in adopting a functional approach to the meaning of possession, and in treating the victim's possession as a different concept from the possession acquired by the thief. We must now examine the decisions on the latter concept.

(2) *The 'possession' acquired by the thief*

The definition of larceny in the Act of 1916 speaks of 'a person who, . . . takes and carries away anything . . . with intent, at the time of such taking, permanently to deprive the owner thereof. . ." The Common Law of larceny required an asportation and an actual physical change of possession, and both requirements are now statutory ('takes[1] and carries away.') But in addition to acquiring possession of the chattel, a thief must form his guilty intention not later than at the moment he acquires possession. Nearly all the difficulties in this aspect of the law of larceny flow from the need for the felonious intention to be contemporaneous with the 'taking', because a man who acquires possession while his mind is innocent cannot generally at Common Law be guilty of larceny even if he subsequently forms a guilty intention and misappropriates the chattel to his own use. (By statute, some exceptions have been made to this rule, *e.g.* larceny by a bailee; at Common Law, the peculiar doctrines of 'breaking bulk'[2] and of 'continuing trespass'[3] have been developed to avoid the operation of this rule in some cases.) Because the intent must be contemporaneous with the taking, the judges have tended wherever possible to postpone the moment of 'taking' until the taker knows what he has in his physical control, and is accordingly in a position to form an intention, whether honest or dishonest, in regard to the thing. In practical life, a person will not form 'an intent permanently to deprive' another of a chattel, until he knows fairly accurately what it is that he is taking or has taken.

The judges, therefore, in the pursuit of the policy of punishing dishonesty wherever possible, have required not only know-

---

[1] At Common Law, 'to take' meant to gain possession of a thing by means of a trespass. Sec. 1 (2) (i) of the Larceny Act, 1916, extends the meaning of 'takes' to cover taking by a trick, by intimidation, and, in some circumstances, under a mistake or by finding.

[2] *The 'Carrier's' Case* (1473), Y.B. 13 Edw. IV, fo. 9, Pasc., pl. 5.

[3] *R.* v. *Riley* (1853), Dearsley C.C. 149; *Ruse* v. *Read*, [1949] 1 K.B. 377; *R.* v. *Kindon* (1957), 41 Cr. App. Rep. 208.

ledge on the part of the taker of the existence of the chattel, but also some knowledge of its main attributes, before he can be said to have 'taken' it. For instance, in *Reg.* v. *Ashwell*[1] the accused asked for the loan of a shilling and received from the prosecutor a coin which they both mistakenly thought was a shilling; some time later, Ashwell found it was a sovereign and immediately determined to misappropriate it for himself and only repay a shilling to the prosecutor. The question whether he was guilty of larceny divided evenly the fourteen judges of the Court for Crown Cases Reserved. Lord Coleridge C.J. said, in favour of upholding the conviction, 'In good sense it seems to me he did not take it till he knew what he had got; and when he knew what he had got, the same instant he stole it.' Ashwell knew from the beginning that he had received a coin, but he did not till later have accurate knowledge of the most important quality or attribute of that coin, namely its value or denomination. In view of the subsequent decision in *R.* v. *Hudson*,[2] it is now probable that Ashwell was properly convicted. Hudson received an envelope not intended for him, and though he retained it unopened for several days, the Court of Criminal Appeal held that he did not 'take' its contents until he opened it and discovered what it contained. The court did not conceal its desire to punish an obviously dishonest person, and this policy clearly influenced the ruling that there was no taking without knowledge.

The latest case is *Russell* v. *Smith*[3] where a lorry, by some mistake, was loaded with 48 sacks instead of 40. After the journey the driver discovered, while unloading, that he had the extra sacks, and he immediately decided dishonestly to keep them for himself. The Divisional Court, on appeal from the justices, held that the 'taking' by the driver occurred only when he discovered he had them, Lord Goddard saying: 'I do not think that a man can take into his possession, or come into possession of a thing of which he has no knowledge.'[4] Such a statement may be correct for the rule in larceny that the thief must 'take'

---

[1] (1885), 16 Q.B.D. 190.   [2] [1943] K.B. 458.   [3] [1958] 1 Q.B. 27.
[4] [1958] 1 Q.B. 27, at pp. 34–35.

the thing, but it does not hold good for all other possessory rules of law. Smith would probably have been held to have had sufficient 'possession or control of or a special property in' the extra sacks for a stranger to be guilty of larceny from him, had the stranger stolen the sacks from the lorry during the journey; Smith's knowledge might not have been vital for his possession were he the innocent victim of a theft.[1]

In the law of larceny, therefore, we have a clear illustration of the way in which English judges have employed possession as a flexible and functional concept, and emphasized different factors in different possessory rules, according to the dictates of justice and social policy. It is submitted that a similar approach will be found in all other possessory rules.

---

[1] In *Russell* v. *Smith* the 'property' was laid in the factory company where the lorry was loaded. However, the 'property' might have been laid in Smith's own employers, who owned and possessed the lorry, on the ground that when the sacks were deliberately placed in the lorry by the factory employees, possession of them passed immediately to the possessor of the lorry. (See *dicta* in *Williams* v *Phillips* (1957), 41 Cr. App. Rep. 5; and *R.* v. *Reed and Another* (1854), 6 Cox 284. The fact that Smith was a servant would not preclude the 'property' being laid in him if a stranger stole the sacks from the lorry. (See *R.* v. *Harding, supra*, p. 101.)

CHAPTER V

Ownership

by A. M. Honoré

OWNERSHIP is one of the characteristic institutions of human society. A people to whom ownership was unknown, or who accorded it a minor place in their arrangements, who meant by *meum* and *tuum* no more than 'what I (or you) presently hold' would live in a world that is not our world. Yet to see why their world would be different, and to assess the plausibility of vaguely conceived schemes to replace 'ownership' by 'public administration', or of vaguely stated claims that the importance of ownership has declined or its character changed in the twentieth century, we need first to have a clear idea of what ownership is.

I propose, therefore, to begin by giving an account of the standard incidents of ownership: *i.e.* those legal rights, duties and other incidents which apply, in the ordinary case, to the person who has the greatest interest in a thing admitted by a mature legal system. To do so will be to analyse the concept of ownership, by which I mean the 'liberal' concept of 'full' individual ownership, rather than any more restricted notion to which the same label may be attached in certain contexts.

Secondly, I propose to say something about the notion of title, about the types of rule which legal systems adopt in order to decide who is to own a thing and, if two or more persons have claims to a thing, how priority between them is to be settled. Thirdly, I touch briefly on some instances of split ownership, in which the standard incidents are divided between two or more persons. Last comes the topic of the restriction of ownership in the social interest and the relation between ownership and public administration. This order of treatment should have the following advantage: once the standard case of full ownership has been depicted the variants and possible alternatives stand out more clearly in contrast, and are easier to understand and assess. On the other hand, this treatment is not meant to prejudge the issue, how far private ownership should stretch and to what extent it should be modified in the public interest. That issue, though it lies outside the scope of this essay, can be understood only with the help of an adequate analysis of the concept of ownership.

I. THE LIBERAL CONCEPT OF OWNERSHIP

If ownership is provisionally defined as the *greatest possible interest in a thing which a mature system of law recognizes*, then it follows that, since all mature systems admit the existence of 'interests' in 'things', all mature systems have, in a sense, a concept of ownership. Indeed, even primitive systems, like that of the Trobriand islanders, have rules by which certain persons, such as the 'owners' of canoes, have greater interests in certain things than anyone else.[1]

For mature legal systems it is possible to make a larger claim. In them certain important legal incidents are found, which are common to different systems. If it were not so, 'He owns that umbrella', said in a purely English context, would mean something different from 'He owns that umbrella', proferred as a translation of 'Ce parapluie est à lui'. Yet, as we know, they mean the same. There is indeed, a substantial similarity in the position of one who 'owns' an umbrella in England, France, Russia, China, and any other modern country one may care to mention. Everywhere the 'owner' can, in the simple uncomplicated case, in which no other person has an interest in the thing, use it, stop others using it, lend it, sell it or leave it by will. Nowhere may he use it to poke his neighbour in the ribs or to knock over his vase. Ownership, *dominium, propriété, Eigentum* and similar words stand not merely for the greatest interest in things in particular systems but for a type of interest with common features transcending particular systems. It must surely be important to know what these common features are?

[1] Malinowsky, *Crime and Custom in Savage Society*, p. 18.

In stressing the importance of such common features, I do not wish to go beyond the claim that these resemblances exist *de facto* and can be explained by the common needs of mankind and the common conditions of human life. It would be rash to assert that the features discussed are *necessarily* common to different mature systems, or that their range and ubiquity proves that what is called 'general jurisprudence' is a reputable pursuit. These assertions may indeed be true, but for my purposes it is enough to show that the standard incidents of ownership do not vary from system to system in the erratic, unpredictable way implied by some writers but, on the contrary, have a tendency to remain constant from place to place and age to age.

Nor must the present thesis be confused with the claim that all systems attach an equal importance to ownership (in the full, liberal sense) or regard the same things as capable of being owned. The latter claim would be patently false. In the Soviet Union, for instance, important assets such as land, businesses and collective farms are in general withdrawn from 'personal ownership' (*viz.* the liberal type of ownership) and subjected to 'government' or 'collective' ownership, which is a different, though related institution.[1] The notion of things 'outside commerce', not subject to private ownership but to special regulation by the state or public authorities, is an ancient one and has retained its importance in modern continental law.[2] Again, there is a case for saying that, in the early middle ages, land in England could not plausibly be said to be 'owned' because the standard incidents of which I shall speak were so divided between lord and tenant that the position of neither presented a sufficient analogy with the paradigm case of owning a thing.[3]

Indeed, in nearly all systems there will be some things to which not all the standard incidents apply, some things which cannot be sold or left by will, some interests which cannot endure beyond a lifetime, some things (flick knives, Colorado

---

[1] Gsovski, *Soviet Civil Law*, p. 569.
[2] Vegting, *Domaine public et res extra commercium.*
[3] Pollock and Maitland, *History of English Law to* 1290, Vol. II, p. 4.

beetles) which it is forbidden to use or to use in certain ways. If the differences between these cases and the paradigm case are striking enough, we shall be tempted to say that the things in question are not or cannot be owned, but it would be a mistake to conclude that the legal systems in which these cases occur do not recognize ownership. Whether a system recognizes ownership, and to what extent it permits ownership (who may own, what may be owned), are widely differing questions. No doubt liberal societies are more inclined than socialist societies to extend the list of items that can be owned, but it does not follow that, when a socialist system permits ownership, or 'personal ownership', it is permitting something different from what is permitted in the corresponding case in a liberal society. It may well be—and all the evidence indeed supports the view—that socialist societies recognize the 'liberal' notion of 'full' ownership, but limit the range of things that can be owned. Perhaps definitions of ownership contained in codes are not a safe guide. Still, it is striking that the French civil code, enacted in an atmosphere of liberal individualism, defines ownership as 'the right of enjoying and disposing of things in the most absolute manner, provided that one abstains from any use forbidden by statute or subordinate legislation';[1] while the Soviet civil code, framed in a socialist context, provides, in very similar language, that 'within the limits laid down by law, the owner has the right to possess, to use and to dispose of his property'.[2] Obviously much here depends on what limits are laid down by law in each system; in fact, so far as articles subject to 'personal ownership' are concerned, the limits in the two systems hardly differ.

One further *caveat*. I set out to describe the incidents of ownership in the simple cases in which one would not hesitate to say 'X owns that thing, that is X's book or house', even though Y may have borrowed it, or Y may be X's tenant. In doing this I do not lose sight of the existence of more complicated cases in which layman and lawyer alike may be puzzled to know which, of two or more persons interested in a thing, to call owner, or whether to say, on the other hand, that neither or

---

[1] *Code civil*, art. 544.   [2] Soviet civil code, art. 58.

none is owner. Just as the rules of a system may so restrict the permissible ways of dealing with certain types of thing that we are inclined to say that such things are not capable of being owned in that system, or can be owned only a sense different from the full, liberal sense we are to investigate, so the rules of a system may provide for the splitting of interests in a type of thing which, in general, is admittedly capable of being owned. Houses can be owned, and there is no conceptual difficulty in locating the ownership of a house let on a short lease. But if *A* lets *B* a house on a lease for 2,000 years it may be very unclear, at least to the layman, whether *A* or *B* or neither should be called owner. (In this case, legal usage designates *A* owner despite the tenuous character of his reversionary right.) Again, can a mortgagor be said to 'own' a house which is mortgaged? (Legal usage here refuses to designate the mortgagee owner despite the potentially indeterminate character of his interest.) No obvious linguistic convention governs the answer to such problems, and, if the rules of a legal system demand an answer, it must be sought in positive law, in the comparative strength of competing analogies with the paradigm case and in the light shed on the problem by the social context.

The fact that there are such cases of split ownership and that they present baffling problems to one who is compelled to fix on one interested person as *the* owner of the thing, does not make it worthless to try to delineate the incidents present in the ordinary, uncomplicated case. On the contrary, such a delineation is essential in order that it may be possible to assess the strength of the analogies in the peripheral cases. What must, however, be recognized at the outset, is that the actual use of 'owner' and 'ownership' extends beyond the standard case now to be described and that to delineate the standard case is here, as with most legal notions, not to provide a code for the use of the word. For instance, the sixteen or so pages of Burrows' *Words and Phrases Judicially Defined*,[1] concerned with the interpretation of the word 'owner' in various statutes, amply reveal how the courts have wrestled with provisions extending the

[1] (1934), Vol. IV, pp. 130–146.

legal meaning of 'owner' beyond the standard cases. But it is important to see that the very existence of such problems of statutory interpretation presupposes that there are paradigm cases in which the interpretation of 'owner' is clear.

Thus where a statute provided[1] that ' "owner" in relation to land, includes every person who jointly or severally whether at law or in equity, is entitled' to the profits of the land etc., Griffith C.J. pointed out that the term 'owner' '*Prima facie* connotes entire dominion. Section 3 [the definition section] extends the meaning so as to take in certain persons who possess some, but not all, of the rights of absolute owners. Although, therefore, the language of the definition is in form inclusive, and not exhaustive, it must be read as if the words "besides the absolute owner" were inserted after "includes".'[2] This presupposes that we know, without the help of an interpretation clause, what is meant by 'absolute owner'. Again, when Jessel M.R. said in a case on the interpretation of the Highways Act, 1835, 'I am clearly of the opinion that the term "owner" means the man in occupation, who may be either the actual owner or else only the occupying tenant',[3] he could not meaningfully have said this unless there were available criteria for the identification of the interest called 'ownership' and so of the 'actual owner' in the majority of cases.

The Standard Incidents

I now list what appear to be the standard incidents of ownership. They may be regarded as necessary ingredients in the notion of ownership, in the sense that, if a system did not admit them, and did not provide for them to be united in a single person, we would conclude that it did not know the liberal concept of ownership, though it might still have a modified version of ownership, either of a primitive or sophisticated sort. But the listed incidents are not individually necessary, though they may be together sufficient, conditions for the person

---

[1] Land Tax Assessment Act, 1910, s. 3.

[2] *Union Trustee Co. of Australia, Ltd.* v. *Land Tax Federal Commission* (1915), 20 C.L.R. 526, at p. 531.

[3] *Woodard* v. *Billericay Harbour Board* (1879), 11 Ch. D.214, at p. 217.

of inherence to be designated 'owner' of a particular thing in a given system. As we have seen, the use of 'owner' will extend to cases in which not all the listed incidents are present.

Ownership comprises the right to possess, the right to use, the right to manage, the right to the income of the thing, the right to the capital, the right to security, the rights or incidents of transmissibility and absence of term, the prohibition of harmful use, liability to execution, and the incident of residuarity: this makes eleven leading incidents. Obviously, there are alternative ways of classifying the incidents; moreover, it is fashionable to speak of ownership as if it were just a bundle of rights, in which case at least two items in the list would have to be omitted.

No doubt the concentration in the same person of the right (liberty)[1] of using as one wishes, the right to exclude others, the power of alienating and an immunity from expropriation is a cardinal feature of the institution. Yet it would be a distortion⁻ —and one of which the eighteenth century, with its over-emphasis on subjective rights, was patently guilty—to speak as if this concentration of patiently garnered rights was the only legally or socially important characteristic of the owner's position. The present analysis, by emphasizing that the owner is subject to characteristic prohibitions and limitations, and that ownership comprises at least one important incident independent of the owner's choice, is an attempt to redress the balance.

(1) *The right to possess*

The right to possess, *viz.* to have exclusive physical control of a thing, or to have such control as the nature of the thing admits, is the foundation on which the whole superstructure of ownership rests. It may be divided into two aspects, the right (claim) to be put in exclusive control of a thing and the right to remain in control, *viz.* the claim that others should not without permission, interfere. Unless a legal system provides some rules and procedures for attaining these ends it cannot be said to protect ownership.

---

[1] In this article I identify rights with claims, liberties etc. For a criticism of this identification see (1960), 34 Tulane L.R. 453.

It is of the essence of the right to possess that it is *in rem* in the sense of availing against persons generally. This does not, of course, mean that an owner is necessarily entitled to exclude everyone from his property. We happily speak of the ownership of land, yet a largish number of officials have the right of entering on private land without the owner's consent, for some limited period and purpose. On the other hand, a general licence so to enter on the 'property' of others would put an end to the institution of landowning as we now know it.

The protection of the right to possess (still using 'possess' in the convenient, though over-simple, sense of 'have exclusive physical control') should be sharply marked off from the protection of mere present possession. To exclude others from what one presently holds is an instinct found in babies and even, as Holmes points out,[1] in animals, of which the seal gives a striking example. To sustain this instinct by legal rules is to protect possession but not, as such, to protect the right to possess and so not to protect ownership. If dispossession without the possessor's consent is, in general, forbidden, the possessor is given a right *in rem*, valid against persons generally, to remain undisturbed, but he has no *right to possess in rem* unless he is entitled to recover from persons generally what he has lost or had taken from him, and to obtain from them what is due to him but not yet handed over. Admittedly there may be borderline cases in which the right to possess is partially recognized, *e.g.* where a thief is entitled to recover from those who oust him and all claiming under them, but not from others.

The protection of the right to possess, and so of one essential element in ownership, is achieved only when there are rules allotting exclusive physical control to one person rather than another, and that not merely on the basis that the person who has such control at the moment is entitled to continue in control. When children understand that Christmas presents go not to the finder but to the child whose name is written on the outside of the parcel, when a primitive tribe has a rule that a dead man's things go not to the first taker but to his son or his sister's

[1] *The Common Law*, p. 213.

son, we know that they have at least an embryonic idea of ownership.

To have worked out the notion of 'having a right to' as distinct from merely 'having', or, if that is too subjective a way of putting it, of rules allocating things to people as opposed to rules merely forbidding forcible taking, was a major intellectual achievement. Without it society would have been impossible. Yet the distinction is apt to be overlooked by English lawyers, who are accustomed to the rule that every adverse possession is a root of title, *i.e.* gives rise to a right to possess,[1] or at least that '*de facto* possession is *prima facie* evidence of seisin in fee and right to possession'.[2]

The owner, then, has characteristically a battery of remedies in order to obtain, keep and, if necessary, get back the thing owned. Remedies such as the actions for ejectment and wrongful detention and the *vindicatio* are designed to enable the plaintiff either to obtain or to get back a thing, or at least to put some pressure on the defendant to hand it over. Others, such as the actions for trespass to land and goods, the Roman possessory interdicts and their modern counterparts are primarily directed towards enabling a present possessor to keep possession. Few of the remedies mentioned are confined to the owner; most of them are available also to persons with a right to possess falling short of ownership, and some to mere possessors. Conversely, there will be cases in which they are not available to the owner, for instance because he has voluntarily parted with possession for a temporary purpose, as by hiring the thing out. The availability of such remedies is clearly not a necessary and sufficient condition of owning a thing; what is necessary, in order that there may be ownership of things at all, is that such remedies shall be available to the owner in the usual case in which no other person has a right to exclude him from the thing.

[1] Pollock & Wright, *Possession in the Common Law* (1888), pp. 91, 95; Wade and Megarry, *The Law of Real Property* (2nd ed.), p. 955.

[2] *N.R.M.A. Insurance, Ltd.* v. *B. & B. Shipping and Marine Salvage Co. (Pty.), Ltd.* (1947), 47 S.C.R. (N.S.W.) 273.

(2) *The right to use*

The present incident and the next two overlap. On a wide interpretation of 'use', management and income fall within use. On a narrow interpretation, 'use' refers to the owner's personal use and enjoyment of the thing owned. On this interpretation it excludes management and income.

The right (liberty) to use at one's discretion has rightly been recognized as a cardinal feature of ownership, and the fact that, as we shall see, certain limitations on use also fall within the standard incidents of ownership does not detract from its importance, since the standard limitations are, in general, rather precisely defined, while the permissible types of use constitute an open list.

(3) *The right to manage*

The right to manage is the right to decide how and by whom the thing owned shall be used. This right depends, legally, on a cluster of powers, chiefly powers of licensing acts which would otherwise be unlawful and powers of contracting: the power to admit others to one's land, to permit others to use one's things, to define the limits of such permission, and to contract effectively in regard to the use (in the literal sense) and exploitation of the thing owned. An owner may not merely sit in his own deck chair but may validly license others to sit in it, lend it, impose conditions on the borrower, direct how it is to be painted or cleaned, contract for it to be mended in a particular way. This is the sphere of management in relation to a simple object like a deck chair. When we consider more complex cases, like the ownership of a business, the complex of powers which make up the right to manage seems still more prominent. The power to direct how resources are to be used and exploited is one of the cardinal types of economic and political power; the owner's legal powers of management are one, but only one possible basis for it. Many observers have drawn attention to the growth of managerial power divorced from legal ownership; in such cases it may be that we should speak of split ownership or redefine our notion of the thing owned. This does not affect the fact that the right to manage is an important element in the notion of ownership; indeed, the fact that we feel doubts in these cases whether the 'legal owner' *really* owns is a testimony to its importance.

Management often takes the form of making contracts relating to the thing owned, whether with servants or agents or independent contractors. This fact, and the growing relative importance of management in comparison with personal use, at least in regard to some types of thing such as businesses, has led some observers to the neat conclusion that, over a wide sphere, *obligatio* has swallowed up *res*.[1] Even if the contrast were an apt one (and, after all, an *obligatio* is a *res*, a chose in action a chose) the sentiment would be exaggerated because many powers of management are exercised otherwise than by way of contract, not to mention powers of alienation. The point would be better made by saying that, in the owner's battery of rights, powers have increased in calibre while liberties have declined.

(4) *The right to the income*

To use or occupy a thing may be regarded as the simplest way of deriving an income from it, of enjoying it. It is, for instance, expressly contemplated by the English income tax legislation that the rent-free use or occupation of a house is a form of income, and only the inconvenience of assessing and collecting the tax presumably prevents the extension of this principle to movables.

Income in the more ordinary sense (fruits, rents, profits) may be thought of as a surrogate of use, a benefit derived from forgoing personal use of a thing and allowing others to use it for reward; as a reward for work done in exploiting the thing; or as the brute product of a thing, made by nature or by other persons. Obviously the line to be drawn between the earned and unearned income from a thing cannot be firmly drawn.

The owner's right to the income, which has always, under one name or another, bulked large in an analysis of his rights,

[1] J. W. Jones, *Forms of Ownership* (1947), 22 Tulane L.R. 83, 93.

has assumed still greater significance with the increased importance of income relative to capital. Legally it takes the form of a claim sometimes *in rem*, sometimes *in personam* to the income. When the latter is in the form of money, the claim before receipt of the money is *in personam;* and since the income from many forms of property, such as shares and trust funds, is in this form, there is another opportunity for introducing the apophthegm that *obligatio* has swallowed up *res*.

(5) *The right to the capital*

The right to the capital consists in the power to alienate the thing and the liberty to consume, waste or destroy the whole or part of it: clearly it has an important economic aspect. The latter liberty need not be regarded as unrestricted; but a general provision requiring things to be conserved in the public interest, so far as not consumed by use in the ordinary way, would perhaps be inconsistent with the liberal idea of ownership.

Most people do not wilfully destroy permanent assets; hence the power of alienation is the more important aspect of the owner's right to the capital of the thing owned. This comprises the power to alienate during life or on death, by way of sale, mortgage, gift or other mode, to alienate a part of the thing and partially to alienate it. The power to alienate may be subdivided into the power to make a valid disposition of the thing and the power to transfer the holder's title (or occasionally a better title) to it. The two usually concur but may be separated. as when *A* has a power of appointment over property held by *B* in trust.[1] Again, in some systems, a sale, mortgage, bequest, etc. may be regarded as valid though the seller or mortgagor cannot give a good title. By giving a good title is meant transferring to the transferee the rights of the owner including his power of alienation.

An owner normally has both the power of disposition and the power of transferring title. Disposition on death is not permitted in many primitive societies but seems to form an essential

[1] Hanbury, *Modern Equity* (1952), p. 114.

element in the mature notion of ownership. The tenacity of the right of testation once it has been recognized is shown by the Soviet experience. The earliest writers were hostile to inheritance, but gradually Soviet law has come to admit that citizens may dispose freely of their 'personal property' on death, subject to limits not unlike those known elsewhere.[1]

(6) *The right to security*

An important aspect of the owner's position is that he should be able to look forward to remaining owner indefinitely if he so chooses and he remains solvent. His right to do so may be called the right to security. Legally, this is in effect an immunity from expropriation, based on rules which provide that, apart from bankruptcy and execution for debt, the transmission of ownership is consensual.

However, a general right to security, availing against others, is consistent with the existence of a power to expropriate or divest in the state or public authorities. From the point of view of security of property, it is important that when expropriation takes place, adequate compensation should be paid; but a general power to expropriate subject to paying compensation would be fatal to the institution of ownership as we know it. Holmes' paradox, that where specific restitution of goods is not a normal remedy,[2] expropriation and wrongful conversion are equivalent, obscures the vital distinction between acts which a legal system permits as rightful and those which it reprobates as wrongful: but if wrongful conversion were general and went unchecked, ownership as we know it would disappear, though damages were regularly paid.

In some systems, as (*semble*) English law, a private individual may destroy another's property without compensation when this is necessary in order to protect his own person or property from a greater danger.[3] Such a rule is consistent with security of property only because of its exceptional character. Again,

---

[1] Constitution of the U.S.S.R., 1936, s. 10; Gsovski, *op. cit.*, p. 620.
[2] Holmes (1897), 10 Harv. L.R. 457, 461.
[3] *Cope* v. *Sharpe*, [1912] 1 K.B. 496; *Cresswell* v. *Sirl*, [1948] 1 K.B. 241.

the state's (or local authority's) power of expropriation is usually limited to certain classes of thing and certain limited purposes. A general power to expropriate any property for any purpose would be inconsistent with the institution of ownership. If, under such a system, compensation were regularly paid, we might say either that ownership was not recognized in that system, or that money alone could be owned, 'money' here meaning a strictly fungible claim on the resources on the community. As we shall see, 'ownership' of such claims is not identical with the ownership of material objects and simple claims.

(7) *The incident of transmissibility*

It is often said that one of the main characteristics of the owner's interest is its 'duration'. In England, at least, the doctrine of estates made lawyers familiar with the notion of the 'duration' of an interest and Maitland, in a luminous metaphor, spoke of estates as 'projected upon the plane of time'.[1]

Yet this notion is by no means as simple as it seems. What is called 'unlimited' duration (*perpétuité*)[2] comprises at least two elements (i) that the interest can be transmitted to the holder's successors and so on *ad infinitum* (The fact that in medieval land law all interests were considered 'temporary'[3] is one reason why the terminology of ownership failed to take root, with consequences which have endured long after the cause has disappeared); (ii) that it is not certain to determine at a future date. These two elements may be called 'transmissibility' and 'absence of term' respectively. We are here concerned with the former.

No one, as Austin points out,[4] can enjoy a thing after he is dead (except vicariously) so that, in a sense, no interest can outlast death. But an interest which is transmissible to the holder's successors (persons designated by or closely related to the holder who obtain the property after him) is more valuable than one which stops with his death. This is so both because on alienation the alienee or, if transmissibility is generally recog-

---

[1] Pollock & Maitland, *op. cit.*, Vol. II, p. 10.
[2] Planiol-Ripert-Esmein, *Traité pratique de droit civil français* (1952), Vol. II, p. 220.
[3] Hargreaves, *Introduction to the Principles of Land Law* (1952), p. 47.
[4] Austin, *Jurisprudence*, 4th ed., (1873), p. 817.

nized, the alienee's successors, are thereby enabled to enjoy the thing after the alienor's death so that a better price can be obtained for the thing, and because, even if alienation were not recognized, the present holder would by the very fact of transmissibility be dispensed *pro tanto* from making provision for his intestate heirs. Hence, for example, the moment when the tenant in fee acquired a heritable (though not yet fully alienable) right was a crucial moment in the evolution of the fee simple. Heritability by the state would not, of course, amount to transmissibility in the present sense: it is assumed that the transmission is in some sense *advantageous* to the transmitter.

Transmissibility can, of course, be admitted, yet stop short at the first, second or third generation of transmittees. The owner's interest is characterized by *indefinite* transmissibility, no limit being placed on the possible number of transmissions, though the nature of the thing may well limit the actual number.

In deference to the conventional view that the exercise of a right must depend on the choice of the holder,[1] I have refrained from calling transmissibility a right. It is, however, clearly something in which the holder has an economic interest, and it may be that the notion of a right requires revision in order to take account of incidents not depending on the holder's choice which are nevertheless of value to him.

(8) *The incident of absence of term*

This is the second part of what is vaguely called 'duration'. The rules of a legal system usually seem to provide for determinate, indeterminate and determinable interests. The first are certain to determine at a future date or on the occurence of a future event which is certain to occur. In this class come leases for however long a term, copyrights, etc. Indeterminate interests are those, such as ownership and easements, to which no term is set. Should the holder live for ever, he would, in the ordinary way, be able to continue in the enjoyment of them for

[1] Hart, *Definition and Theory in Jurisprudence* (1953), p. 16; (1954), 70 L.Q.R. 49.

ever. Since human beings are mortal, he will in practice only be able to enjoy them for a limited period, after which the fate of his interest depends on its transmissibility. Again, since human beings are mortal, interests for life, whether of the holder of another, must be regarded as determinate. The notion of an indeterminate interest, in the full sense, therefore requires the notion of transmissibility, but, if the latter were not recognized, there would still be value to the holder in the fact that his interest was not due to determine on a fixed date or on the occurence of some contingency, like a general election, which is certain to occur sooner or later.

On inspection it will be found that what I have called indeterminate interests are really determinable. The rules of legal systems always provide some contingencies such as bankruptcy, sale in execution, or state expropriation on which the holder of an interest may lose it. It is true that in most of these cases the interest is technically said to be transmitted to a successor (*e.g.*, a trustee in bankruptcy) whereas in the case of determinable interests the interest is not so transmitted. Yet the substance of the matter is that the present holder may lose his interest in certain events. It is never, therefore, certain that, if the present holder and his successors so choose, the interest will never determine as long as the thing remains in existence. The notion of indeterminate interests can only be saved by regarding the purchaser in insolvency or execution, or the state, as succeeding to the same interest as that had by the previous holder. This is an implausible way of looking at the matter, because the expropriability and executability of a thing is not an incident of value to the owner, but a restriction on the owner's rights imposed in the social interest. It seems better, therefore, to deny the existence of indeterminate interests and to classify those which are not determinate according to the number and character of the contingencies on which they will determine. This affords a justification for speaking of a 'determinable fee', of 'fiduciary ownership' etc., for these do not differ essentially from 'full ownership', determinable on bankruptcy or expropriation.

(9) *The prohibition of harmful use*

An owner's liberty to use and manage the thing owned as he chooses is in mature systems of law, as in primitive systems, subject to the condition that uses harmful to other members of society are forbidden. There may, indeed, be much dispute over what is to count as 'harm' and to what extent give and take demands that minor inconvenience between neighbours shall be tolerated. Nevertheless, at least for material objects, one can always point to abuses which a legal system will not allow.

I may use my car freely but not in order to run my neighbour down, or to demolish his gate, or even to go on his land if he protests; nor may I drive uninsured. I may build on my land as I choose, but not in such a way that my building collapses on my neighbour's land. I may let off fireworks on Guy Fawkes night, but not in such a way as to set fire to my neighbour's house. These and similar limitations on the use of things are so familiar and so obviously essential to the existence of an orderly community that they are not often thought of as incidents of ownership; yet, without them 'ownership' would be a destructive force.

(10) *Liability to execution*

Of a somewhat similar character is the liability of the owner's interest to be taken away from him for debt, either by execution of a judgment debt or on insolvency. Without such a general liability the growth of credit would be impeded and ownership would, again, be an instrument by which the owner could defraud his creditors. This incident, therefore, which may be called *executability*, seems to constitute one of the standard ingredients of the liberal idea of ownership.

It is a question whether any other limitations on ownership imposed in the social interest should be regarded as among its standard incidents. A good case can certainly be made for listing *liability to tax* and *expropriability by the state* as such. Although it is often convenient to contrast taxes on property with taxes on persons, all tax must ultimately be taken from something owned, whether a material object or a fund or a chose in action. A general rule exempting the owners of things from paying tax from those things would therefore make taxation impracticable. But it may be thought that to state the matter in this way is to obliterate the useful contrast between taxes on what is owned and taxes on what is earned. Although therefore, a society could not continue to exist without taxation, and although the amount of tax is commonly dependent on what the taxpayer owns or earns, and must be paid from his assets, I should not wish to press the case for the inclusion of liability to tax as a standard incident of ownership. Much the same will hold good of expropriability; for though some state or public expropriation takes place in every society, and though it is not easy to see how administration could continue without it, it tends to be restricted to special classes of property. We are left with the thought that it is, perhaps, a characteristic of ownership that the owner's claims are ultimately postponed to the claims of the public authority, even if only indirectly, in that the thing owned may, within defined limits, be taken from the owner in order to pay the expenses of running the state or to provide it with essential facilities.

Ownership and Lesser Interests

The interest of which the standard incidents have been depicted is usually described as the *greatest* interest in a thing recognized by the law and is contrasted with lesser interests (easements, short leases, licences, special property, mere detention). It is worth while looking a little more closely at this distinction, for it partly depends on a point that the foregoing analysis has not brought to light.

I must emphasize that we are not now concerned with the topic of split ownership—cases where the standard incidents are so divided as to raise a doubt which of two or more persons interested should be called owner. We are dealing with those simpler cases in which the existence of *B*'s interest in a thing, though it restricts *A*'s rights, does not call in question *A*'s ownership of the thing.

The first point that strikes us is that each of the standard incidents of ownership can apply to the holder of a lesser interest in property. The bailee has possession of, and often the right to possess, the goods bailed. The managing director of a company has the right of managing it. The life tenant or usufructuary of a house is entitled to the income from it. The donee of a power of appointment is entitled to dispose of the capital subject to the power. The holder of an easement has a transmissible and non-determinate right in the land subject to the easement. Yet, without more, we feel no temptation to say that the bailee owns the thing, the managing director the company, the life tenant the house, the donee the capital, or the easement holder the land. What criteria do we use in designating these as 'lesser interests'?

One suggested view is that the rights of the holder of a lesser interest can be enumerated while the 'owner's' cannot.[1] This rests on a fallacy about enumeration. The privileges, for instance, exercisable over a thing do not together constitute a finite number of permissible actions. The 'owner' and the lessee alike may do an indefinite number and variety of actions, *viz.* any action not forbidden by a rule of the legal system.

A second view is that the criterion used is the fact that, at least as regards *some* incidents, the holder of the lesser interest has more restricted rights than the owner. The lessee's interest is determinate, the 'owner's' merely determinable. But, conversely, the lessee has the right to possess and manage the property and take its income; in these respects the 'owner's' interest is, for the time being, more restricted than his own. Nor will it help to say that the 'owner's' rights are more extensive than those of the holder of a lesser interest as regards *most* of the incidents listed, for, in such cases as lease, this would lead to the conclusion that the lessee has as much claim to be called owner as the reversioner.

A third suggestion is that some one incident is taken as the criterion. It is possible, however, for all the listed rights, to put

---

[1] J. von Gierke, *Sachenrecht* (1948), p. 67. *Cf.*, Markby, *Elements of Law considered with reference to Principles of General Jurisprudence* (6th ed.), pp. 157–158.

examples which would lead to the opposite result from that sanctioned by usage. If *A* lets *B* a car on hire, *B* possesses it but *A* 'owns' it. The holder of a life interest or usufruct manages and takes the income of the thing, but the *dominus* or reversioner 'owns' it. When trust property is subject to a power of appointment, the donee of the power can dispose of it but the trustee 'owns' it. When property is subject to a *fideicommissum*, the fiduciary has no transmissible right (unless the *fideicommissum* fails), yet he is 'owner' while the fideicommissary may, exceptionally, have such a right. A person who holds an interest *in diem* may 'own', while one who has a potentially indeterminate interest *ex die* does not as yet do so.

Besides these examples, where any of the suggested criteria would give a result at variance with actual lay and legal usage, there are many others where the rights in question apply to both or neither of the persons holding an interest in the thing. For instance, some writers appear to treat 'duration'[1] as the criterion for distinguishing between ownership and lesser interests. Yet the holder of an easement, like the 'owner' of land, has a transmissible and indeterminate right over it, while, *per contra*, neither the 'owner' nor the licensee of a copyright has an indeterminate right.

It would be easy but tedious to list examples for the other rights; clearly, if a criterion is to be found, it must be sought elsewhere. A hopeful avenue of inquiry seems to be the following: what happens on the determination of the various interests in the thing under consideration? This brings us to a further standard incident of ownership, *viz.* its residuary character.

(11) *Residuary Character*

A legal system might recognize interests in things less than ownership and might have a rule that, on the determination of such interests, the rights in question lapsed and could be exercised by no one, or by the first person to exercise them after their lapse. There might be leases and easements; yet, on their ex-

---

[1] *Cf.*, Turner, *Some Reflections on Ownership in English Law* (1941), 19 Can. B.R. 342.

tinction, no one would be entitled to exercise rights similar to those of the former lessee or of the holder of the easement. This would be unlike any system known to us and I think we should be driven to say that in such a system the institution of ownership did not extend to any thing in which limited interests existed. In such things there would, paradoxically, be interests less than ownership but no ownership.

This fantasy is intended to bring out the point that it is characteristic of ownership than an owner has a residuary right in the thing owned. In practice, legal systems have rules providing that on the lapse of an interest rights, including liberties, analogous to the rights formerly vested in the holder of the interest, vest in or are exercisable by someone else, who may be said to acquire the 'corresponding rights'. Of course, the 'corresponding rights' are not the same rights as were formerly vested in the holder of the interest. The easement holder had a right to exclude the owner; now the owner has a right to exclude the easement holder. The latter right is not identical with, but corresponds to, the former.

It is true that corresponding rights do not always arise when an interest is determined. Sometimes, when ownership is abandoned, no corresponding right vests in another; the thing is simply *res derelicta*. Sometimes, on the other hand, when ownership is abandoned, a new ownership vests in the state, as is the case in South Africa when land has been abandoned.

It seems, however, a safe generalization that, whenever an interest less than ownership terminates, legal systems always provide for corresponding rights to vest in another. When easements terminate, the 'owner' can exercise the corresponding rights, and when bailments terminate, the same is true. It looks as if we have found a simple explanation of the usage we are investigating, but this turns out to be but another deceptive short cut. For it is not a sufficient condition of *A*'s being the owner of a thing that, on the determination of *B*'s interest in it, corresponding rights vest in or are exercisable by *A*. On the determination of a sub-lease, the rights in question become exercisable by the lessee, not by the 'owner' of the property.

Can we then say that the 'owner' is the ultimate residuary? When the sub-lessee's interest determines the lessee acquires the corresponding rights; but when the lessee's right determines the 'owner' acquires these rights. Hence the 'owner' appears to be identified as the ultimate residuary. The difficulty is that the series may be continued, for on the determination of the 'owner's' interest the state may acquire the corresponding rights; is the state's interest ownership or a mere expectancy?

A warning is here necessary. We are approaching the troubled waters of split ownership. Puzzles about the location of ownership are often generated by the fact that an ultimate residuary right is not coupled with present alienability or with the other standard incidents we have listed. Was the feudal lord's right of escheat ownership or merely an expectancy? When land was given in *emphyteusis*, was the *emphyteuta* or the reversioner owner? Other puzzles are created by cases of cross-residuarity. When property is held subject to a *fideicommissum* in the modern law, the fideicommissary benefits from the lapse of the fiduciary's rights and *vice versa*; so which is really residuary?

We are of course here concerned not with the puzzles of split ownership but with simple cases in which the existence of *B*'s lesser interest in a thing is clearly consistent with *A*'s owning it. To explain the usage in such cases it is helpful to point out that it is a necessary but not sufficient condition of *A*'s being owner that, either immediately or ultimately, the extinction of other interests would enure for his benefit. In the end, it turns out that residuarity is merely one of the standard incidents of ownership, important no doubt, but not entitled to any special status.

The Thing Owned

'To own' is transitive; the object of ownership is always spoken of as a 'thing' in the legal sense, a *res*. There is, clearly, a close connexion between the idea of ownership and the idea of things owned, as is shown by the use of words such as 'property' to designate both. We ought, apparently, to be able to throw some light on ownership by investigating 'things'.

Outside the law, external material objects are thought of as the prime examples of things and, in this sense, things are contrasted with persons. But, in a wide sense, any object of discourse may be called a thing—events, states, emotions, actions, processes are all things. The extra-legal use of 'thing' is therefore not likely to help us in finding out what can be owned.

In the law we find the following position. As regards external material objects, it is natural to speak of ownership. A person 'owns' a book, house or car. The terminology of ownership is also extended to some things other than material objects. A person may 'own' a copyright, leasehold property, goodwill, a business, patent rights. In these cases the analogy with the incidents of the ownership of external material objects is a close one.

In other cases the holder of a right is said to 'have' rather than own the interest in question. Thus, one 'has' an easement or a chose in action or a reputation. Here the analogy with the ownership of material objects is less strong or, as in the case of easements, the alternative expression is adopted to avoid confusion with the ownership of the material object to which the right relates.

In other cases again, we speak not of 'having' a thing but of 'having a right' to or in something. Thus, a person does not either 'own' or 'have' his body or liberty. He has a right to bodily security or liberty. Here the analogy with the ownership of a thing is tenuous; thus, these rights are inalienable. Finally, there are interests which the law refuses to recognize: one does not own, have or have a right to them. An example in English law is privacy.

In any viable society we shall expect certain interests (having a house, clothes, food, preserving one's body from harm) to be protected, but, as regards many other interests, (copyright, reputation, privacy, shares) there will be nothing absurd in a system which does not protect them, though it may be an inconvenient system. There will be no way of telling, apart from knowing the details of a system, whether such interests are protected and, *a fortiori*, no way of telling whether they are conceived as consisting in the ownership of things. Apart from the basic interests mentioned, protection of an interest is not merely the recognition of a social necessity. The meaning of the words 'right' or 'thing' will not help one to guess what the decision has been or is likely to be.

Much the same may be said of the difference between simple rights and interests conceived in terms of ownership. A person is not, in most systems, regarded as owning his body, reputation, skill, honour or dignity. At most he has a simple right to these things, which are therefore not legally 'things'. By a 'simple right', I mean one which is protected by law but is not alienable or transmissible. Now it may be that the doctrine that one does not own one's body, etc. is influenced by the linguistic fact that such aspects of one's person do not fall within the prime class of things, external material objects. But a more likely explanation is simply that it has been thought undesirable that a person should alienate his body, skill or reputation, as this would be to interfere with human freedom. When human beings were regarded as alienable and ownable they were, of course, also regarded as being legally things: and it is quite easy to conceive arrangements under which one could, for instance, lease one's reputation or one's skill for a term of years, so that the lessee could sue for infringements of the lessor's good name or for the fruits of his work. It may, indeed, be argued that contracts for the assignment of goodwill and contracts of service are examples of at least partial alienations of these interests.

However that may be, it is clear that to stare at the meaning of the word 'thing' will not tell us which protected interests are conceived in terms of ownership. When the legislature or courts think that an interest should be alienable and transmissible they will *rei*-fy it and say that it can be owned, that it is property. They will not say that it can be owned and is a *res* because of a prior conviction that it falls within the appropriate definition of 'thing'. The investigation of 'things' seems to peter out in a false trail.

A more promising approach is to try to classify the things

that can be owned. An obvious classification is into material objects and things that are not material objects (incorporeals). According to one school of thought, this division is so important that only corporeals can really be owned; according to another, it is so unimportant that we ought always to speak of owning rights over material objects, never of owning the objects themselves; in this way we shall keep in mind the parallel with the ownership of incorporeal rights.

Both schools propose a departure from lay and legal usage which stands in need of justification. The former has little to commend it. Consider the difference between 'owning' land and 'owning' (having) an easement over land. The first counts as the ownership of a material object, the second of an incorporeal. Yet their incidents are in every way similar and, in both cases, include the right to exclude others from interfering with or obstructing a particular physical thing, a right which at first sight might seem to differentiate the ownership of material objects from the ownership of incorporeals. It is true that, when we come to consider claims, we find cases in which either there is no right to exclude others or no right to exclude them from a particular physical thing.

Copyright is an example of one type of claim. It involves the right to prevent others publishing, etc. one's written work without consent, and hence a sort of right to exclude others; but this right does not relate to a particular physical thing, a particular book. It relates to all material objects which have certain characteristics, *viz.* that they are copies of the work in question. Again, it is not clear that the incident of prohibition of harmful use applies in a straighforward way to copyrights: on the other hand convincing analogues of the other standard incidents are to be found. Thus it may be said that the notion of ownership applies to copyrights in an extended and somewhat weaker sense than that in which it applies to material objects and interests in them.

Debts due and other choses in action present an example of another type of claim. Here the claim is to the performance of some positive act. No right to exclude others is involved, and, as in the case of copyrights, no question of harmful use arises. On the other hand, incidents such as alienability (nowadays) and transmissibility do apply to choses in action. Hence the ownership of choses in action is to be understood in a still weaker sense than that of copyrights.

It seems, therefore, as if a more useful classification of things owned than that into corporeals and incorporeals would be into material objects and rights in them, claims, and collections of objects and claims. Slightly expanding this, we get the following list:

(*a*) Material objects and interests in material objects;
(*b*) Claims, and interests in claims;
(*c*) Fixed collections of material objects, claims or both;
(*d*) Variable collections of material objects, claims or both;
(*d*) Funds.

The list is self-explanatory, 'claims' being understood to exclude such claims as amount to interests in material objects. The introduction of fixed and variable collections is necessary in order to accommodate the ownership of estates, businesses, etc. either frozen at a point of time (fixed collection) such as the date of a person's death, or varying from time to time, as in the case of the spouses' 'ownership' of a joint estate when they are married in community of property. A 'fund' is the monetary equivalent of a collection of things or claims or both.

It is a commonplace that the ownership of funds has become of great importance in the twentieth century. With this development a new twist has been given to the notion of ownership, and one which is inherent in the notion of owning a variable collection of things.

A variable collection of things may be owned and managed like a particular thing but, as a matter of convenience, lesser interests in and claims to the collection are not construed as giving the holder powers of management or security against the alienation of particular items in the collection. Such claims are in effect claims to the income and/or capital of a fund which may vary in value and will in any case be composed of varying items. They are claims on the fund, not claims on the items, and they may well be divorced from what in any case is notionally separable, the management of the individual items

The modern world presents us with many examples where the ownership of property consists in claims on a variable collection or fund. Of the former the interest of a wife married in community of property is a striking instance. She has no power of managing the community assets and her claim is restricted to whatever items may be found in the collection of community assets on the dissolution of the marriage. Another example is the ownership by members of an unincorporated association of the association's assets. Prominent instances of the latter are the ownership of shares, the ownership of interests in trust funds and floating charges: all the instances of *Gesamthandseigentum* in German law fall into one of these classes.[1]

Such claims on collections and funds present a still remoter analogy with the ownership of interests in material objects than the simple claims previously considered. The incidents of possession, management, and the prohibition of harmful use apply, if at all, in a sketchy form. Alienability, transmissibility, income and (sometimes) capital rights remain. Since, among forms of property holding, claims on collections and funds are now of outstanding importance economically, we might either say that, over a wide field, the character of things owned has altered or that the character of ownership has altered. I see no reason for preferring one form of expression to the other; our investigation has revealed, what we began by suspecting, that the notions of ownership and of the thing owned are interdependent. We are left, not with an inclination to adopt a terminology which confines ownership to material objects, but with an understanding of a certain shift in meaning as ownership is applied to different classes of things owned.

It remains to consider the view that the thing owned should always be spoken of as a right. This is certainly an odd-looking proposal, since 'owning' in ordinary use involves 'having certain rights to' a thing. If, therefore, we are to substitute for

[1] Palandt, *Bürgerliches Gesetzbuch* (1956), p. 806.

'owning a pen' 'owning certain rights in a pen', it would seem to follow the owner should correctly be said to have certain rights in certain rights in a pen; but why stop at the second order of rights?

Of course, the force of the proposal is a protest against the habit of thinking of the ownership of a thing, particularly a material object, as if it consisted only in a relation between a person and a thing, and not at all in relations between the owner and other persons. Yet to speak always of owning rights rather than things would be doubly misleading. Ownership, as we have seen, is not just a bundle of rights, as it is no help towards understanding our society to speak as if it were. Secondly, the idiom which directly couples the owner with the thing owned is far from pointless; where the right to exclude others exists, there is indeed (legally) a very special relation between the holder of the right and the thing, and this is a rational way of marking it.[1]

II. TITLE

It is not enough for a legal system to recognize the possibility of people owning things. There must be rules laying down how ownership is acquired and lost and how claims to a thing are to rank *inter se*. This brings us to the notion of title, a word which is used in two main senses. First, it refers to the conditions of fact which must be fulfilled in order that a person may acquire a claim to a thing. In this sense, delivery, registration, seizure and succession on death may be titles to the ownership of property. 'Mode of acquisition' or 'mode of loss' will do as well for this meaning as 'title'; so I use 'title' in the second sense.

This is the sense in which a title to a thing is a claim, valid against persons generally though not necessarily against everyone, to the possession of the thing. It is true that in ordinary legal usage 'title' involves a great deal more than this; it implies, for instance, a power of alienating the holder's interest and the transmissibility of that interest. The restricted sense I have given to 'title' is, however, adequate for the present discussion.

---

[1] *Cf.*, G. P. Wilson, *Jurisprudence and the Discussion of Ownership* (1957), Camb. L.J. 216.

Clearly every owner has a title to the thing owned, provided that the thing admits of being possessed; even if it does not admit of this, there will be prior and posterior claims to the thing, as in the case of choses in action, and the owner will have such a claim. It is also clear that several persons may have titles to the same thing; thus, a mere possessor has, under some systems of law, a better right to possess than any later possessor of the thing not deriving title from an earlier possessor. Taking possession is regarded under such systems as a mode of acquiring a right to possess, valid against persons generally, not merely against a trespasser or disseisor. Hence there may be problems of priority of title. What is not, at first sight, clear is whether the name 'owner' should be confined to the person with the best title to a thing out of all possible claimants (*the* title, a *good* title) or whether we should in such cases speak of two or more 'owners' of the thing ranking in a certain order.

Modes of Acquisition

These obviously vary from system to system. It is often thought that light can be thrown on the concept of possession by a study of the conditions for acquiring possession; ought not the same procedure to be fruitful in the study of ownership? Holmes, following a general theory about the analysis of legal concepts, approaches the matter in this way,[1] but without yielding more than a catalogue of modes of acquisition. On the other hand, some writers who wish to justify the institution of ownership as a fair one, in spite of the apparent injustice involved in excluding all save the owner from the thing owned, argue that, though there are various modes of derivative acquisition, there is only one mode of original acquisition, namely taking possession.[2] They go on to say that the labour involved in taking or making the thing justifies the taker in retaining it against subsequent claimants and transmitting it to others.

The argument is certainly not, apart from its other defects, consistent with positive law. Thus, in South Africa, land cannot be acquired by *occupatio* but only (apart from irrelevant ex-

[1] *The Common Law*, p. 245.　　[2] Locke, *Second Treatise on Civil Government*, ch. 5, s. 26.

ceptions) by Government grant, statute or thirty years' prescription. The truth is that modes of acquisition, original and
derivative, are many and various; one of the functions of
expressions such as 'he is owner' is precisely to draw similar
legal conclusions from varying states of fact.[1]

If, therefore, we are to seek moral reasons why particular
persons ought to own particular things we shall need different
reasons for different modes of acquisition; and derivative modes
of acquisition stand in need of justification as much as original.
There are in fact good reasons why the commonest modes of
original acquisition (making and taking) and of derivative
acquisition (consent and debt) should be recognized. If these
are thought morally satisfactory, we have arrived at a justification for the adoption by a legal system of certain modes of
acquisition; what we have not found is a justification for the
institution of ownership. I do not, of course, wish to imply that
none can be found.

Modes of Loss

Once derivative modes of acquisition are recognized, modes
of loss or extinction must also be recognized. These give little
difficulty when the loss is with the consent of the previous owner
or through his debt, but a good deal when the system admits, as
many systems do, the possibility of acquiring title or barring a
prior title by lapse of time or, as in English Land Law, of acquiring a 'title' in the sense defined above, albeit imperfect, by the
simple act of squatting or dispossessing the present holder.

In such cases the later acquisition may have the effect either
of divesting the earlier or of creating a second, concurrent title:
in the latter event, the two titles may continue indefinitely to
run concurrently, or the earlier may lapse or become unenforceable after a period of time.

One or Many Titles

This is a convenient point at which to try to classify legal
systems according to the number of independent titles which

[1] This is overlooked by A. Ross, *Tû-Tû* (1956–7), 70 Harv. L.R. 812.

they permit. By 'independent' I mean 'not derived from a common source'.

In the simplest type of system only a single independent title is possible. Such a system may be called unititular. Under it, if the title to a thing is in *A*, no title to it can be acquired (independently) by *B*, except by a process which divests *A*. There is only one 'root of title' for each thing, and the present title can ultimately be traced back to that root.

In some ways a unititular system is simple, but it may seem to leave unprotected persons whose interests are deserving of protection. It does not provide for the grading of claims to a thing; it proceeds on the view that only one claim is worthy of protection against persons generally, and that other claims need not be recognized, save, perhaps, that a person in possession may be protected against a trespasser or disseisor, a fact which, as we have seen, does not by itself give the possessor a title. A unititular system may be conservative in its working, if acquisition without the consent of the previous owner is made difficult, or may be 'active' and may favour enterprise, or even banditry, if acquisition without the consent of the previous owner is easy.

Classical Roman law at first sight approximates to the 'active' unititular system, Justinian's law to the 'conservative' version, since the period for acquiring by usucapion or prescription and so divesting the previous owner was increased in the latter case. But on a closer examination the Roman system looks conservative at all periods; the mere thief or trespasser and their successors are never favoured, because nothing stolen or taken by force can be acquired in this way, and the owner of such things can never be divested against his will.[1]

It may be thought that the statement that Roman law was substantially unititular is inconsistent with the distinction between Quiritary and 'bonitary' ownership. This is true only so far as 'defeasible' bonitary owners are concerned. The Quiritary and bonitary 'owners' did not hold by independent titles where the 'bonitary' ownership was indefeasible. The

---

[1] To this Cod. 7.39.8 makes a small exception.

praetorian, 'bonitary' owner derived title from the Quiritary owner. The division between the two is a case of split ownership, not of independent titles. The *bona fide possessor in via usucapiendi* also had a title, a type of 'bonitary' ownership, defeasible only by the true owner; this is, perhaps, the only exception in Roman law to the rule that there was only one title. When the periods of usucapion were short, it was not an exception of much importance; after a year or two there was, once again, only a single title. As the periods were increased the exception grew in importance. Roman law held to the theory that, in such cases, there was only one *dominus*.

Under a unititular system one way of ascertaining the true owner is by tracing title to the original acquirer. With land, especially, this is seldom practicable. The remedy may lie in rules either of substance or procedure. A substantive rule creating a mode of acquisition which has a divesting effect may meet the need, especially if the period is fairly short. A ruthless form of divesting is found in French law, where the maxim that possession of movables is equivalent to title is interpreted to mean that, if a bailee of goods delivers them by way of sale, gift, etc. to another, he thereby divests the title of the bailor, leaving him to his action for damages against the bailee.

In Roman law, given the rule that theft or violent dispossession was a bar to acquisition running with the thing, it was theoretically necessary to trace title to the original source in order to see whether a 'vice' affected the property. If therefore the difficulty of proof of title is, as Hargreaves asserts,[1] a reason against adopting the terminology of ownership, his argument would apply with as much force to Roman and modern Civil Law as to English law.

In practice, in modern systems based on Roman law, rules of evidence help to overcome the practical difficulties. Possession, unless otherwise explained, is regarded as evidence of ownership and an earlier possession is regarded as better evidence of ownership than a later, independent possession. Registration of

---

[1] Hargreaves, "Terminology and Title in Ejectment" (1940), 56 L.Q.R. 376, 377.

title is really an evidentiary device of the same order. In most systems registration does not have a divesting effect;[1] the register may be rectified at the instance of the true owner (or, in a multititular system, someone with a better title than the registered owner). The register merely makes it possible to discover without difficulty who is presumptively owner.

With unititular systems we may contrast multititular systems. As we have seen, these turn on the possibility of acquiring title without the consent of the present owner of a thing by a process which does not have a divesting effect. Such systems may take either a 'conservative' or an 'active' form. In the former the earlier titles continue to be valid indefinitely or for a very long time. In the latter either the right or the remedy is barred after a relatively short period. Again, if the title of a thief or trespasser is recognized, the system is thereby rendered more 'active'.

The English system as regards both land and chattels falls into the multititular category. As regards land, a title could and can be acquired without the consent of the previous owner by mere disseisin or dispossession.[2] It was a principle of the medieval law that a disseisor *ipso facto* acquired an estate in fee, albeit a tortious estate. 'Every fee simple is not *legitimum*, for a disseisor, abator, intruder, usurper, etc. have a fee simple, but it is not a lawful fee'.[3] In the modern law it seems that a dispossession adverse to the present holder gives the trespasser or squatter an estate in fee simple;[4] despite Holdsworth,[5] every adverse possession is a root of title,[6] though the title may lapse on abandonment.[7]

Such ease of acquisition is consistent with a unititular system. Thus in the early land law disseisin had a divesting effect; the disseisee had a mere right of entry, which might be tolled,

---

[1] Wade and Megarry, *The Law of Real Property* (2nd ed.), p. 960 n. 33.
[2] Littleton, *Tenures*, ss. 473, 519, 520; *Asher* v. *Whitlock* (1865), L.R. 1 Q.B. 1; *Allen* v. *Roughley* (1955), 94 C.L.R. 98.
[3] Coke on *Littleton*, 2a; see also *ibid.*, 297a.
[4] Lightwood, *The Time Limit of Actions*, p. 125.
[5] *History of English Law*, Vol. VII, p. 64.
[6] Some authorities go no further than to say that possession is *prima facie* evidence of seisin in fee and so of a title: *Allen* v. *Roughley* (*supra*), *per* Dixon J., at p. 109.
[7] *Allen* v. *Roughley* (*supra*), *per* Williams J., at p. 118.

and was inalienable. Since the nineteenth-century reforms the disseisee or his modern equivalent can alienate his interest *inter vivos* or on death and it descends to his personal representatives.[1] Hence, as Megarry and Wade say, when *S* dispossesses *O*, '*S*'s possession gives all the rights and powers of ownership: *S* has, in fact, a legal estate, a fee simple absolute in possession. But so also has *O*, until such time as his title is extinguished by limitation. There is no absurdity of speaking of two or more adverse estates in the land, for their validity is relative.'[2]

If, then, *S* and *O* both have fees simple, shall we say that both are owners of the land? Or shall we call *S*, the present possessor, alone owner, but say that his ownership may be divested; or, again, that *O*, since his claim is ultimately entitled to prevail, is alone owner? One cannot expect clear criteria for answering such questions. *S*, however, has every incident of ownership except security against divesting, while *O* has every such incident except present enjoyment. There is much to be said, therefore, for treating them as independent owners rather than as persons sharing a single, split ownership.

On the other hand, it may be argued that, in view of such puzzles, it would be better not to speak of the ownership of land in English law at all. This argument ignores the many straightforward cases in which there is a single tenant in fee simple and no competing title.

Hargreaves, who argues against speaking of 'ownership' in English land law, relies on the fact that in actions for the recovery of land the plaintiff need only prove a better title than the defendant not that his title is the best of all possible titles.[3] Now a multititular system must have rules for enabling the holders of titles to recover possession and for regulating priorities between the holders of competing titles. There will not, therefore, be any prodecural need in such a system to provide a special remedy (*e.g.*, a *vindicatio*) for the person with the best title. The holder of the best title can make use of the remedies

---

[1] Cheshire, *Modern Law of Real Property* (8th ed.), p. 30.
[2] Wade and Megarry, *The Law of Real Property* (2nd ed.), p. 958.
[3] *Terminology and Title in Ejectment* (1940), 56 L.Q.R. 376, 377.

(*e.g.*, ejectment) available to those with *a title*. The point of such a system is that proof of any title will suffice except against a person who can show a better. But, of course, if priorities are regulated someone must have top priority; *maius ius* implies *maximum ius*. Surely the holder of *maximum ius*, at least, cannot be denied the title of owner? It will, however, be never necessary, though always sufficient, when he claims the possession of land, for him to prove that he has *maximum ius*.

English land law exhibits a highly 'active' system of regulating title, owing to the relatively short period of limitation coupled with the recognition of the disseisor's title. Sociological writers may detect in this the *mores* of the Germanic tribes who invaded Britain; but as the twelve year period of limitatian is a modern innovation, the system has not always been as 'active' as it now is.

The English law of title to chattels is also multititular. It is not clear, however, that a thief acquires title except against a later wrongdoer[1]; hence the rules for chattels are in some ways less 'active' than for land. Divesting, may however, take place either by limitation or by certain consensual dispositions (sale in market overt, sale by factors). The Sale of Goods Act makes a sharp distinction between the holder of *the title*, who can give a 'good title' to the goods and the holders of lesser titles.[2] Only the former can make a valid disposition of the thing by way of sale. Hence there is no temptation to speak of goods as having more than one independent owner.

From what has been said, it emerges that multititular systems are more flexible than unititular systems, though they are not necessarily more 'active'. The difference between these two ways of regulating title has often been construed as a difference between two conceptions of ownership. This, I suggest, is a mistake. The only difference of importance between the place of ownership in the two schemes is procedural: what has to be proved in an action. But whether a plaintiff must prove that he is owner, and what is to be understood by ownership, are entirely distinct questions.

[1] *Buckley* v. *Gross* (1863), 3 B. & S. 566.   [2] Sale of Goods Act, 1893, ss. 21–23.

III. SPLIT OWNERSHIP

Space does not permit more than a few brief remarks on the subject of split ownership and the fragments (*Eigentumssplitter*) created by splitting. Historically, there have been many reasons for separating the standard incidents into two or more parcels; indeed, historically speaking, the metaphor of 'splitting' may mislead, for in some cases full ownership has been built up from the fragments, not *vice versa*. Thus, the alienable, heritable and indefeasible fee simple was evolved from the inalienable and intransmissible tenancy in fee, subject to onerous incidents of tenure.

But looked at from the point of view of their social function, the various cases of splitting fall into two main classes. Many of them are directed towards maintaining intact a physical thing or collection or, in more modern times, a fund, in order that this asset may serve a family or a business[1] or an association over a substantial period. In this class fall such examples of splitting as concurrent interests in property (joint tenancy, tenancy in common, co-ownership, the interest of spouses in a community estate, the interest of members of an unincorporated association in the property of the association); and the ownership of property by juristic persons (corporations sole, *Stiftungen*, the state, joint stock companies). Secondly, splitting may serve the purpose of specialization, by separating management from the enjoyment of income and/or disposition of the capital; the beneficiary obtains the advantage of expert management of the property but also runs some risk. In this second class fall such devices as trusts, the Dutch *bewind* (administration), and incorporated companies.

Most of these institutions have been carefully analysed by specialist writers. Some of them present problems to a lawyer who has to work with a rule that every thing must have one and only one independent 'owner'. Ought we, for instance, to speak of 'equitable ownership' or only of 'equitable interests'? In answer to such questions generalities are unhelpful. If the

---

[1] Gower, *Principles of Modern Company Law* (1954), p. 10.

context is one in which stress is laid on income rights we may
be tempted to speak of 'equitable ownership' but, if powers of
alienation are in question, the holder of the legal estate will
alone qualify (if anyone) to be called owner.

There is, however, one device, formerly used mainly to keep
a thing or fund in a family over a period, which has not been
analysed as carefully as it deserves. This is the device of the
estate. Its originality has been exaggerated by some, minimized
by others. Considering it in its mature form, it provides for the
present alienability of an indefinite number of successive interests in a thing, of which, however, not more than one may be a
fee simple. Only one of these, obviously, can be presently vested
in possession. It further provides for the creation of limited
interests which may extend beyond a lifetime, such as estates
tail. Finally, it provides for certain rules of descent to regulate
the devolution of the thing in the cases where the interest is
regarded as extending beyond a lifetime, *e.g.* again in the case
of an entail. These are interesting devices, though not in every
way successful. For instance, the freedom thereby given to
property owners to impose fetters on future generations turned
out to be excessive, and counteracting devices such as the barring of entails were found desirable to redress the balance.

It is important, however, to see that to speak of the ownership of estates, of 'many things each with its owner',[1] rather
than the ownership of land or funds does not of itself constitute
an original contribution to our legal resources. It would be
quite possible, indeed, to reproduce *all* the important features
of the doctrine of estates in the terminology of Roman and
civilian systems. We have only to think of a set of rules whereby (i) all usufructs and other *iura in re aliena* are freely alienable,
(ii) an indefinite number of successive vested usufructs may
co-exist (As regards all but one, *dies cedit sed nondum venit*), (iii)
multiple usufructs extending beyond a lifetime may be created
and (iv) these are of various types, to which names are given,
and for each a particular mode of devolution and termination
is prescribed. Such a scheme would incorporate all the inno-

[1] Pollock and Maitland, *op. cit.*, p. 4.

vations introduced by the doctrine of estates. Would there, however, be any point, if it were introduced, in continuing to distinguish between *dominium* and *iura in re aliena*?

Clearly there would. The distinction would still neatly fit a vast mass of cases, in which the complexities of successive and multiple usufructs were absent, and also most cases in which they were present. But when multiple usufructs were introduced which might extend to an indefinite succession of usufructuaries (corresponding to entails) it would come to seem rather pointless to continue to call the ultimate reversioner *dominus*, because of the uncertainty that he would ever come into possesssion. There would, indeed, be an inclination to call the 'usufructuary-in-tail' *dominus*. But, obviously, at this limit, it would be clearer to abandon the terminology of ownership and speak simply of *A* as having a 'usufruct-in-tail', and of *B* as having a 'reversion'. Only at this limit, however, would the contrast between *dominum* and *iura in re aliena* fade and its utility disappear.

There does not, then, seem any good reason why the introduction of the doctrine of estates should lead us to abandon the terminology of ownership; the puzzles it presents in peripheral cases are like those presented by other forms of split ownership in such cases, and may, of course, lead a lawyer, very reasonably, not to use the contrast of ownership with lesser interests *in those cases*.

IV. SOCIAL CONTROL

'Absolute' is perhaps the most ambiguous word met in discussions of ownership. Sometimes it is used to deny the 'temporary' (intransmissible or determinate) character of an interest,[1] sometimes to deny its defeasible character (liable to be divested by another, liable to escheat or forfeiture),[2] sometimes to emphasize its exemption from social control.

In the last sense, ownership has never been absolute. Even in the most individualistic ages of Rome and the United States, it

[1] Hargreaves, *Introduction to the Principles of Land Law* (1952), p. 44.
[2] Hargreaves, *op. cit.*, p. 46.

has had a social aspect. This has usually been expressed in such incidents of ownership as the prohibition of harmful use, liability to execution for debt, to taxation and to expropriation by the public authority.

Emphasis on the social aspect of ownership has, however, varied from age to age. Those 'sacred and inviolable' rights, which, according to the *Declaration of the Rights of Man*, no one could be forced to cede except for *public necessity*[1] have become, in French law, liable to expropriation on grounds of *public utility*[2] and subject to a general doctrine forbidding 'abuse'. According to the liberal conception of ownership, there is a sharp distinction between government and ownership, *imperium* and *dominium*. Though, in a loose sense, the state may be said to have an 'eminent domain' over at least the land comprising its territory, this does not carry with it rights to possess, enjoy or alienate it, so that the sense in which the state is owner is very loose indeed. The interest of the state, according to this conception, is confined to powers of expropriation and a minimum of restrictive regulation, together with the expectancy of acquiring property as *bona vacantia* or by escheat in a few rather remote contingencies.

Socialism has led to a revised view of the relation between government and ownership, at least as regards some important types of property,[3] such as land and businesses. This means, in practice, that the owner's privileges of using and powers of managing a thing as he wishes have been curtailed and that the social interest in the productive use of things has been affirmed by legislation. Negatively, this process has meant that, in the interests of health and comfort, many substances cannot be used at all or can only be used in certain ways. The sale of drugs is minutely controlled, only smokeless fuel may be used in certain areas, garden hoses may not be used at certain periods. Such instances, multiplied a thousand fold, have come to seem so natural that we hardly realize that the social interest in the use of things, the conservation of resources and in the

---

[1] *Declaration of the Rights of Man*, art. 17.   [2] Code civil, art. 545.
[3] Friedmann, *Law and Social Change in Contemporary Britain* (1951), ch. 2.

details of manufacturing processes is a modern, though it is also a primitive, conception.

Positive control by the state shades into prohibition. The positive duty to exploit one's property in a socially beneficial way, as opposed to the prohibition of a harmful exploitation, has not been generally imposed or its implications fully worked out. The British Agriculture Act imposed an obligation on farmers to observe the rules of good husbandry;[1] the owners of patents can in certain cases be compelled to allow their exploitation.[2] According to the Russian civil law book of 1944, the state has a general right to order forfeiture of property in case of mismanagement; there is also a general prohibition on the use of property to exploit others.[3]

A different form of state control is exercised by drawing a distinction between different types of ownership. In Russia the ownership of collective farmers, of handicraftsmen and of the Government are all treated as differing from 'personal ownership' and from one another.[4] The difference lies, of course, in the right of officials to interfere in the management of the former categories and in state regulation of income rights deriving from the property; also in differing rules about alienation. In this way the sphere of operation of ownership in the liberal sense is narrowed and a form of state participation in management substituted in the remaining sphere.

A third form of social control consists in the exercise by officials of the management of things in the 'private' ownership of the state. Such arrangements present the form but not the substance of ownership in the liberal sense. Management and enjoyment are split, and political control, directly or indirectly, is exercised over the allocation of resources and the uses to which the thing owned is put. The nationalized industries in the United Kingdom follow this pattern of control.

Fourthly, social control may be exercised by a restriction on the type of thing that is subject to ownership by persons other

---

[1] Agriculture Act, 1947, ss. 9–11. The Agriculture Act, 1958, Second Schedule, repealed s. 9.

[2] Patents and Designs Act, 1949, s. 16.

[3] Gsovski, *op. cit.*, p. 557.   [4] Gsovski, *op. cit.*, p. 569.

than the state, as in the Russian building lease, where the building is owned by a private individual, the land remaining in
state ownership.[1] In effect, this restricts the privileges of the
building owner in the general interest.

It remains to be seen which combination of these techniques
will prove most effective and most acceptable to the people who
have to operate them. So far, they have not, singly or together,
reached the point in any country at which they could be
said to have displaced the liberal conception of ownership and
replaced it by a social conception. In practice the two overlap,
and operate side by side, together with various types of split
ownership and ownership of funds which diverge, to a greater
or less extent, from the standard instances depicted in the first
Section. The final picture is that of a set of related institutions
of great complexity which are best studied against the background of the basic model—a single human being owning, in the
full liberal sense, a single material thing.

[1] Gsovski, *op. cit.*, p. 580.

CHAPTER VI

The *Ratio Decidendi* of a Case and the Doctrine of Binding Precedent

by A. W. B. Simpson

WHAT do we mean when we say that a court is bound by an earlier decision, and how is it that the binding element in a decided case is identified? These two questions are clearly fundamental if we are to understand the working of the English doctrine of precedent, and they have been discussed and illuminated by a considerable body of writing. Yet there remains a widespread difference of opinion amongst writers who have attempted to provide answers. In this there is a certain oddity, for the lawyers who have written on the subject would no doubt all argue a point of the Common Law according to the same conventions, or more or less so; the source of their disagreement is not that they differ in their knowledge of how the legal game is played, of how cases are cited and used to bolster up a legal argument; rather it springs from a difficulty in describing and analysing one particular aspect of legal technique in a generally satisfactory way. When this is the case we have a jurisprudential rather than a legal problem. Now there are a number of rules connected with the doctrine of precedent which do not by themselves give rise to any jurisprudential problems.[1] Such are the rules which tell us which courts are bound by which decisions, when a decision may be said to have been given *per incuriam*, and so on. This essay is not directly concerned with these rules, though it will from time to time be useful to refer to them; the analytical difficulties are met when we go deeper

---

[1] For an account of these see Salmond, *Jurisprudence* (11th ed.), ch. VII and VIII.

and instead of asking, for example, whether the House of Lords is bound by its own decisions, we ask what it means to say that the House is so bound, and what being bound by precedent involves.

THE IMPLICATIONS OF THE WORD 'BINDING'

For a start let us consider the word *binding* itself, which is always a source of puzzlement wherever it appears in legal theory. Inevitably it conjures up associations with the literal use of the term. This has been the source of a recurrent feature of writings on the judicial process—an uneasiness in recognizing, at one and the same time, a doctrine of binding precedent and a creative power to make new law vested in the English judges. Examples of this are common enough, and in different hands the desire to deny that judges are mere machines, 'fettered' by case law, takes different forms. Lord Wright wonders 'How this perpetual process of change can be reconciled with the principle of authority and the rule of *stare decisis*.'[1] Professor Stone tells us that 'The question whether a court is "bound" by a single precedent must remain largely meaningless, with respect, however earnestly it continues to be discussed by courts and text-book writers.'[2]

Sir Carleton Allen is led into paradox, and writes, 'We say that he (a judge) is bound by the decisions of higher courts; and so he undoubtedly is. But the superior court does not impose fetters upon him; he places the fetters on his own hands. He has to decide whether the case cited to him is truly apposite to the circumstances in question and whether it accurately embodies the principle which he is seeking. The humblest judicial officer has to decide for himself whether he is or is not bound . . .'[3] Such an account, for all its striking plausibility, becomes more mystifying on every reading. Then there is the solution of the gap. Judges, it is said, make law only where there are areas of no-law. Thus Dr. Goodhart writes,

---

[1] *Legal Essays and Addresses*, p. xvi.
[2] *The Province and Function of Law*, p. 188, n. 223.
[3] *Law in the Making* (6th ed.), p. 276.

'when a vacant space has been closed by a precedent, then no further development is possible.'[1] Finally we may note the tendency in some writers to solve the apparent conflict between the growth of the common law and the doctrine of binding precedent by treating the whole doctrine of precedent as 'a fiction', a 'myth', or a 'device' which conceals legal change and the exercise of judicial discretion. An illustration of this tendency may be taken from a recent text-book, where it is said, 'The arguments outlined above would indicate that the division between *ratio* and *dicta* is in fact mainly a device employed by subsequent courts for the adoption or rejection of doctrine expressed in previous cases, according to the inclinations of the subsequent court.'[2] No doubt if this really is so, the whole doctrine of binding precedent is indeed something of a fantasy.

The very real difficulties which have provoked all these attempts to explain and understand the doctrine of precedent can be made less oppressive if the initial step is taken of considering what it means to say that the House of Lords, for instance, is *bound by its own decisions*. Being bound clearly implies the existence of some sort of obligation, and the content of the obligation may be quite simply stated. The House, we may say, is under an obligation to *follow* or *distinguish* its own earlier decisions, except where the various exceptions to the general rule apply. To this obligation practical convenience imposes some limitations; the obligation to distinguish only arises in relation to those cases which are arguably relevant to the issue which the House has to decide. Distinguishing is essentially a way of replying to arguments which are being rejected, and it would be pointless to reject arguments which have never been advanced either by counsel, or by judges in lower courts.

THE STATUS OF RULES OF PRECEDENT

But although it is not difficult to say what the content of the obligation is, and to cite authorities which illustrate this content,

---

[1] *Precedent in English and Continental Law* (1934), 50 L.Q.R. 40, at p. 50.
[2] Dias and Hughes, *Jurisprudence*, p. 81.

it has been argued that there is an inherent logical difficulty in showing that the House of Lords is under any obligation at all. Dr. Williams has maintained[1] the view that cases about the doctrine of precedent do no more than report or record certain regularities of conduct, and that they do not impose legal obligations, or state what are legal obligations. He supports this point of view by an analysis of the normal lawyer's method of justifying the assertion that the House of Lords is bound by its own decisions, which is to cite the case of *London Street Tramways, Ltd.* v. *London County Council*[2] as authority for the proposition. Such a method of justification is, he says, question-begging, for it assumes what must be proved. The doctrine of precedent cannot 'pull itself up by its own bootstraps'. And conversely, as he admits, an argument that the House is not bound by its own decisions is certain to be question-begging too. Thus it is mistaken to think of the doctrine of precedent as a body of legal rules which impose legal obligations on courts; the doctrine must consist only in a set of propositions (which may be true or false) about what the judges in various courts as a matter of fact do. Thus cases on the doctrine of precedent can only sensibly be cited as evidence of certain facts of judicial behaviour.

Certainly it is true to say that cases on the doctrine of precedent can be used as evidence of certain regularities of conduct; so indeed can cases on any branch of the law. But when cases are cited in legal arguments and in judgments to provide support for arguments, and justifications for decisions, they are not (and this again is a matter of fact) being used as evidence of historical facts. The function of these arguments and decisions is not to increase knowledge of the truth, but to show what ought to be done by judges and to justify what judges have decided to do. In short, cases are used to indicate standards of conduct, and cases on the doctrine of precedent, such as *London Street Tramways, Ltd.* v. *London County Council*, are used to indicate standards of conduct for judges. Since this is the function which these cases do in fact perform, one is

---

[1] Salmond, *Jurisprudence* (11th ed.), pp. 187–188.   [2] [1898] A.C. 375.

naturally suspicious of a theory which would say that some principle of formal logic invalidates their use in this familiar way.

In essence, the problem which is raised by Dr. Williams' conundrum is this—how can the House put itself under a legal obligation by simply saying that it is under a legal obligation? Only, it would seem, if there exists some rule which confers upon the House a power or competence to impose such an obligation upon itself. What binding authority is there for saying that such a rule of competence exists? There appears to be none; yet such a rule of competence seems to be logically prior to any declaration or imposition of an obligation in exercise of the power. When Dr. Williams asks for authority for the rule that the House of Lords is bound by its own decisions he is asking for binding authority for the rule of competence, and he correctly denies that the decision in the *London Street Tramways* case furnishes such authority. But, in seeking authority, he is seeking too much, for he misconceives the function of binding authorities in legal argument. They do not serve as proofs of the existence of law-making competence, but only as proofs of the way in which a law-making power has been exercised in fact, granted the existence of such power. Thus it is that there is a purpose in a lawyer's citation of the *London Street Tramways* case (though a limited purpose) as authority for the rule that the House is bound by its own decisions, for the case shows *what the rule is*; it shows what obligation has been imposed upon the House, granted initially that the House has a power to impose obligations upon itself.

Now the most usual reason for citing the *London Street Tramways* case is to justify an argument about a specific case—to show, for example, that the House is bound by the decision in *Rylands* v. *Fletcher*.[1] In such an instance there is no circularity in the method of justification. It is only when the case is cited to justify an argument that *London Street Tramways, Ltd.* v. *London County Council* is binding that Dr. Williams finds the justification circular. But are those who use such an argument rightly

[1] (1868), L.R. 3 H.L. 330.

accused of circularity or question-begging? The reasoning can
be set out thus:

(1) The House of Lords has a power to make rulings about
the status of its own decisions, whether they are binding
or not.

(2) In *London Street Tramways, Ltd.* v. *London County Council*
the House in exercise of this power ruled that all its own
decisions, unless given *per incuriam* or in ignorance of a
Statute, are binding.

(3) The decision in *London Street Tramways* is a decision of the
House of Lords and is therefore binding.

The argument does not assume what it seeks to prove; it assumes that the House has a power to rule whether its decisions
are binding or not binding, and proves that they are binding.
What it does not prove is that the House has this power.

Nor is there any need to confuse the question—'Is the House
of Lords at present under an obligation to treat its own earlier
decisions as binding?'—with the quite separate question—
'Has the House of Lords a power to reverse its decision in
London Street Tramways, Ltd. v. *London County Council*?' The reason
why these two questions are confused is partly because an
analogy is seen between a Court and a single person, and partly
because of the strong temptation to interpret the statement
'the rule that the House is bound by its own decisions is binding
upon the House' as if it meant 'the rule that the House is bound
is unalterable by the House'. These two sources of confusion are
closely connected. Suppose that there was a legal system in
which Smith was given by statute a power to impose legal
obligations upon himself by simple declaration and to alter
them by simple declaration. There would be a temptation to
say that this would lead to a nonsensical position—how could
one say that Smith was ever under an obligation to do anything, when he could absolve himself from his obligation at
will? If one thinks of the House of Lords in the same way the
temptation is the same; at first sight declarations of obligations
in such circumstances seem to be shams, better characterized as

declarations of intentions or statements of practice. But even in Smith's case it might still be reasonable to accept that his declarations really did impose legal obligations until he went through the simple formality of making contrary declarations; at least he had to go through some sort of procedure. When we speak of the House of Lords having a power to impose obligations upon itself the situation is much more complex. The statement is one which requires filling out. In the first place, 'the House' is a term for a body of fluctuating membership, and the obligation breaks up into an indefinite number of obligations imposed upon an indefinitely large though defined class of people. The declaration of the obligation was the consequence of majority action, and this presupposes a rule which requires a majority decision. If the obligation can be modified or destroyed, this too will require the observance of a special procedure. There is indeed no more reason to deny the possibility of the House of Lords imposing an obligation upon itself than there is reason to deny that the members of the Legislature might do the same—for example if they were to pass a statute saying that they should be liable to a fine if they took bribes during a session.

For much the same reasons the contention that the rule 'that the House of Lords is bound by its own decision' is itself a binding rule—which only means that it is a rule which imposes an obligation as opposed to some sort or rule which does not— ought not to be confused with the contention that the rule is unalterable by the House. What precisely the powers of the House of Lords are in this matter can hardly be said to be settled. For although the assumption is made that the House of Lords has a power to lay down rules (so long at least as they do not conflict with a statute) about the obligations which rest upon it, there has been to date no particular need to delineate with great precision the precise scope of this power; all that can be shown is that a power of vague scope does exist. The way in which it can be shown that the power, or, to look at it in another way, the rule of competence exists, is by showing that a rule or set of rules made in purported exercise of this power have as a matter of fact been recognized as obligatory. In this particular instance the rule that the House of Lords is bound by its own decisions has secured this recognition both by judges sitting in the House of Lords, by members of the legal profession and to a limited extent by other members of our society; perhaps more important than this is the fact that there has been no substantial body of opinion which denies the obligatory quality of the rule. It is only by pointing to facts of this sort that it is possible to support a claim that there is such a power vested in the House of Lords.

THE CONTENT OF THE RULE THAT THE HOUSE OF LORDS IS BOUND BY ITS OWN DECISIONS

It has been suggested that the content of the obligation which rests upon the House can be expressed in terms of *following* and *distinguishing*, and it may be that following and distinguishing cases turn out to be the very ways in which the creation of law by judges usually takes place in the common law system, so that the apparent conflict between 'being bound' and 'making law' is not a real conflict. At the same time, a small, but important, historical point may become easier to understand. We all know that the doctrine of binding precedent is not very old; the rule that the House of Lords is bound by its own decisions was only settled in 1898. Yet, in spite of the acknowledged importance of the ruling in *London Street Tramways, Ltd. v. London County Council* in that year, it is difficult to detect any sharp breach of continuity in the development of the common law before and after that date. To some this might seem to be evidence of the mythical nature of the doctrine. To others it might evidence widespread evasion of the effects of the decision. There is, however, a simpler explanation. All that the House lost after 1898, and all that other courts which are bound have lost, is the power to refuse to follow a limited number of earlier decisions *without distinguishing them*. Such a power was very rarely exercised before 1898; its loss was not therefore very momentous, for the development of new Common Law only rarely took place through the exercise of such a power.

CASE LAW AND LEGISLATIVE POWERS

In order to follow or distinguish a case it is necessary to discover what was decided in that case about the law, or, to put it another way, it is necessary that we should know how to extract rules from cases. Indeed a very usual way of stating the doctrine of binding precedent takes the form of saying that a court which is bound by an earlier decision is not generally allowed to dispute the rule or rules of law laid down in that earlier case. Thus Lord Halsbury said in the *London Street Tramways case*,[1] 'A decision of this House once given upon a point of law is conclusive upon this House afterwards . . .' So it is that courts which have power to bind other courts have a power to give rulings upon points of law which have some degree of finality; the ruling given not only may be accepted, but must be accepted by some other courts. Such rulings vary very much in the width of their implications. When they are of great doctrinal or practical importance we often employ a special terminology to indicate this, and speak of 'The rule in *Rylands* v. *Fletcher*' or 'The rule in *Tulk* v. *Moxhay*'. Other rulings are of less importance, sometimes because they do no more than state what any lawyer would have stated to be the law, and sometimes because they deal with fragmentary points of law. We can draw a rough and ready distinction between the activity of a court which makes law and the activity of a court which merely applies existing law to new circumstances, and since the novelty of a ruling alone never affects its validity under the doctrine of precedent, it never becomes crucial to state this distinction with great precision, if indeed it is possible to do so. We do, however, recognize that many cases, especially those which go to appeal, add something to the *corpus* of rules of the legal system, or to our understanding of those rules, and the power to give binding rulings is therefore in some ways akin to the parliamentary power of legislation. The end product of judicial legislation is a body of rules, definitions, exceptions, and so on, which can, like the law governing the sale of goods, be enacted

[1] [1898] A.C. 375, at p. 381.

in statutory form. Since we find no difficulty in thinking of the Sale of Goods Act, 1893, as the result of an act of legislation, there is no need to find difficulty in thinking of the previous Common Law of the sale of goods as the result of a number of acts of judicial legislation, though it would of course be very misleading to forget the numerous and important differences between the law-making of judges and the law-making of Parliament. But notwithstanding these differences it is important to bear in mind that what is sought in a decided case is an answer to the question 'In what way did a court exercise its power to add to the rules of the legal system?' just as in a statute one seeks an answer to the question 'In what way did Parliament exercise its power to add to the rules of the legal system?'

Now when this question is asked in relation to Parliament, there is normally no difficulty in giving an answer; one simply purchases a copy of an Act of Parliament. Possible difficulties are resolved by the existence of a sacred text, and by the fact that the power of Parliamentary legislation is so wide—perhaps only limited by some formal requirements—so that we are only occasionally forced to consider whether a particular provision is *intra vires* the constitutional power of Parliament. Given the text, we can say what is the rule; for saying what the rule is merely involves citing the text. The existence of an indisputable text of a statutory rule is in marked contrast to the lack of such a text in the case of Common Law rules, and many of the difficulties which surround the use of common law rules spring from this peculiarity.

Now with statute any difficulties about the use of a rule are treated as problems of interpretation; we know what the statute *says* though we may have some doubt about what was intended by the words and expressions used, or about what meaning is to be given to this or that provision, so that disputes about the interpretation can arise. What is at issue in such a dispute is what ought to be done, and since this issue is to be resolved in conformity with the rules of the legal system, and statutory rules have a fixed verbal formulation, the conventions of linguistic usage are obviously going to play a considerable part in its resolution. In cases where there is no relevant statutory rule, and the rule has to be drawn from cases, and not from a statute, the absence of an unalterable verbal formulation of the rule reduces the importance of the conventions of language, and makes it less natural to talk of 'interpretation', though sometimes the courts do behave just as they do with a statute, when, for some reason or another, a common law rule has achieved a settled formulation. But this is rather exceptional.[1] The consequence is that problems of applicability which arise in the courts about Common Law rules cannot be solved by interpretation—that is by a process of reasoning which attaches particular importance to linguistic considerations—for there is no text to interpret. Solved they have to be, however, but by other types of reasoning. So it is that usually arguments as to whether an earlier case should be followed or distinguished do not rest primarily upon linguistic grounds; they rest rather upon the use of analogy, and upon the discovery of factual similarity and difference between cases. But just as difficulties of *interpretation*, which seem to be difficulties about words, are really difficulties about the applicability of rules to facts, so also are many difficulties involved in the use of precedent. Thus even if there is a measure of agreement about the *ratio* of an earlier case, an agreement, that is, as to what rule can be extracted from it, there may still be difficulty in the second task which confronts a court in using precedents—the task of deciding whether the rule does or does not fit the case before the court. Neither being bound by statute, nor being bound by cases, absolves a court from this second task; indeed it is only when a person or a court is to some degree or other bound by a rule that the second task becomes necessary at all. *Distinguishing* cases, which consists in giving reasons why a rule in a case ought not to be followed or applied in a later case, is often conceived to be an indication that courts are not 'really' bound; in truth, earlier cases are distinguished, and have to be distinguished, just because they are binding, so that they ought

---

[1] An example is provided by the rule in *Indermaur* v. *Dames* (1866), L.R. 1 C.P. 274.

to be followed unless a reason can be given for not following them; in much the same way courts have to interpret statutes just because statutes are binding.

The comparison between parliamentary and judicial legislation leads on to a second point. When we ask in what way Parliament exercised its power to formulate a rule of the legal system, it is the existence of a text which enables an answer to be given without initial difficulty, except in rare and anomalous circumstances, and the lack of such a text which lies at the root of many of the difficulties when the same question is asked in relation to the judicial power of legislation. There is a natural temptation to seek for some technique for determining the *ratio decidendi* of a case which will repair the initial absence of a formal text: some formula such as 'read a Queen's Printer's copy', which works well enough for Parliament. There is a temptation to feel that there ought to be some formula, if only we could find it; after all the whole doctrine of precedent depends upon the conception of the *ratio decidendi*, and it seems somehow absurd to accept the doctrine of precedent if we have to admit that we are not able to say what is the *ratio decidendi* of a particular case. The difficulty may perhaps be solved if it is realized that there are really two problems involved in the use of cases. The first is the problem of *defining* the *ratio decidendi*, that is to say defining what is meant by 'the *ratio* of a case'. A satisfactory definition will indicate what a lawyer is to look for in his case. The second is the problem of *determining* the *ratio decidendi*. This is the problem of how to look, and not the problem of what to look for. It would indeed be odd if it was not possible to formulate a satisfactory *definition* of the expression '*ratio decidendi* of a case'; indeed, failure here would indicate that it was high time to abandon the conception. It is quite another matter to suppose that there ought to be one technique or one set of rules, or one formula, which will serve as a general solution for the problem of determining what precisely is the *ratio* of a particular case. There may indeed be as many ways of finding the *ratio* of a case as there are ways of finding a lost cat; certainly the *ratio* of some cases seems as elusive.

DEFINING THE RATIO DECIDENDI OF A CASE

In *defining* the *ratio decidendi* of a case, then, we must seek for a definition which will serve as an answer to the question 'What am I to look for?' For purely legal purposes we may take it for granted that we should look in cases for a rule or rules of some kind or other. Furthermore the term *ratio decidendi* is normally used to refer to some binding rule (or rules) which is to be found in decided cases—some rule which a later court (appropriately placed in the hierarchy) cannot generally question. Bearing all this in mind, a possible defining technique is to elucidate the judicial power to make binding rules, and to tell our questioner to seek for a rule (or rules) made within the ambit of this power —such a rule (or rules) will constitute the *ratio* of the case. This method of definition will have an obvious advantage, for it will be closely related to the purpose for which the conception of the *ratio decidendi* has been developed. For the conception only serves to point the distinction between the rule-making of judges which is *intra vires* a power to make binding rules, and the rule-making of judges which is *ultra vires* this power. Furthermore the method suggested closely resembles the normal defining technique adopted to isolate the product of other law-making activities—for example, Acts of Parliament. And finally it leads to a very orthodox and unstartling result, for it is not in the least a novel technique.

What then are the bounds upon the power of rule-making which is vested in judges? The most important limitation is to be found in the principle which denies them the power to make binding rules except when those rules are relevant to the determination of actual litigation before the court in which they are empowered to sit. Historically this limitation dates from the seventeenth century, when it became recognized that a court ought not to give official opinions upon hypothetical problems—a convention which has become refined and elaborated since then. As this convention came to be accepted an obvious corollary develops; there must be some principle which has the effect of reducing the importance of enunciations of the law which have in fact been delivered by judges—either accidentally or deliberately—upon hypothetical issues. Thus the conception of *obiter dicta* grows up; *obiter dicta* are in some sense *ultra vires* enunciations of law. The distinction between such *dicta* and the elusive *ratio decidendi* is in essence a distinction between relevance and irrelevance, and much of the difficulty in elucidating the conception of the *ratio decidendi* arises from attempts to give a precise meaning to relevance in this context. Without some criterion of relevance the judicial power of rule-making seems to have no limit, and in a country wedded to the conception of the rule of law there is naturally a desire to state with precision where the limit lies.

Limitations upon a rule-making power may be formal or substantial; they may restrict the way in which rules are made, and they may restrict what rules are made. The power vested in the judges is subject to both kinds of limitation, but the concept of the *ratio decidendi* seems to embody only a formal limitation. This is that only a rule (or rules) *acted upon in court* can rank as a binding rule. Once this primary condition is satisfied the rule will so rank, *unless* one of the various exceptions to the doctrine of precedent apply—for example the *per incuriam* rule. The rule becomes binding, subject to exceptions. The fact that the rule has been acted upon is the hallmark of relevance, and this may no doubt be expressed in a variety of different ways; thus we talk of 'the rule applied', 'the reason for the decision', 'the grounds upon which the decision rested', 'the basis of the decision', and there is no particular advantage in adopting one of these formulations rather than another, for they are but variations upon a single theme. All state the primary formal limitation upon the judicial power, or, to put it another way, all state the manner and form in which the judicial power is exercised. They thus serve as definitions of the source of law under discussion—the *rationes decidendi* of cases—in much the same way as similar 'manner and form' statements of the parliamentary power serve to define what a statute is.

But, however we *define* the *ratio decidendi* of a case, we encounter difficulties in applying our definition which are much greater than those which accompany parliamentary law-making. The rule-making procedure of Parliament operates on a text—a definite and settled verbal formulation of a rule or body of rules—and it is to the rules so drafted that legal validity is attached. With case law it is different; we do not require the courts to draft the rules upon which they act. Even where a judge does take some peculiar care to formulate a rule accurately and precisely, we do not usually treat such a formulation in the same way as a section in a statute, for the prerogative of judges is not to confer binding force upon a rule by formulating it and submitting the formulated rule to some procedure, but rather to decide cases by acting upon rules, without settling for the future the verbal form of the rule on the basis of a single application of it. The minimum required before a judge may be said to act upon a legal rule is that

(*a*) He should have a rule in mind when he decides to act. This does not mean that he should have in mind a precise formulation of a rule; a person may act upon a rule without thinking out a draft of the rule.

(*b*) He should decide that the rule is applicable—that is to say he should decide that some fact or set of facts should by subsumed under the rule, and this will involve a task of classification.

(*c*) He should deliberately so conduct himself that his conduct conforms to the conduct prescribed by the rule.

In everyday life this acting upon a rule may be quite a casual process; in the judicial process the convention is that the judge should 'show his working', and this produces a reflective 'acting upon a rule' not so often met with outside the law and other special fields. And with this reflective 'acting upon rules' which is characteristic of the judicial process goes the custom which the courts have adopted of justifying the action taken by an opinion delivered openly in court, which opinion provides the best possible evidence of the rule upon which the court did act. It will be noted that to say that a person acted upon a rule is not to assert anything about the psychological motivation of his action. Recognition of this has wide implications in legal theory. Furthermore, in general, a person may act upon a rule notwithstanding the fact that he may himself be the originator of the rule, as will sometimes be the case in judicial decisions. There is therefore no need to deny that the courts act upon rules simply because it is believed that the courts 'make up the rules as they go along'. If I make it a rule to have a bath before breakfast I can act upon the rule, and if someone was seeking to deny that I had acted upon it, he would not convince me simply by saying that I had made the rule myself.

THE 'WIDTH' OF RULES EXTRACTED FROM CASES

There are a number of writers (and judges) who have not been happy to say that the *ratio decidendi* of a case is simply the rule (or rules) upon which the court acted; they have wished to impose some limit upon the width of such a rule. Hence there have arisen attempts to define the *ratio* of a case as the principle or rule of law which was *necessary* for the decision; many variant forms of this sort of definition have been attempted from time to time. Criticism has been levelled at the use of the notion of necessity in this context, and it has been pointed out that there is no principle of logical necessity which enables one to say that a particular formulation of a rule was more general than was required to justify a particular decision, or, for that matter, not general enough.[1] A variation of the same idea is found in the writings of those who have defined the *ratio* as *the rule or rules which the judge in a particular case thought to be necessary.* But again it is difficult to see the force of any logical necessity which would guide the judge in deciding what precise rule *was* necessary. Yet there is a point in these attempts to deny that any rule acted upon by a court, however formulated, cannot be questioned by a subsequent court which happens to be bound by the earlier decision, and it is important to examine what underlies these attempts.

In essence it is a desire to impose upon the law-making power of the courts a narrow conception of relevance. The court

---

[1] See Stone, *Province and Function of Law*, p. 186, *et seq.*

should not in formulating and enunciating legal rules go beyond the immediate requirements of the case which is before them. If this is our convention we must have some idea of what is required of judges. Surely what this is can be explained by saying that they are required to justify their decision by showing that they have acted upon one or more rules of the legal system. Now whatever rule of the legal system is used as a justification that rule will be capable of embracing situations different in some respects from the situation confronting the court; otherwise it would not be a rule. Furthermore, many rules of the Common Law are extremely wide and general, and if a court has acted upon a wide rule it can hardly be accused of irrelevance if it chooses to justify a decision by reference to such a rule; the relevant rule is just that rule which was acted upon, be it wide or narrow in scope, although a narrower rule would have justified the same action. Of course a judge may be criticized by a superior court or by a court which is not bound by his decision upon the ground that he stated a rule too widely, but the ground of such criticism will be that he stated a rule *wrongly* not that he stated it irrelevantly. It is just the fact that the rule stated is relevant (and thus not *obiter*) which makes it important to correct the supposed error.

THE INCOMPLETE NATURE OF CASE-LAW RULES

If, however, the word 'sufficient' is used in place of the word 'necessary' the point of substance involved would become clearer. In order to act upon a rule it had been said that a judge need not have any precise formulation of the rule in mind. All he needs is a sufficiently precise idea of the scope of the rule for his immediate purpose. There may be exceptions to the rule too, which he would like to introduce were he codifying a branch of the law, but which he need not have in mind since they do not affect the particular problem which confronts him for decision. This is often so in the courts; the point was made a long time ago by Lord Nottingham.[1]

---

[1] In the *Duke of Norfolk's Case* (1681), 3 Ch. Cas. 49, he said 'It hath been urged at the bar where will you stop if you do not stop at Childe and Bayly's

A resolution to act upon a rule which the actor does not consider himself at liberty to change is one thing if the actor commits himself to a set formulation of the rule, which purports to be exhaustive, and quite another if he does not. In the first instance his future freedom of action is limited primarily by linguistic conventions; he breaks his resolution if he does not apply the rule when ordinary linguistic conventions would indicate that he ought to have applied it. Only when such considerations are neutral is he at liberty to pay attention to considerations of purpose and policy. If he is not committed to a set formulation the situation is different; he can build up the exhaustive formulation of the rule as occasion demands, introducing modifications and qualifications as he goes along. He cannot be charged with a breach of his resolution unless he is inconsistent, as he would be if he introduced a particular qualification in one instance after having rejected the opportunity to introduce it on an earlier occasion, when it would have affected the action he took.

So it is that every 'borderline' case adds something to the precision of a legal rule, by bringing to the judge's notice circumstances which make it necessary to refine, modify or qualify the rule, but no case brings this process to an end. When the courts handle precedents they do not treat the formulations of law in earlier cases as exhaustive formulations, but as formulations which were sufficiently exhaustive in the context in which they were made, and sufficiently precisely framed. It is not that a judge by convention should state a rule of law as narrowly as he can when he delivers judgment, but rather that he is not expected to state a rule with the completeness of a statutory draftsman, and thus it is always open to later courts to introduce exceptions which he did not mention—either because such exceptions did not occur to him, or because he deliberately abstained from stating an exception which, as a

Case? I answer, I will stop anywhere when any inconvenience appears, nowhere before. It is not yet resolved what are the utmost bounds of limiting a contingent fee upon a fee: and it is not necessary to declare what are the utmost bounds to the springing trust of a term, for whensoever the bounds of reason or convenience are exceeded, the law will quickly be known.'

matter of fact, he would have stated and acted upon if the facts of the case before him had been different from what they were. Case-law rules derived from judicial statements of law are thus treated by the courts as incomplete things. And in practice judges do not claim completeness for their statements of rules and exceptions; indeed they frequently go out of their way, when stating a rule, to say that there may well be exceptions to the rule which they have not mentioned, or about which the have formed no clear opinion. Furthermore judges are not expected to formulate the rule or exception upon which they have acted with the precision expected of the draftsman of a text. Thus in many judgments there is no passage which can be enthusiastically underlined and quoted in the headnote as the statement of the *ratio decidendi*, or put as it stands into a codifying statute; the style of many judgments forbids this. Sometimes however a judge does purport to state in precise language the rule upon which he acted; many of the great leading cases contain just such formulations. But even in such cases the formulation of the rule by the judge is not, and cannot be, treated as precisely the same as a statutory rule, where every word is sacred.

This is so because of a number of factors. To start with, the formulation is invariably embedded in the rest of the judgment, so that there may be in the rest of the judgment passages which reveal the judge's intended meaning more clearly than his careful formulation taken in isolation. More important perhaps is the fact that a case-law rule, if formulated, is formulated and applied at the same time; in *Rylands* v. *Fletcher* we have not only a carefully stated rule but also an example of 'non-natural user', of a thing 'likely to do mischief if it escapes' and 'an accumulation'; these illustrations may justify a later reformulation of the rule—a selection of different words not designed to alter the rule but rather to bring out rather better or rather more clearly the meaning which it is believed an earlier court intended to convey by the words used, or to resolve an ambiguity or vagueness which becomes apparent in a later case but which was not apparent when the rule was originally formulated. Again a formulation of a rule in a judgment serves a justificatory purpose which is quite different from the purpose served by the formulation of a rule in a statute, and the choice of words is inevitably influenced by a desire to leave no doubt as to the applicability of the rule to the case before the judge; it is sensible enough for the courts to retain a somewhat greater freedom in dealing with rules enunciated in such circumstances than they enjoy in relation to statutory rules. But the extent of this freedom is not very great, and judicial practice in general reflects little more than reluctance to be over-impressed by short passages lifted out of judgments.

Thus we may say that the judicial power of rule-making is limited in two ways. Rules, and exceptions to rules, may only be made if they are simultaneously acted upon, and no judge can do what Parliament can do, and introduce into the body of the law an exhaustive and unalterable formulation of a rule— he cannot confine his successors to mere interpretation. Neither of these two limitations impose any restriction upon the content of a rule; the restrictions of a substantial nature which do exist are not embodied in the conception of the *ratio decidendi* of a case. When we have decided what the *ratio* of a case is, we have still to decide whether the case was rightly or wrongly decided, or decided for the wrong reason; for example the rule acted upon may contravene statute, or be at variance with the rule which can be extracted from the binding decision of a higher court. It is the exceptions to the doctrine of binding precedent and the system of appeals which impose restrictions upon the content of the rules upon which the courts can confer binding authority; the *ratio* of a case is only binding if it is not inconsistent with statute, or inconsistent with the *ratio* of another decision.

The conception of sufficiency has another aspect. The reason why a judge enunciates the rule of law upon which he acts is that the rule justifies his action; not any rule will serve as a justification, but only a rule which is acceptable as a rule of the legal system. If, as frequently happens when a Common Law rule is relied upon, there is room for doubt as to whether the rule which the judge relies upon is a Common Law rule or not, then not only must the rule be stated to justify the decision but the rule in its turn be justified by reference to earlier precedents or other 'authorities'. This need for secondary justification will itself have an effect upon what is or is not a sufficient statement of the rule. Thus to justify the rule acted upon in *Grant* v. *Australian Knitting Mills*[1] by reference to *Donoghue* v. *Stevenson*[2] requires the statement of a rule at least wide enough to embrace both cases; a rule about the liability of a manufacturer of foodstuffs could not be so justified.

DETERMINING THE RATIO DECIDENDI OF A CASE

The problem of *determining* the *ratio* of a particular case is quite separate from the problem of *defining* the *ratio*, of saying in general what the expression *ratio decidendi* means. Cases do not follow a set pattern; some judgments are rambling and obscure; others are short and precise. Sometimes no judgment is given, and sometimes judgments are badly or inadequately reported. There is no such thing as a common form judgment, and thus it is intrinsically unlikely that any simple rule of thumb will enable us to discover the rule or rules upon which the court acted. Naturally a rule enunciated by a judge as the rule upon which he acted will be the best guide of all to the *ratio*; at the other end of the scale the absence of any judgment at all reduces the search to guesswork. There is not, and there cannot be, one single technique which can be utilized by a lawyer to solve a problem of communication of this sort. To imagine that there is seems to be as mistaken as to imagine, for example, that some technique is discoverable which could be applied to the pages of Hansard in order to determine the reason why a particular politician voted one way or the other. To search for a satisfying answer to the question 'How do I determine the *ratio decidendi* of a case?' is to search for a phantom.

The tendency has been, however, for the difficulty of the task of determining the *ratio* of a case to be exaggerated. In a large number of instances it is not particularly difficult to

[1] [1936] A.C. 85.   [2] [1932] A.C. 562.

arrive at a satisfactory formulation of the *ratio*—it is the exception for the writers of headnotes to be criticized rather than the rule—but it is frequently difficult to decide whether the rule derived from an earlier case applies in a later case. No technique of determining the *ratio* would in any way reduce this difficulty which is just as acutely felt with the interpretation of statute; the problem is an unavoidable one. If anything, deciding whether to apply case-law rules is easier, for at least the earlier decision does provide an example of the application of the rule which may be of assistance, and this cannot be said of statutes before they have been considered in the courts. There is also a tendency to confuse the definition of the *ratio* with its determination, with the result that extremely unsatisfactory and paradoxical theories are produced to deal with the consequential difficulties. The *reductio ad absurdum* of this confusion is to be found expressed in the theory that the *ratio decidendi* of a case is a rule which is constructed by a later court when called upon to consider the case. To *define* the *ratio* in this way is surely perverse—if it were correct to do so a number of oddities would follow. For example it would be a contradiction to say that a court had misunderstood an earlier case's *ratio*, for by definition this could not be so; it could neither be understood nor misunderstood; confronted with two variant judicial decisions as to the *ratio* of an earlier case one would have to say that the case had two different *rationes decidendi*; analyses of cases which had not yet been considered by a court would have to be portrayed as prophecies as to what in the future would be the *ratio decidendi* of a case already decided. Incongruities of this sort could easily be multiplied. Closely related to this perverse theory is the view that any attempt to determine the *ratio decidendi* of a single case is fatuous—an opinion which has some adherents. If it were really true that it is *a priori* impossible to determine the *ratio* of an isolated case (as opposed to its being merely difficult) it would seem to follow that there is no such thing as the *ratio* of a single case; to be consistent it would be necessary to maintain that in an isolated decision a court cannot for some reason be said to act upon a rule, but that if we take a group of court decisions collectively it becomes possible to say that in each one the court did act upon a rule. There seems to be a paradox here. It may be that those who take the view that rules cannot be extracted from single cases, but only from groups of cases, are confusing *acting upon* rules (which is what lawyers are interested in) and mere *conformity* to regularities or regular patterns of behaviour (which interests natural scientists). A single instance of acting upon a rule may well enable us to be certain as we can be of the rule; a single instance of behaviour provides a poor basis for inductive reasoning as to a regularity or pattern of behaviour to which that behaviour conformed, if indeed it provides any basis at all.

KNOWING WHAT THE LAW IS

Yet in these paradoxical theories there is an important element of truth. It is easier to tell *what the law is* on a topic if we have a group of cases, easier, for example to expound 'the rule in *Rylands* v. *Fletcher*' (meaning not the *ratio* of that case, but the whole body of rules on liability for escapes) now that we have a large number of decisions in which that leading decision has been discussed; many of the points which were uncertain at first have been cleared up since. In part this is because of the peculiarity of Common Law rules, which cannot be stated exhaustively in any one case, but only sufficiently; thus later courts can and do introduce qualifications and exceptions to deal with circumstances which were not in issue before. The growth of exceptions to liability under *Rylands* v. *Fletcher* is an obvious example of this process. But the cases which have introduced exceptions and defences do not increase our knowledge of the *ratio* of *Rylands* v. *Fletcher*; they add to our knowledge of the law generally. In part, groups of cases help more because of the very nature of rules, which, even if they achieve a set formulation (which Common Law rules do not achieve), require continuous interpretation, and thus breed subsidiary rules. This is what happens to statutory rules just as much as to Common Law rules, and just as a decision upon the interpretation of an Act of Parliament may resolve a doubt as to what the law is upon a topic, so can a decision upon the interpretation of a case resolve a similar doubt. This does not make it necessary to say that a statute which has never been interpreted by the courts is an empty, meaningless thing, or that a case which has never been considered by a court does not have a *ratio decidendi*, which it is quite sensible to seek to discover.

The use of cases to provide authority for propositions of law is greatly assisted by another factor. It is very unusual for cases to be cited as authority for extensive doctrinal propositions, but only for isolated points of law which were treated as arguable by the litigant's professional advisers. It has been strikingly said that a large body of case law treats not of rules, but of 'rule-fragments'.[1] A whole body of customary terminology has grown up to express this fact. Lord Coke speaks of 'the great doubt in the case', modern lawyers of 'the point which was decided in . . .', 'the question which was raised . . .', 'the matter in issue . . .' and so on. We talk far more frequently of what was decided in a case than we talk of the *ratio decidendi* of a case. Lawyers are not usually confronted with the problem of extracting anything which can be regarded as a complete rule from a case, but only with the much simpler task of deciding what question of law was asked and answered in a case, and how it was answered. Since both the form of the arguments and the form of the judgments concentrate, often at great length, upon these isolated points, it is not normally particularly difficult to see what they are and how they were resolved; the most usual problem with precedents is not that of discovering what was decided in an earlier case, but in deciding whether a ruling in an earlier case ought or ought not to be applied in a slightly different situation which has arisen subsequently.

FOLLOWING AND DISTINGUISHING CASES

This leads on to a discussion of following and distinguishing. The reasoning involved in these two processes depends upon the recognition of similarity and dissimilarity between cases;

---

[1] The expression is used by Professor Montrose; see *Judicial Law Making and Law Applying* (1956), Butterworth's S.A.L.R. 187, at p. 191.

as Levi has put it: 'The finding of similarity or difference is the key step in the legal process.'[1] When an earlier case is followed the judge subsumes the situation which confronts him under the rule upon which the judge acted in the earlier case; he does not perform a merely passive rôle; it is he and not the earlier judge who makes the decision. Much less is he a merely passive instrument when he distinguishes by emphasizing some dissimilarity between the two cases which justifies him in refusing to follow. Indeed the development of the law is normally brought about by just these two activities, as any perusal of the law reports indicates; refusal to follow without distinguishing plays a very subsidiary part in the development of the law. This process of change appears to produce a paradox. The legal process is conceived of as conditioned by rules, yet in a sense the rules change from case to case; the very point in having a system of rules to ensure consistency in decision seems to be frustrated if the rules themselves lack fixity.

In the case of statutory rules it is not so difficult to resolve this paradox. The area of choice left to the judge by a statutory rule is dictated by the inherent vagueness in the language in which the rule is formulated; the rule is muzzy at the edges. It is as though a man were told to cut a piece of wire 1.5 cms. long $\pm$ .05; however conscientiously he complies with this request he can only cut it to a certain degree of accuracy, and he will have done as he is told if he keeps within the tolerance permitted. It would be an illusion to imagine that he could be given so precise a specification that no tolerance was permitted, for he could not comply with such a specification even if it could be given to him. But with Common Law rules this analogy is not complete. It is not as though the Common Law consisted in a body of unchanging rules, whose inherent vagueness leaves the courts with a limited (though extensive) area of choice whose boundary does not alter, like our wire cutter, for the rules themselves appear to alter. The difference perhaps lies in the way in which Common Law rules, besides suffering from the vagueness

---

[1] *An Introduction to Legal Reasoning*, p. 2. Levi gives a very full account of reasoning by analogy, to which I am greatly indebted.

inevitably associated with rules, do not acquire binding force through a single act of legislation, but by a series of related legislative acts; it is not so much that Common Law continuously changes, but rather that the Common Law is continuously built up from the *rationes decidendi* of a series of cases. The body of law which we call the rule in *Rylands* v. *Fletcher* was not created in 1868 as the result of one law-making act; it represents the results of a series of such acts, a series which is still being continued. Unless and until the law of torts is codified there can never come a point when the formulation of this body of law is frozen into a fixed and complete verbal form, which would restrict the activities of subsequent judges to mere interpretation; in this lies the primary difference between statutory rules and Common Law rules.

If this characteristic of Common Law rules is appreciated the apparent antithesis between the continuous development of the common law and the acceptance of the doctrine of *stare decisis* becomes unreal. *Stare decisis* does not require the judges to limit themselves to interpreting rules whose verbal expression is fixed, nor does it require them to behave as if at any one moment in time the power of making rules by acting upon them which their predecessors enjoyed had suddenly been taken away from them. What it does require is that at any one time a court's power to make law is limited by the rule that it should follow or distinguish earlier binding decisions, and by the rule that the court's own decision may in the future be either followed or distinguished.

'DISTINGUISHING' AND 'BEING BOUND'

The introduction of exceptions and qualifications to rules of law by distinguishing is often treated as if it showed that courts are not *really* bound by earlier decisions, or that courts use the doctrine of precedent as an almost fraudulent device for cloaking the fact that they do very much as they please in deciding cases. To some extent this notion arises from a failure to appreciate what is meant by saying that a court is bound by earlier decisions. To some extent it arises from giving the word 'bound' a too literal meaning, and imagining that being bound by case law involves some sort of psychological compulsion which removes the need for decision or the possibility of choice, in the way in which being bound by cords involves a physical compulsion. There is a further factor which encourages this sort of argument. It is said that courts sometimes distinguish two cases by emphasizing some circumstances in the earlier case which the judge in the earlier case did not think important or material, and using this fact to justify the drawing of a distinction between the two cases, and the implication is that this is in some way objectionable, or at least indicative of some sort of intellectual sharp practice. But is it? Suppose a College Dean has a power to make and enforce rules of conduct in his College, and that he does not publish a set of carefully drafted rules, but applies a rough and ready doctrine of precedent. He fines Jones £5, and explains to him that he has done so because Jones kept Miss Doe, his girl friend, in the College until 9.30, and that he has always fined undergraduates £5 if they allow ladies to stay in College after 9 p.m. Two days later he discovers that Smith allowed Miss Styles to remain in until 9.10 p.m. because she had been stung by a bee and was in considerable pain. It would surely be justifiable for the Dean to excuse Smith, and distinguish his earlier decision, without having to show that in Jones' case he had emphasized the rude health of Miss Doe, or treated it as in any way material to the issue of Jones' guilt. For what he does in Smith's case is not to pretend that he previously regarded Miss Doe's health as material—which would be untrue—but only that in Smith's case he finds a circumstance which makes it very different from Jones' case, which is not in the least untrue, and indeed quite sensible of him. Distinguishing in the law can be explained in precisely the same way, without its being regarded as a suspicious or spurious 'way round' the doctrine of precedent.

It if were true however that a case could always be distinguished, in any meaningful sense of 'could', it would then be hard to maintain that a court which was bound by a precedent case was in any way restricted by the doctrine of precedent.

Now when one is talking in this context of what judges can and cannot do under the rules of the legal system one is not making simple statements of fact, of what is as a matter of fact humanly possible. If one were, it would be true to say that a case can always be distinguished, for this would only amount to saying that two cases will always involve some factual difference, which it is possible for a judge to point out. From this it does not follow that it is always permissible for a judge to distinguish a case; that he can do so whilst conforming to the rules of the legal system, or that he can do so without becoming liable to be criticized for having acted improperly. Distinguishing does not simply involve pointing out a factual distinction between two cases; it involves further the use of this factual distinction as a justification for refusal to follow the earlier case; thus a particular example of distinguishing can be criticized without denying that there is a factual difference between two cases. In the example which has been used it is clear that not any factual difference will justify our Dean if he declines to follow his own previous decision: it would hardly do for him to say that Miss Styles is a young lady of extraordinary ugliness, whilst Miss Doe was not. It would indeed be as hopeless to attempt to catalogue the possible justifications of distinguishing as it would be hopeless to catalogue the factors which influence the making of law and recommend it to a nation. But when, for example, the case of *Nichols* v. *Marsland*[1] was distinguished from *Rylands* v. *Fletcher*[2] upon the ground that the escape was caused by an act of God, the court's acceptance of this distinction did involve some recognition of some justificatory principle of morality, justice, social policy or commonsense which was external to the law, and this will generally be found to be the case when law is made. For though the making of law may be justified by legal rules which permit the making of law by this or that person upon this or that occasion, the content of the law which is so made requires a different type of justification.

[1] (1876), 2 Ex. D.1.   [2] (1868), L.R. 3 H.L. 330.

CHAPTER VII

Logic in the Law

by A. G. Guest

MOST people suspect, even if they do not know, that lawyers reason in a peculiar way. In the case of the *Prohibitions del Roy* in 1607[1], when James I attempted to interfere personally in the administration of justice, Coke C.J. reproved the intervention of that monarch, saying that 'causes . . . are not to be decided by natural reason but by the artificial reason and judgment of law'. Today it is still recognized that there is an esoteric quality about the type or reasoning which is required for the unravelling of cases, but it is a controversial issue as to how far this reasoning involves the use, or abuse, or neglect of logic.

UNPOPULARITY OF LOGIC

On the threshold of our inquiry we are bound to remark that logic as an instrument of legal reasoning has grown unpopular of late.[2] Any attempt to rehabilitate it is therefore unlikely to be received with a great deal of sympathy. The chief objection to logic in the law is usually expressed in the form that logical thought processes are rigid and inflexible whereas legal reasoning is empirical and discretionary. 'The life of the law has not been logic: it has been experience.'[3] 'In any contact between life and logic, it is not logic that is successful.'[4] Such familiar statements underline the distrust which most common lawyers rightly feel towards any type of reasoning which would force

---

[1] (1607), 12 Co. Rep. 63.
[2] See, for example, Frank, *Law and the Modern Mind, passim.*; Konstam (1944), 60 L.Q.R. 232; Lloyd (1948), 64 L.Q.R. 468; Stone, *Province and Function of Law,* ch. VI, VII.
[3] Holmes, *The Common Law*, p. 1.
[4] Laski, *Studies in the Problem of Sovereignty*, p. 201.

them into the straightjacket of legal determinism and compel them to apply 'clock-work' reasoning without any consideration of the moral or social considerations involved. In particular, this general distrust is supported by three specific arguments: that decisions cannot be arrived at simply by deduction from existing legal principles, that legal rules are too fluid and uncertain to support any logical inferences which could be drawn from them, and that the whole conception of law as a single, unitary, logically consistent system is at least an impractical ideal, if not an illusory fetish.

It must be admitted that, at first sight, there is considerable truth in these contentions. It is clear that there are many other sources of decision besides simple deductions from existing principles, and that consequently such deductions do not necessarily follow as a matter of law. The pre-existence of a body of legal rules does not eliminate discretion on the part of the judge whether or not he should apply them, and he is always entitled to keep his eye on other sources of law—on the ethical code of the community, on social justice, on history—in arriving at his decision. Whether or not we go so far as to assert that legal certainty and the whole doctrine of precedent are themselves illusory, it is nevertheless evident that the complexity of the issues presented to him and the wealth of competing analogies frequently allow a judge to make his own constructive choice without resort to strict deduction from existing legal rules.

A realization of this fact provokes the further observation that propositions of law are not based, like those of Euclidean geometry, upon fixed axioms or postulates, but upon concepts of a linguistic and jurisprudential nature which may be indefinite and change in the course of time. As far as case law is concerned, these propositions are to found in the *rationes decidendi* of previous cases and, as Cardozo J. has said,[5] 'Cases do not unfold their principles for the asking'. Where a statute is in question, its provisions are frequently no less obscure. The words of the statute will require interpretation and in this semantic process the same flexibility of decision remains. If there can be some

---

[5] *The Nature of the Judicial Process*, p. 29.

dispute as to whether an underground petrol storage tank is a 'building or structure',[1] whether a car park to which the public has access is a 'road',[2] and whether a costermonger's barrow is a 'place',[3] how much more indeterminate are such words as 'reasonable', 'suitable' and 'negligent'? These words are subject to so many psychological and sociological overtones that it is surprising that individual judges are able to reach any agreement as to their use at all.

It is therefore impossible, so it has been argued, in view of this state of flux, to conceive of logical symmetry in a legal system in the sense that it must be a logical and coherent whole, propositions being derived one from the other and without conflict. Indeed, some judges have expressly repudiated any such ideal. 'Your Lordships' said Lord Macmillan in *Read* v. *J. Lyons & Co., Ltd.*,[4] 'are not called upon to rationalize the law of England'. But even if we conceive that a judge's functions are somewhat wider than this, it is clear that the law is not a logically monistic system in fact, being full of paradoxes and contradictions. We experience a pleasant surprise when it proves capable of even a small amount of consistency. It would be wrong, however, to attribute this degree of consistency necessarily to the dictates of logic, for its coherence may be due to other extra-logical factors.

THE PLACE OF LOGIC

While admitting these criticisms, it may legitimately be asked whether they really affect the question of the place of logic in the law.[5] For logic does not purport to determine the content of the premises on which it works; nor does it purport to decide from which premises we should begin or in any way disable our choice; it does not seek to provide us with a self-sufficient and self-perpetuating system liberated from all contradictions; it does not even purport to determine the truth or falsity of the propositions advanced. Logic is concerned merely to demonstrate

---

[1] *Shell-Mex and B.P., Ltd.* v. *Holyoak (Valuation Officer)*, [1958] 1 W.L.R. 331.
[2] *Griffin* v. *Squires*, [1958] 1 W.L.R. 1106.
[3] *Kahn* v. *Newberry*, [1959] 2 Q.B.1.   [4] [1947] A.C. 156, at p. 175.
[5] See Jensen, *The Nature of Legal Argument*, pp. 8–10; Hart (1958), 71 Harvard L.R. 593, at p. 610.

the correctness or incorrectness of the deductions or inferences made, and, although it may be necessary for this purpose to inquire into the logical form of the propositions advanced, it is not necessary to assert their truth or to define the sources from which they are to be drawn. There may, for example, be correct deductions from untrue premisses, and, so far as inductive reasoning is concerned, the conclusion is one of the relative probability (or improbability) of a hypothesis as inferred from the observation of individual instances.

When, therefore, we are supposedly confronted with a choice between 'logic' and 'life', or between 'logic' and 'experience', it is necessary to inquire closely whether it really is logic which we are being asked to discard. In *Hynes* v. *New York Central Railroad Co.*,[1] for example, Cardozo J. rejected 'dry logic' in favour of a more empirical approach. The deceased, a boy aged sixteen, was killed by the fall of a high tension wire from the defendants' railway. At the time of the accident he was standing on a springboard which was attached to the defendants' land, but which projected over the Hudson River. The deceased had no right to be on the springboard, and the defendants contended that he was a trespasser to whom they would not be liable for mere negligence. They relied on the proposition, familiar to the law of real property, that whatever is attached to the land forms part of the land, and argued that the springboard, being attached to their land, formed part of it. The deceased being on the defendants' land without their permission was therefore a trespasser. Cardozo J., however, preferred to emphasize the public ownership of the surrounding air space and water, and he deprecated 'the extension of a maxim or a definition with relentless disregard of the consequences to a "dryly logical extreme".'

But the real question in this case is not one of logic at all. What is being contested is not any deduction from the proposition that 'whatever is attached to the land forms part of the land' but the meaning to be attached to the words 'part of the land'. Nevertheless in his book *The Province and Function of Law*,[2]

[1] (1921), 231 N.Y. 229.   [2] At p. 141.

Professor Stone appears to think that the rejection of logic lies in the abandonment by the judge of 'the implied assumption that all propositions of all parts of the law must be logically consistent with each other'. Yet it is clear that when Cardozo J. refused to allow the transfer of this proposition without any qualification from the law of real property to that of torts he no more created any *logical* inconsistency than if, in ordinary speech, we distinguished between the word 'man' as applied to the present Lord Chancellor, the man who broke the bank at Monte Carlo, or the man on the Clapham omnibus. All he is saying is that things which are attached to the land do not form 'part of the land'—at any rate for the purposes of the law of negligence—when they project over or into space to which the public have access. This does not involve any rejection of logic.

Similarly in the case of *Whiteley* v. *Chappell*,[1] the accused was charged with having 'personated a person entitled to vote'. It was proved that he had filled in a voting paper in the name of a man who was dead. He was acquitted of the offence charged. This decision is frequently cited as a glaring example of 'automatic' reasoning. The use of 'dry logic' is contrasted unfavourably with a judicial discretion based upon discovering the true intent of the legislature. But the issue in this case was simply one of the interpretation of the words 'personating' and 'entitled to vote'. It was, in fact, one of semantics.

As a final illustration we may take the celebrated *dictum* of Lord Halsbury in *Quinn* v. *Leathem*,[2] where he said, 'a case is only authority for what it actually decides. I entirely deny that it can be quoted for a proposition that may seem to follow logically from it. Such a mode of reasoning assumes that the law is necessarily a logical code, whereas every lawyer must acknowledge that the law is not always logical at all'. An examination of his speech, however, will reveal that Lord Halsbury had in mind two points: first, that the facts in the case of *Allen* v. *Flood*[3] differed materially from those in the case under consideration, and, secondly, that he rejected the interpretation given by Palles

---

[1] (1868), L.R. 4 Q.B. 147, construing 14 & 15 Vict., c. 105, s. 3.
[2] [1901] A.C. 495, at p. 506.   [3] [1898] A.C. 1.

C.B. of *Allen* v. *Flood* in the Divisional Court. The Lord Chief Baron had assumed that the earlier case laid down the principle that there could be no tort unless there had first been a violation of a legal right—some act which would have been actionable whatever the motive and whether or not there was any conspiracy. Such a proposition was, of course, much too wide. Again however, no question of logic was involved. The principle enunciated by Palles C.B. was not the product of any logical deduction from the facts and decision in *Allen* v. *Flood*, but consisted of his own formulation of the *ratio decidendi* of that case. Many decisions which have similarly been criticized (or supported) on the ground of an alleged conflict between logic and law thus involve no such conflict at all.

THE MEANING OF LOGIC

What do we mean by logic? Too often discussion of this subject has centred around the rather barren controversy whether legal reasoning is deductive or inductive in form.[1] In this dispute, both sides have assumed that by deductive logic is meant the most simple form of the Aristotelian syllogism: All S is P; x is an instance of S; therefore x is an instance of P. It should be realized, however, that there are many more deductive inferences which may be made even in traditional or Aristotelian logic. For example, there is the logic of alternatives, of compound propositions, and of relationships. Modern logicians have also demonstrated that it is not possible to assume that the rules of logic merely govern the relationship between propositions and do not have any influence upon their factors. Propositions may not always be of the same logical form and so will possess different logical properties in their application. The analysis of these properties is also proper to the study of logic. Any criticism, therefore, which is based solely on the inadequacy of the Aristotelian syllogism must be discounted.[2] It would not be possible to confine any type of reasoning within so narrow a compass.

[1] Jensen, *op. cit.*, p. 10.

[2] Paton, *Jurisprudence* (2nd ed.), p. 151; Allen, *Law in the Making* (6th ed.), p. 157; Cardozo, *The Nature of the Judicial Process*, p. 22.

We must expect the position to be far more complicated. We must expect legal reasoning to be partly deductive and partly inductive, partly reasoning by analogy and partly the product of intuition, emotion or prejudice. In fact, legal reasoning will range over all the possible forms of human argument. 'Lawyers do not possess, and do not claim to possess, a monopoly of the art of dialectic'.[1] In this essay, however, it is not contended that all legal reasoning involves the use of logic. All that is asserted is that logic can and does play some part in legal thought processes, and that certain objections which have been taken to its use in the law are not well founded. It will therefore be sufficient for the moment to produce some familiar examples of deductive reasoning (in the sense of the application of a general rule to a particular instance) and to inquire whether or not they can be cast in a logical form.

Deductive Reasoning

Let us take the words of a penal statute, in this case the Representation of the People Act, 1949, s. 52: 'Any person shall be guilty of an offence if, at a parliamentary or local government election, he fraudulently takes out of the polling station any ballot paper'.[2] Here the legal process consists in the application of a fixed and ascertained rule to the facts of a particular case. The section of the statute constitutes the major premiss, the minor being 'X (the accused) at a parliamentary or local government election fraudently took out of a polling station a ballot paper.' This, it will be seen, comprises the words of the indictment. If the minor premiss is true, the offence is made out and X will be found guilty.

In most cases, of course, the main argument will turn upon the meaning of the major premiss, or upon the truth of the minor. In the trial court the inquiry will be: Did the accused take a ballot paper out of the polling station, and with what intent? In an appellate court the question may well be argued: What is meant by 'fraudulently', 'polling station' or 'ballot paper'? If the facts are ascertained and the dispute is merely

[1] Allen, *Law in the Making* (6th ed.), p. 271.   [2] 12 & 13 Geo. VI, c. 68.

one of interpretation or is a dispute as to the subsumption of the facts under a given rule (as, for example, where the court has to decide whether a spoiled ballot paper is a ballot paper for the purposes of this section, or whether the accused's conduct in law amounts to fraud), the legal process is quite different. It is, as Professor Wisdom has said, 'a presenting and re-presenting of those features of the case which *severally co-operate* in favour of the conclusion, in favour of saying what the reasoner wishes said, in favour of calling the situation by the name which he wishes to call it'.[1] The process of argument here is not one of deductive reasoning. 'The reasons are like the legs of a chair, not the links of a chain'.

An examination of the terms used is, however, necessary in all cases where words are to be employed in logical argument. It is only in this way that material fallacies can be avoided. The terms must be minutely examined in order to ascertain whether or not they are being used in an exactly identical sense. In the appellate courts, the judges are frequently called upon to conduct this examination, and counsel argue for different interpretations. Yet their argument is ultimately directed to this end: that the court should be persuaded to apply to the facts elicited for them by counsel that rule which counsel hope will produce the most favourable conclusion for their clients. At the end of their deliberations counsel expect that the judges will be able (or unable) to apply the language of the major premiss to that of the minor, and to reach a conclusion. In the lower courts, however, the words of the statute may be quite simply and literally applied to the case in hand.

It is this process of application which has been termed deductive, and we are concerned to inquire whether or not it is also logical.

Normative Statements

One immediate difficulty has been pointed out by Castberg:[2] Can binding conclusions be drawn from statements with nor-

---

[1] 'Gods', an essay in *Essays on Logic and Language* (1951), p. 195.
[2] *Problems of Legal Philosophy* (2nd ed.), p. 52; Jensen, *op. cit.*, p. 18.

mative contents? If we take the proposition 'All negroes are curly-haired' (All *S* is *P*), the predicate 'curly-haired' is descriptive of the subject 'negroes'. If the proposition is admitted, certain other propositions follow logically from it *e.g.* that no negroes are not curly-haired. If it is denied, this will similarly involve certain logical inferences *e.g.* that some negroes are not curly-haired. But in the case of legal rules such as the section of the Representation of the People Act, 1949, already cited, the predicate 'guilty of an offence' is not descriptive of the subject 'ballot-paper-takers'. The relationship between the two parts of the proposition depends upon the injunctive 'shall' which prescribes what shall be the case and does not describe simply what is. The content of normative propositions is therefore more readily comparable with that of causal propositions of the form 'If *p*, then *q*' *e.g.* 'If a match is applied to gunpowder, then an explosion will occur'. But again there is this difference in that normative propositions say what ought to be the case and do not predict what will be so.

Some jurists regard them as a species of command. If this view were correct, it would raise serious difficulties in relation to the logical inferences to be drawn from legal propositions. The logic of imperative propositions, that is of commands and prohibitions, is by no means settled and there is considerable doubt as to how far deductions can properly be made from them.[1] Kelsen has consistently maintained that legal rules are in fact commands addressed to the courts enjoining them to act in a certain way if certain conditions are satisfied. Thus, in the example cited, upon proof that the accused took out of the polling station a ballot paper, the courts are commanded to apply certain sanctions to the wrongdoer. In fact, however, it is highly artificial to regard legal rules merely as commands, and such a view scarcely corresponds with a realistic examination of any developed legal system. Legal rules are not normative in the sense that they are commands or injunctions. Like moral rules they constitute a standard of conduct to be accepted and observed. It is interesting to note the oblique way in which penal

[1] Jensen, *op. cit.*, p. 19.

statutes are normally framed. They do not say 'If a man steals, he shall be (or ought to be) punished'. They merely enact that if he does a certain act or acts 'he shall be guilty of an offence', or 'he shall be liable to a term of imprisonment not exceeding three months'. The language used would more convincingly suggest that a legal norm in the form set out above simply specifies the conditions under which certain consequences are permitted to happen.

Other legal propositions are indicative in form, for instance, the rule that 'the performance of an existing duty to the promisor is no consideration for a promise'. Kelsen would presumably explain this as a command, directed to the court, prohibiting them from enforcing any contract for which the consideration was the performance of an existing duty to the promisor. This, however, would be as if we were to regard the rules of cricket as commands addressed to the scorer prescribing what action he is to take if one of the batsmen is caught. The real force of such a rule is that it establishes a particular convention of how the game is to be played. Its validity lies not so much in the coercion of the scorer's pencil as in its acceptance by the players.

A legal system involves a *corpus* of legal rules, consisting of normative propositions of a more or less general kind. These set up certain standards for, and regulate the conduct of, the natural persons who participate in the legal system. The formulation of these normative propositions rests upon the assumption that it will be socially beneficial for individual persons to act, or refrain from acting, in accordance with the rule. They have therefore to be applied to individual instances. As Castberg says:[1] 'No well ordered life in common is possible unless certain valuations are more or less clearly formulated in normative statements, which are "observed", *i.e.* made concrete by logical conclusions (subsumptions), and carried out in the concrete situations'. When this is realized, there is less difficulty about the logic of normative propositions, for it is a social fact that we do thus reason from the general norm to the particular instance.

[1] *Op. cit.*, p. 53.

What has in fact caused the difficulty is that legal propositions are not 'true' or 'false' in the same sense that factual propositions such as 'All negroes have curly hair' are true or false. The justification for their assertion is quite different. Where propositions are put forward concerning objects which exist in nature, such as 'negroes' or 'curly hair', it is possible to explain these terms by pointing to actual specimens or representations of these objects. The truth or falsity of the propositions may similarly be demonstrated in appropriate cases by resort to observation. But where propositions concerning abstract ideas are involved it is not possible in the same way to point to specimens or representations of, say, a 'misfortune' or 'generosity'. Nor can propositions containing such ideas be proved or disproved by the same method as those containing concrete terms. If we take the two propositions 'All misfortunes are fortuitous' and 'Generosity is a misfortune', we cannot simply deduce that 'Generosity is fortuitous' without first at least inquiring whether or not the word 'misfortune' is being used in an identical sense in both the major and the minor premiss. The meaning of this word cannot be determined except by asking, 'In what circumstances would it be significant to say that generosity is a misfortune?' And, secondly, 'In those circumstances, would the word "misfortune" be used in the same sense as it would be used if the circumstances which justify the proposition "All misfortunes are fortuitous" were to be satisfied?' In most cases, this inquiry will launch us into significance, if not the truth, of the propositions.

Legal propositions usually involve abstract as well as concrete ideas. Concepts such as 'possession', 'consideration', and 'part of the land' have no real existence in the world of nature, although they apply to it. The process of the elucidation and verification of legal propositions is still further complicated by the fact that they are normative and not indicative in form. Consequently, they must be critically and minutely examined lest material fallacies creep in. Such difficulties, however, are not peculiar to legal thinking. They also apply, for example, to such statements as 'Man is descended from the ape', and 'Personal misfortunes are not a fit subject for public entertainment'.

The 'Judicial Hunch'

A second objection to the use of logic in the law may be put in the form of the 'judicial hunch': Although legal reasoning may, in certain circumstances, be put into a deductive form, this does not necessarily show that the conclusions which are in fact drawn from legal propositions are deductive in fact. The so-called reasoning may be no more than a judicial reflex, or an intuitive or emotional reaction.[1] We carry in our minds a number of indefinite moral and other generalizations to which we resort almost unconsciously in a concrete situation. When a judge decides a case, his reflex may be instinctive. A good judge, so it has been said, arrives at his conclusion first and gives his reasons after.

In certain cases, this will undoubtedly be so; but a more accurate appraisal of the 'judicial hunch' is given by Sir Carleton Allen in his *Law in the Making*.[2] 'This only means' he says, 'that a judge who is steeped in the law can often discern the principle which governs the situation before he can cite the exact authorities which support it; and, indeed, this is an experience common not only to judges but to all well-trained lawyers. But this is not to say that the judge is dependant on 'hunch', in the sense of inspiration or supra-rational intuition; his mind is working in accordance with long training and experience, and there is nothing at all remarkable in the fact that he can see the picture before he has filled in all the details'.

Also the comparison with the intuitive application of moral norms is not entirely satisfactory, for the object of the legal process is decision, and there has to be a reasoned justification of the decision made. Many legal decisions, for example those in the law of real property, are very largely devoid of any moral or social ideals; they rest entirely upon the application of legal rules. There is therefore no intuitive generalization to which resort can be made.

---

[1] Simmel, *Das Individuelle Gesetz, Logos*, p. 117; Frank, *Law and the Modern Mind, passim.*; Jensen, *op. cit.*, p. 17; Cohen (1916), 29 Harv. L.R. 622, at p. 628.
[2] (6th ed.), p. 334.

In his selection of competing propositions and in his consideration of the propriety of subsuming a particular case under a certain general rule, a judge is not, of course, guided by logic. He is guided by insight and experience. But in his application of the proposition selected, and in his testing of its implications before he adopts it, he uses a deductive form of reasoning in order to discover its potentialities. The directive force of a principle may be exercised along the line of logical progression, and a judge must always keep in mind the effect which his decision will have on the general structure of the law.

Induction

The Common Law is, for the most part, not a codified law. We can only arrive at principles by the examination of decided cases. We do this by drawing generalizations from the cases, and it is commonly asserted that his process involves the use of inductive logic.

Inductive reasoning looks at a number of different instances of S and finds that they have P in common. Its logical form is, 'All observed negroes have curly hair; therefore all negroes have curly hair'. Or it looks at causal connexions and determines the conditions under which certain events occur. We observe that p and q repeatedly occur together; we therefore infer that 'If p, then q': 'If acid is applied to litmus paper, it turns red'. Scientific reasoning is of this kind. From a series of data a hypothesis is formulated; the hypothesis is then tested (verified) experimentally. Indeed, one of the most successful ways of verifying a hypothesis is by predicting successfully the outcome of an experimental reproduction of the causative factors.

But scientific reasoning and legal thinking are quite distinct. The object of a scientific inquiry is discovery; the object of a legal inquiry is decision.[1] When a judge examines previous cases in an effort to find a common principle, he does not do so in order to frame a hypothesis which he will verify by the outcome of the case which is presented for decision. Let us take, for

---

[1] Dickinson (1931), 79 Univ. of Pennsylvania L.R. 833; Jensen, *op. cit.*, p. 29; Goodhart (1931), 47 L.Q.R. 118, 138.

example, the case of a penalty clause in a contract. From an examination of previous cases, the judge concludes that penalty clauses in a contract are unenforceable. But this is not an observation of the same kind as 'If acid is applied to litmus, it turns red'. What he observes is that, in previous cases, the courts have *decided* that penalty clauses have this characteristic.[1] He has himself now to decide whether or not this penalty clause is unenforceable. His decision is not like the generalization about a chemical reaction. The judge does not predict that he will decide one way or the other on the strength of his observations. He 'follows' previous decisions, but he does not turn out the answer like an automatic machine.

Again, his decision is not like that of a scientific experiment. He does not employ the case before him as a means of testing the validity of the principle which he has extracted from previous authorities. It is not as if he were using the present case in order to prove or disprove the enforceability of penalty clauses. He may, of course, test a particular past decision by showing that it is inconsistent with other decisions which lay down a general principle; or he may test a principle dialectically by showing that it does not conform with the decisions. But he does not use the decision which he is making to test the validity of the principle.

Perhaps the position is best summed up by Dickinson,[2] 'Scientific thought', he says, 'concerns itself with analysing and classifying the elements of given fact-situations and determining their relations to one another for the purpose of acquiring ability to predict the relations between these elements if recurring in a future situation. This procedure involves the same basic thought-processes which are involved in the procedure of judicial thinking,—the isolation of identities, their formulation in general propositions, and the application of these propositions to specific situations. Here, however, the resemblance ends'.

Legal or normative thinking is therefore quite different from the type of reasoning employed in the sciences; and if we equate induction with scientific reasoning, it is clear that legal thinking

---

[1] Dickinson, *op. cit.*, at p. 850.   [2] *Ibid.*, at p. 860.

is not inductive. On the other hand, an examination of Aristotle's definition of induction will reveal that he considered it to be the leading (ἐπαγωγή) of a person from one truth to another—the passage from a number of particular instances to a general conclusion.[1] He does not use the term in the same technical way that he uses συλλογισμός (syllogism) as a term of art in the deductive process. He thinks of induction as a form of argument in which a person is brought to believe in a general conclusion without supposing that the conclusion is certain.[2]

When a judge examines a number of cases and notices that they have some feature in common, he finds it convenient to abstract this feature and to formulate some general principle or 'concept'. The concept is subsequently applied to the case in hand. This process by which the principle is abstracted and applied may be termed 'inductive' in the Aristotelian sense, although it would not satisfy the stricter requirements of scientific induction.

Analogy

Legal thinking however, is seldom cast so simply in the form of induction and deduction. There is a natural tendency to short-circuit the process of abstraction and application, and, while working within the freedom of a general rule, to argue more empirically from case to case. This type of reasoning is that by analogy, or as Aristotle terms it, 'by example'.

Suppose, for instance, we wish to prove that causing vibrations to escape from one's property is a nuisance. We must assume that any act which interferes with the use and enjoyment of neighbouring land is a nuisance. Evidence of this is obtained from similar cases *e.g.* that causing smoke or smells to escape is a nuisance. Since, then, any act which interferes with the use or enjoyment of neighbouring land is a nuisance, and to cause vibrations to escape is such an act of interference, the conclusion is that causing vibrations to escape is a nuisance. 'To argue by example' says Aristotle,[3] 'is neither like reasoning

---

[1] Aristotle, *Analytica Priora* (Ross's ed.), 23. 68b, 15.
[2] *Ibid.*, Intro., p. 48.   [3] Aristotle, *op. cit.*, 24, 69a, 13.

from part to whole, nor like reasoning from whole to part, but rather reasoning from part to part, when both particulars are subordinate to the same term, and one of them is known'.

Such a process of reasoning is so familiar to lawyers that it needs no further illustration. Indeed, it is central to all common law thinking. The interesting point of this process is that the comparison of instances itself produces the rule. In the above example, the assumption that 'any act which interferes with the use and enjoyment of neighbouring land is a nuisance' is not axiomatic. It is assumed expressly in order to embrace the particular instances within a common classification. On the other hand, there is not a completely full and free choice as to what this assumption may be. It must be consistent with the general pattern of that branch of the law. Levi has lucidly described the situation as follows:[1] 'The problem for the law is: When will it be just to treat different cases as though they were the same? A working legal system must . . . be willing to pick out key similarities and to reason from them to the justice of applying a common classification. The existence of some facts in common brings into play the general rule'.

In subsequent cases the common classification may have to be qualified, or restricted, or extended, to meet the new situations which emerge. 'The kind of reasoning involved in the legal process is one in which the classification changes as the classification is made'.[2] It is therefore quite true to say that the law is, to this extent, uncertain. Since the classification does 'move' in the course of time, no one can predict with absolute certainty the exact assumption upon which the application of an argument by analogy will be based. The assumption is, however, not simply a matter of guesswork. Just as in a game of chess there are rules which restrict the movement of the pieces, so too in legal reasoning the judges work within certain rather ill-defined conventions. These conventions are largely a matter of judicial experience, and they perhaps mean no more than that a judge can distinguish between a 'good' and a 'bad' legal argument. But any major violation of these conventions would

---

[1] *An Introduction to Legal Reasoning* (1949), p. 2.   [2] Levi, *op. cit.*, p. 3.

cause such an upheaval in accepted assumptions that it would destroy the game.

In *Stone* v. *Boreham*,[1] for example, the defendant was the owner of a motor-van equipped as a mobile shop. He sold a packet of tea to a customer on a Sunday. He was charged with carrying on retail trade at a place on a Sunday, contrary to sections 47 and 58 of the Shops Act, 1950. In a previous case, however, it had been held that a motor-van was not a 'place' within the meaning of the Act. So counsel for the prosecution sought to argue that the piece of road on which the van stood might be regarded as the place. The Divisional Court rejected this argument on the ground that it would be 'fanciful' and 'artificial' to distinguish between the van itself and the place on which the van stood. On the other hand, in *Read* v. *J. Lyons & Co., Ltd.*[2] the House of Lords was quite prepared to draw a distinction between injuries which occurred on, and injuries which occurred off, the premises for the purpose of applying the rule in *Rylands* v. *Fletcher*.[3] In this case, however, the distinction could be justified by an analogy with the law of nuisance, and so it could not be said to be purely 'fanciful', even though it might seem from certain aspects to be somewhat artificial.

It may therefore be said that the distinguishing (*i.e.* restriction) of an existing classification without real justification, so as to exclude the argument by analogy, is seldom acceptable. The same may also be said of any fundamental change in the existing rule. In *Pillans* v. *Van Mierop*,[4] for example, Lord Mansfield attempted the introduction of the idea that consideration was only evidentiary in the formation of a contract, and sought to explain previous cases in the light of this new principle. The innovation was shortly disapproved by the House of Lords. Similarly in *Williams* v. *Williams*,[5] Denning L.J. (as he then was) 'reformulated' the rule that the performance of an existing general duty is no consideration for a promise. He would seek to establish that future cases should be decided analogically under the general assumption that the performance of such a

---

[1] [1959] 1 Q.B.1.   [2] [1947] A.C. 156.   [3] (1868), L.R. 3 H.L. 330.
[4] (1765), 3 Burr. 1663.   [5] [1957] 1 W.L.R. 148.

duty is a consideration provided that it is not contrary to public policy. It remains to be seen whether this will also meet the same fate. On the other hand, in the course of its history, the celebrated rule in *Tulk* v. *Moxhay*[1] has changed its character very considerably. Being based originally on the fact of notice by the party acquiring the land subject to the covenant, it subsequently assumed the additional requirement that there should be in existence a dominant and servient tenement.[2]

It is not possible to lay down in advance to what extent and in what way a legal classification will move or change. But in all legal thinking it is perhaps a sense of what may or may not be achieved by the use of induction and analogy which is the hallmark of the experienced common lawyer.

THE LIMITATIONS OF LOGIC

The usefulness of logic in the law is inhibited by the fact that the concepts which are formulated from an examination of previous cases are often so imprecisely expressed that by far the most important task of the judge is to discover, clarify, and define the concepts involved. Some concepts in the law maintain their position solely by the fact that they are so vague and general as to allow the judges to subsume, or to refuse to subsume, individual cases within the rule virtually without any form of conceptual restraint. Examples may be found in the 'natural user of land' test in *Rylands* v. *Fletcher*,[3] and in the 'particular'[4] or 'general'[5] application of the concept of a duty of care in negligence. Others have moved to such a high level of abstraction that at times it may seem to be unprofitable even to try to generalize about their existence. Instances are provided in the case of 'Ownership' and 'Possession' earlier in this book. Faced with such material, as Dickinson says,[6] 'the question of how to determine whether a rule applies to the case, or conversely the propriety of subsuming the case under the rule, is

---

[1] (1848), 2 Ph. 774. [2] *London County Council* v. *Allen*, [1914] 3 K.B. 642.
[3] (1868), L.R. 3 H.L. 330. [4] *Hay (or Bourhill)* v. *Young*, [1943] A.C. 92.
[5] *Carmarthenshire County Council* v. *Lewis*, [1955] A.C. 549.
[6] (1931), 79 Univ. of Pennsylvania L.R. 1052, at p. 1061; Castberg, *op. cit.*, p. 63; Hart (1958), Harv. L.R. 593, at p. 610.

always the point of central difficulty. It may therefore be admitted that much of the traditional body of logic has little light to shed on some of the most pressing problems of legal thought . . .'

Very occasionally, but only very occasionally, judges have expressed their reasoning in a syllogistic form. Mr. Lloyd has drawn our attention to two cases in which this was so.[1] In *Stuart* v. *Diplock*,[2] Bowen L.J. re-stated counsel's argument in the form of a syllogism in order to show that it contained the fallacy of the undistributed middle. In *Lewis* v. *Bell*,[3] the same technique was used by Simonds J., where the fallacy pointed out was that there was no middle term at all. In neither of these cases, however, were counsel's original submissions put in this form, and the judge 'was doing no more than knocking down a skittle that he had been at some pains himself to erect'.[4] Similarly, in a more recent case, *Ex parte Mwenya*,[5] where the applicant applied for a writ of *habeas corpus* to issue to a British Protectorate, Romer L.J. began his judgment with a logical flourish. 'The essential contention of the Crown', he said 'on the preliminary issue, which was argued before us, may be expressed syllogistically as follows: The writ of *habeas corpus* will in no circumstances issue into any British Protectorate; Northern Rhodesia is a British Protectorate; therefore the writ will not issue into Northern Rhodesia. There is no difficulty with regard to the second premise of this syllogism . . . . The difficulty, in my judgment, lies in the first premise'.

It would, however, scarcely be prudent to assert any general pattern of 'syllogistic' reasoning in reliance upon these few instances. Nor, indeed, would it be any more convincing to point to any general 'inductive' pattern relying upon statements such as, for example, that of Brett L.J. in *Heaven* v. *Pender*.[6] In that celebrated case, a workman employed by an independent contractor was injured by the collapse of scaffolding which had been negligently erected by the defendant. The Court of Appeal

[1] (1948), 64 L.Q.R. 468.   [2] (1889), 43 Ch. D. 343, at p. 352.
[3] [1940] Ch. 345, at p. 350, 351.   [4] Lloyd (1948), 64 L.Q.R. 468, at p. 481.
[5] [1960] 1 Q.B. 241, at p. 303.   [6] (1883), 11 Q.B.D. 503, at p. 509.

decided that the defendant owed him a duty to take care, and
in his search for a general principle upon which to base liability,
Brett L.J. said, 'The logic of inductive reasoning requires that
where two major propositions lead to exactly similar minor
premisses there must be a more remote and larger premiss
which embraces both of the major propositions.' These words
have been taken to be merely 'a scholastic exercise',[1] but there
is something more in them than this comment would allow.
Logic is here being used as an instrument of persuasion. Although 'the art of thinking must not be confused with logic',[2]
it is true to say, as Professor Ryle does in his *Philosophical
Arguments*,[3] that 'arguments are effective as weapons only if
they are logically cogent, and if they are so they reveal connexions, the disclosure of which is not the less necessary to the
discovery of truth for being also handy in the discomfiture of
opponents. The love of truth is not incongruous with a passion
for correcting the erring.'

LOGICAL STRUCTURE

Arguments need not be cast in a strictly syllogistic form, provided that they exhibit a logical structure. In the dialectic of
the law, logic has an important part to play at a stage when a
suggested rule has to be tested in order to discover whether or
not its adoption will involve the contradiction of already established legal principles. When a rule is tentatively asserted as
an explanation of existing cases, it is not always possible to
attend immediately to the logical consequences involved in its
enunciation. In *Mersey Docks & Transport Co., Ltd.* v. *Rea, Ltd.*,[4]
Scrutton L.J. expressed the opinion that the House of Lords'
case of *Elder Dempster & Co., Ltd.* v. *Paterson, Zochonis & Co.,
Ltd.*[5] had established a principle of 'vicarious immunity' of an
agent in English law. An agent, he said, while carrying out a
contract, is entitled to any immunity which may be possessed
by his principal. In subsequent cases, however, decisions were

---

[1] Fifoot, *Judge and Jurist in the Reign of Victoria* (1959), p. 37.
[2] Stebbing, *Modern Introduction to Logic*, p. 493.   [3] (1945), p. 5.
[4] (1925), 21 Ll. L. Rep. 375.   [5] [1924] A.C. 522.

reached without reference to this principle,[1] and it came to be realized that his rule could not be applied deductively to the facts of these later cases without producing an inconsistent result. Eventually the rule was discarded.[2] In this type of situation logic may be used to detect contradictions and to iron out inconsistencies, to test hypotheses and to discover similarities.

Thus even if the conception of law as a logically monistic system cannot be supported, it is clear that social considerations cannot, by themselves, without the aid of a logical and legal technique, produce any system of ordered jurisprudence.[3] 'Given a mass of particulars', said Cardozo J.[4] 'a congeries of judgments on related topics, the principle that unifies and rationalizes them has a tendency . . . to project and extend itself to new cases within the limits of its capacity to unify and rationalize'. As an example, it is possible to cite the instance of the deserted wife's right to occupy the matrimonial home.[5] Originally developed from that licence which any wife has to stay in the matrimonial home during the subsistence of the marriage, it took on an irrevocable character from a generous interpretation of section 17 of the Married Women's Property Act, 1882. It was used successively to enable her to claim the continuing benefits of her husband's protected tenancy under the Rent Acts,[6] and to prevent her from being evicted by her husband.[7] Eventually, in *Bendall* v. *McWhirter*,[8] the principle was formulated that her right was an equity, or equitable interest, which bound all but a *bona fide* purchaser for value. In this final stage, it took on the character of a recognizable legal concept, which could then be applied in accordance with existing legal rules.

Again, in the case of the doctrine of the 'fundamental breach' of a contract,[9] the progenitors of this principle can be discerned in such diverse fields as that of bailment,[10] the carriage of goods

---

[1] *Cosgrove* v. *Horsfall* (1945), 62 T.L.R. 140; *Adler* v. *Dickson*, [1955] 1 Q.B. 158.
[2] *Midland Silicones, Ltd.* v. *Scruttons, Ltd.*, [1959] 2 Q.B. 171.
[3] Cohen (1916), 29 Harv. L.R. 622.   [4] *The Nature of the Judicial Process*, p. 31.
[5] See Megarry (1952), 68 L.Q.R. 379.   [6] *Brown* v. *Draper*, [1944] K.B. 309.
[7] *Bramwell* v. *Bramwell*, [1942] 1 K.B. 370.   [8] [1952] 2 Q.B. 466.
[9] See Melville (1956), 19 M.L.R. 26.   [10] *Lilley* v. *Doubleday* (1881), 7 Q.B.D. 510.

by sea,[1] and the sale of goods by description.[2] This 'congeries of judgments' was unified by the enunciation of a doctrine, which, in its turn, could be re-applied so as to defeat even the most carefully drafted exemption clause. No one, it is now said, can excuse himself from the performance of his fundamental obligations under a contract.

The law can never succeed in becoming a completely logical system, not can it ever be said that logic will help us to discover what propositions should be selected or what their true content should be. But logic acts as a kind of geography,[3] explaining the directive force of propositions and their relationship one with the other. There was a time when the law of torts could have been said to be no more than 'chaos with a full index'. The achievements which have been made in the field of analysing and testing legal principles in this, as in other branches of the law, have been due in no small measure to the use of this 'geographical' technique. In this sense logic can never be entirely disregarded in the judicial process.

[1] *Hain Steamship Co., Ltd.* v. *Tate & Lyle, Ltd.* (1936), 52 T.L.R. 617.
[2] *Pinnock Brothers* v. *Lewis and Peat, Ltd.*, [1923] 1 K.B. 690.
[3] Ryle, *Philosophical Arguments*, p. 10.

CHAPTER VIII

Sovereignty

by R. F. V. Heuston

THE doctrine of parliamentary sovereignty is almost entirely the work of Oxford men. It was once thought that Edward Coke might have had something to do with it, but this is no longer believed even in Cambridge.[1] We may start with Thomas Hobbes of Magdalen Hall, who in 'the greatest, perhaps the sole, masterpiece of political philosophy written in the English language',[2] explained to a country weary of civil wars that its sole hope of salvation lay in complete submission to Leviathan. The tale was taken up by Blackstone, the first of the many Fellows of All Souls who were to devote their talents to draping the attorney's mantle about the shoulders of arbitrary power. 'What the parliament doth, no power on earth can undo',[3] wrote the great commentator, and his successor as Vinerian Professor, Albert Venn Dicey, developed these two points in a manner which generations of undergraduates never forgot: Parliament can do anything, and there is no person or body in the kingdom with power to set its acts aside. Yet even the high priests of the mystery[4] had their doubts: even within All Souls there were moments of agonizing reappraisal. Thus the holders of the Vinerian chair were not always consistent with each other or even with themselves. At the inmost centre of English legal education there were ominous signs of fission. Blackstone was obliged to express doubts concerning the effect of statutes contrary to the

---

[1] Jennings, *The Law and the Constitution* (5th ed., 1959), Appendix III.

[2] Oakeshott, *Hobbes's Leviathan* (1949), p. viii.

[3] Bl. Comm., Vol. I, p. 161. Note the continuance of the medieval notion that Parliament is an event rather than an institution.

[4] I am indebted to Mr. Geoffrey Marshall, who in his valuable *Sovereignty in the Commonwealth*, reminds me of what I had forgotten—that I had used this phrase some years ago in 32 J.C.L. 116.

law of God, or 'impossible to be performed', or with 'absurd consequences manifestly contradictory to common reason', and reprobated those who talked about 'the omnipotence of parliament' for using 'a figure rather too bold'.[1] Dicey, having emphasized the full scope of parliamentary sovereignty with all his peculiar clarity and eloquence, then tried to explain why Parliament did not enact legislation utterly at variance with the decent feelings of Victorian Englishmen of the upper middle-class. Why did not Parliament command all blue-eyed babies to be killed? This was the question asked by Leslie Stephen in his characteristically trenchant style. Dicey answered him thus: because there are both internal and external limits to parliamentary sovereignty. The internal limit is the fact that members of Parliament are not usually men of outrageous views: the external limit is the possibility that the English electorate would not obey such a statute. If the reasoning is not entirely convincing, it is at least more persuasive than that in the curiously tortuous chapter in which Dicey tried to prove that the doctrines of parliamentary sovereignty and the rule of law are not mutually contradictory.[2] Unfortunately as the years went by the Vinerian Professor became involved in deeper and deeper confusions. In 1885 it may have been possible to affirm that members of Parliament could be trusted not to vote for revolutionary proposals; but in 1913, when the Home Rule Bill was about to become law, the truth was only too plain to an ardent Unionist, such as Dicey had become when Chamberlain had split the Liberal Party in 1886. At first Dicey sought for some means within the boundaries of the constitution for preventing Parliament from exercising the powers which he had ascribed to it in his Liberal days, and made some very ill-advised suggestions about the power of the monarch to force a dissolution or refuse his assent to the Bill; but eventually in desperation he jettisoned the constitution and pledged himself to armed resistance to lawful authority: he signed the Ulster Covenant.

Then there was the Warden. Sir William Anson had once

---

[1] Bl. Comm., Vol. I, pp. 91, 160.
[2] *The Law of the Constitution* (10th ed., 1959), ch. 13.

stated the orthodox doctrine with his accustomed bland precision: 'Parliament therefore is omnipotent to change, but cannot bind itself not to change, the constitution of which it forms a part'.[1] But he too was aghast at the prospect of being taken literally by a parliamentary majority composed of the sons of nonconformist manufacturers and Irish peasants, and in a letter to *The Times* argued that 'Our only safeguard against such a disaster is to be found in the exercise of the prerogatives of the Crown'.[2] Although he would not actually pledge himself to civil disobedience (he was after all a Privy Counsellor), he viewed with a tolerant eye the prospect of Dicey's departure from the common room to join his fellow-covenanters on the battlefields of Fermanagh and Tyrone. From his study the learned author of the polished volumes on the Law and Custom of the Constitution defied with vehemence the wishes of Parliament and people: 'If the covenanters meet [the Home Rule Act] with armed resistance, I for one believe, with a conviction which no results of a referendum or a general election can alter that they are justified in their resistance'.[3]

Then there was the Regius Professor of Civil Law. James Bryce had not regarded the duties of his chair as precluding him from accepting office as Under-Secretary of State for War under a Liberal government—for, although of Ulster descent, he was, inexplicably, a Home Ruler. When not occupied with politics or the pandects he also wrote copiously on jurisprudence; as far back as 1857 he had been described (by a contemporary at Trinity) as 'that awful Scotch fellow who outwrote everybody'.[4] In 1886 he put forward a view which perplexed not only Dicey and Anson but also many humbler students: Parliament, he said, was completely sovereign—subject to one limitation: it could not bind its successors. He also attempted to explain the reluctance of Parliament to pass outrageous legislation by drawing a distinction between legal and political sovereignty. This has not met with the approval of such authorities as Sir

---

[1] *Law and Custom of the Constitution*, Vol. I, p. 8.
[2] *The Times*, 31 March, 1914.
[3] Henson, *Sir William Anson* (1919), p. 148.
[4] *Dictionary of National Biography*, 1922–30, p. 128.

Ivor Jennings and Professor C. H. McIlwain, who have remarked that to a lawyer 'political sovereignty' is a perfectly
meaningless phrase; for in the law sovereignty means authority
not might.

Next came the Chichele Professor of International Law. Sir
Thomas Erskine Holland discharged the duties of his chair
mainly by letters to *The Times* which 'were frequently of
assistance in steadying public opinion in times of excitement'.[1]
But he too found time to write on jurisprudence. He revised the
thirteenth edition of his textbook in 1924 no less than forty-four
years after its first publication. It might have been expected
that in a work avowedly founded on Austinian principles he
would have referred to some of these difficulties. But 'it is
indicative of his serene confidence in the strength of the position he had adopted that in the latest edition he hardly refers
to any criticisms more recent than that of Sir Henry Maine'.[2]
The reader who vainly scans his pages in the hope of enlight-
enment may still reflect that he was 'a well-known figure in
university politics . . . generally on the losing side . . . Yet even
the majority who over-ruled his arguments often knew that he
stood courageously for a point of view which is too apt to be
neglected in the hustle of modern university business.'[3] Another
member of this remarkable group of men was William Geldart,
who had been elected (amidst some surprise) Vinerian Professor when Dicey retired in 1909. It is not easy to trace his
opinions on these important topics, for apart from a popular
work in the Home University Library (described by Professor
Hanbury as 'a perfect little gem') in which there is a colourless
reference to the orthodox doctrine, he published almost nothing. 'The object dearest to his heart was the achievement of
equality between the sexes in all advantages and amenities of the
University; and it was in no small degree due to his untiring
efforts . . . that at the present day nobody remembers that a
"female problem" ever existed.'[4] He was also known to hold

[1] Pearce Higgins, 'Sir Thomas Erskine Holland' (1926), 42 L.Q.R. 471, at
p. 472.
[2] Brierly (1926), 42 L.Q.R., at p. 477.   [3] *Ibid.*, at p. 476.
[4] Hanbury, *The Vinerian Chair* (1958), p. 165.

rather 'advanced' views about the position of trade unions: he would not, in short, have gone quite so far as to say that they should be treated as criminal conspiracies. No doubt the others suspected him of Liberal sympathies and feeling outnumbered with Bryce away as ambassador in Washington he thought it prudent to keep silent.

If then we take our stand at about the year 1930 we survey a confusing scene. It is generally agreed that Parliament is a sovereign body which can repeal or amend by way of a simple majority in both houses even the most time-honoured principles of the constitution. This principle is, however established more by a series of *obiter dicta* by eminent persons, whether sitting on the bench or in the professorial study, than by any judicial decision of binding authority. Indeed, if we confine ourselves to the law reports, it has never been decided either that Parliament is a sovereign body or that one of its acts cannot be challenged.[1] Further, the moral validity of the principle has been doubted—often by the same persons who expounded it. But by 1940 a new doctrine has begun to make considerable headway—a doctrine which has the attraction of being couched in the calm, hard, tightly-knit style of the common lawyer rather than in the vague and emotional language of the political scientist. The concept of sovereignty, as a result of a cautious and subtle re-examination from within its own four corners, as it were, has been shown to be at once more complex and less terrifying than had been thought. It appears that the lawyer can, without reservation or evasion, subscribe not only to the unlimited power of Parliament, but also to the possibility of legal restraints upon (at least) the mode of user of that power. So Anglican a solution cannot fail to be agreeable to many.

A SUMMARY OF THE NEW THEORY

It is suggested that the new view can be summarized thus:

(1) Sovereignty is a legal concept; the rules which identify the sovereign and prescribe its composition and functions are logically prior to it.

[1] Jennings, *The Law and the Constitution*, p. 155.

(2) There is a distinction between rules which govern, on the one hand, (*a*) the composition, and (*b*) the procedure, and, on the other hand, (*c*) the area of power, of a sovereign legislature.

(3) The courts have jurisdiction to question the validity of an alleged act of Parliament on grounds 2(*a*) and 2(*b*), but not on ground 2(*c*).

(4) This jurisdiction is exercisable either before or after the royal assent has been signified—in the former case by way of injunction, in the latter by way of declaratory judgment.

SOVEREIGNTY IS A LEGAL CONCEPT

The first proposition means that sovereignty is a concept which expresses the relationship between Parliament and the courts. The courts will accept as finally authoritative any document which is in truth the authentic expression of the sovereign's will. As Richard Latham of All Souls wrote, in the most brilliant contribution to the literature of English constitutional law since Dicey, 'When the purported sovereign is anyone but a single actual person, the designation of him must include the statement of rules for the ascertainment of his will, and these rules, since their observance is a condition of the validity of his legislation, are Rules of Law logically prior to him.'[1] To quote Latham again: 'It is not impossible to ascertain the will of an individual without the aid of rules: he may be presumed to mean what he says, and he cannot say more than one thing at a time. But the extraction of a precise expression of will from a multiplicity of human beings is, despite all the realists say, an artificial process and one which cannot be accomplished without arbitrary rules. It is therefore an incomplete statement to say that in a state such and such an assembly of human beings is sovereign. It can only be sovereign when acting in a certain way prescribed by law. At least some rudimentary manner and form is demanded of it: the simultaneous incoherent cry of a rabble, small or large, cannot be law, for it is unintelligible. The

---

[1] *The Law and the Commonwealth* (1949), p. 523.

minimum would be rules prescribing some sort of majority—
simple, plurality, absolute majority, unanimity or some arbitrary portion—coupled with rules for the election of a chairman.'[1] Or, as Dr. Beinart puts it shortly, the rules 'define the
sovereign, not sovereignty'.[2] It has been discovered that we
have been asking the wrong sort of question. Instead of asking
'What can Parliament do?' or 'Can Parliament bind its
successors?' we should rather ask 'How is Parliament composed?', or 'How does Parliament express its will?'

In the United Kingdom the rules on this matter are so simple
and have been accepted without question for so long that it is
sometimes forgotten that they are rules of law. At Common
Law they are simply two: First, Parliament is composed of three
component parts, the Queen, the House of Lords, and the
House of Commons, and each of these component parts must
record its assent separately.[3] Secondly, there must be words of
enactment, though probably they need not be in any particular
form;[4] otherwise there would be nothing to distinguish the
document from a set of resolutions passed by either House.[5] If
these rules are to be altered it can only be in accordance with
their own terms.

[1] Latham, 'What is an Act of Parliament?' (1939) King's Counsel 152. (This
important and little-known article does not appear in Sir Keith Hancock's list of
Latham's publications in the 1949 reprint of *The Law and the Commonwealth*.) The
point that the rules which identify the sovereign are as important as the institution
so identified can be proved quite simply: where is the sovereign between the
dissolution of one parliament and the election of another?

[2] 'Parliament and the Courts' (1954) Butterworth's *South African Law Review*
134, at p. 136, n. 37. Those who have read Dr. Beinart's article will realize how
much I owe to it. *Cf.*, Hood Phillips, *Constitutional Law* (4th ed.), p. 56: 'This is
not a matter of limitation, but of identification.'

[3] Maitland, *Constitutional History*, p. 381; E. C. S. Wade, in Dicey, *The Law of
the Constitution* (10th ed.), p. xli. It seems better to put it like this, rather than to
say that each House must sit separately, for all Acts are done by the Queen-in-
Parliament.

[4] Apart from cases to which the Parliament Acts, 1911–49, apply. (*Quaere*,
what would be the effect of the omission of the statutory form in such a case?) It
should be noted (1) that the enacting clause does not speak of the House of Lords
and the House of Commons, but of the Lords Spiritual and Temporal and Commons; (2) that the enacting clause cannot itself be passed by either House, but is
added later—no doubt on the authority of the Clerk of the Parliaments.

[5] *The Prince's Case* (1606), 8 Co. Rep. 481; Halpin v. *Attorney-General*, [1936] I.R.
226.

THE DISTINCTION BETWEEN POWER AND PROCEDURE

The second and third propositions can conveniently be discussed together. There is no need to rehearse here the familiar examples which prove that there is no restriction on the area or ambit of the power of Parliament. It is 'so transcendent that it cannot be confined either for persons, or places, or causes'.[1] There is only one judicial decision which squarely denies this doctrine, the recent Scottish case of *MacCormick* v. *Lord Advocate*.[2] In this case the court refused to interdict H.M Ministers from issuing a proclamation in which the Queen was styled 'Elizabeth II of the United Kingdom of Great Britain and Northern Ireland.' It had little difficulty in holding that it had no jurisdiction to determine whether governmental acts of this type did or did not conform to the Act of Union, 1707. The interest of the case lies in the fact that the Lord Advocate, the Rt. Hon. J. M. Clyde, expressly conceded in argument that Parliament 'could not' repeal or alter such of the provisions of that Act as were stated to be 'fundamental and unalterable for all time coming.'[3] The Lord President, Lord Cooper, approved and extended this statement. He said that he was unable to see why the Parliament of the United Kingdom should have inherited all the characteristics of the English, and none of the characteristics of the Scottish, Parliament. But he also said that even if Parliament did legislate in breach of the fundamental provisions, there was no court with jurisdiction to hold such legislation invalid. There are no doubt certain foreign countries where this is so—excess of legislative authority is regarded as a matter between the legislature and the electors. But this has never been the English view. With us the constitution is a matter of private, not of public law. In any event, the remarks in the judgment, of which it might be said that if they had not been made by Lord Cooper, they would not have been believed,

---

[1] Co. Inst., 4, 36.   [2] 1953 S.C. 396.

[3] At first sight it may seem surprising that a member of Dicey's old college (Trinity) should have made such an admission; but Mr. Clyde was influenced by the doubts Dicey had expressed in his later *Thoughts on the Scottish Union*.

may be disregarded as completely contrary to the whole tenor of English authorities on the point.

We may now turn to the cases which establish that the courts have jurisdiction to question the validity of an alleged Act of Parliament on the ground that the relevant rules prescribing the composition and procedure of the sovereign body have not been observed, with the result that the measure in question is not in truth that which it purports to be. There are three cases—one from Ireland, one from Australia, and one from South Africa. They will be described in turn and then it will be shown that the arguments deduced from them can be applied to the United Kingdom.

The first case is *R. (O'Brien)* v. *Military Governor, N.D.U. Internment Camp*,[1] a decision of the old Irish Court of Appeal (Molony C.J. and Ronan L.J.) in the interregnum between the establishment of the Irish Free State and the setting up of the new courts authorized by the Constitution of 1922. Mrs. O'Brien, who had admittedly been detained without trial by the army authorities for some six months, had applied to O'Connor M.R. for a writ of *habeas corpus*. The application was opposed successfully on the ground that a state of war or armed rebellion existed and that therefore the jurisdiction of the ordinary courts to interfere with the military *durante bello* was ousted according to the well recognized rules on martial law. An affidavit by 'Gearoid Ó Súilleaváin, of General Headquarters, Parkgate Street, in the County of the City of Dublin, Lieutenant-General, aged 21 years and upwards,' recited in detail the episodes of civil commotion upon which the army relied to prove this contention. On appeal this decision was reversed. Molony C.J. said: 'I am satisfied that it has not been proved that a state of war or armed rebellion at present exists in the City of Dublin. There is, no doubt, a certain amount of disorder, and the presence of the military may be sometimes required for the purpose of assisting the police in the maintenance of order or the protection of buildings. Parliament is, however, sitting without interruption: every court is functioning, writs

[1] [1924] 1 I.R. 32.

are duly served and executed, and while it may be sometimes necessary that the civil administration should be aided by military force, it by no means follows that in every case where military aid is necessary a state of war or armed rebellion can be said to exist.'[1] Ronan L.J. thought that the court should make an order for the immediate release of the prisoner, but as the Attorney-General claimed the right to make a return to the writ the court eventually ordered the writ to issue returnable the following morning, Thursday, 2 August, 1923. The events of the next twenty-four hours must have caused Molony C.J. to regret not only that he had not accepted Ronan L.J.'s suggestion, but also that he himself should have cited the fact that Parliament was still in session to prove that a state of war did not exist. For within a few hours of the judgment being delivered the Government had secured the passage through both Houses of, and the Governor-General's assent to, a measure entitled the Public Safety (Emergency Powers) Act, 1923. This authorized the Minister of Defence to make an order for the detention without trial of any person whose continuance at liberty he thought would endanger the public safety, and such an order was made in respect of Mrs. O'Brien in the early hours of Thursday morning. So when the Attorney-General appeared in court at 11 a.m. he produced not only Mrs. O'Brien, which was expected, but also the Act and the order made under it, which was not. Her counsel was able to argue, however, that the Act was invalid on the ground that it contravened Article 47 of the Constitution, which in effect enabled certain machinery for a referendum to be set in motion within seven days of the passage of a Bill unless both Houses had resolved that it was immediately necessary for the preservation of the public peace or safety. The Government had acted with such haste that they had omitted to secure those declarations. Article 47 did not expressly provide that the Governor-General should not signify the royal assent

---

[1] *Ibid.*, at p. 42. Students of martial law will appreciate that this part of the case is of the greatest significance, for apart from the dubious decision in *Egan* v. *Macready*, [1921] 1 I.R. 280 it is the only reported case in which the court has refused to accept the contention of the military that a state of war existed sufficient to justify the proclamation of martial law.

until either the expiry of seven days or the passage of a declaration, but this was clearly its intent.

The sympathies of the court were not with the Attorney-General, as is shown by the following brisk interchange:

The Attorney-General: [The Act] had received the assent of the Governor-General, and the court was bound to assume that it had been properly converted from the Bill stage to the Act stage. Consequently the court was bound by it and was not concerned with considerations as to whether the Act was only passed the previous day or not. If an Act were produced in England with the king's assent, no court would entertain such considerations for a moment.

Ronan L.J.: The question is, what is the true construction of Article 47 of the Constitution. You have no declaration here by both Houses that this Bill was necessary for the immediate preservation of the public peace.

The Attorney-General: It is not for your lordships to impeach the assent which has been given by the Governor-General.

Molony C.J.: Two things are admitted in this case. The first is that this particular measure only passed both Houses yesterday. The second is that no declaration was made.

The Attorney-General: I do not admit that there was no declaration.

Molony C.J.: You will have to prove your declaration.

The court finally held that the measure could not be relied upon as a valid statute and ordered the immediate release of the applicant.[1] The decision clearly establishes that a court is not bound to assume that a measure 'has been properly converted from the Bill stage to the Act stage.'

The next case is the familiar one of *Attorney-General for New South Wales* v. *Trethowan*.[2] In 1929 the legislature of New South Wales had enacted that the Legislative Council (the upper house) should not be abolished except by a Bill which,

---

[1] The Government's reply was to secure the passage through both houses the same day of the Public Safety (Emergency Powers) (No. 2) Act, 1923, which was identical in terms with the first measure, but this time accompanied by the declarations requisite under Article 47 to preserve it from judicial review.

[2] (1931), 44 C.L.R. 394; [1932] A.C. 526.

before being presented to the Governor for the royal assent, should be approved by the electors at a referendum. Further, this requirement of a referendum might not itself be repealed except by the same process. In 1931 a new government took office and secured the passage through both Houses of two Bills: one purported to repeal the requirement of a referendum and the other to abolish the Legislative Council. It was admitted that the bills were about to be presented for the royal assent without any prior referendum. Two members of the Legislative Council sought and obtained from the Supreme Court a declaration that the proposed action was illegal and an injunction to restrain the Bills being presented to the Governor before they had been submitted to a referendum. This judgment was upheld on appeal both in the High Court of Australia and the Judicial Committee of the Privy Council. The *ratio decidendi* was that section 5 of the Colonial Laws Validity Act, 1865, which gives to a colonial legislature full power to legislate for the constitution, powers and procedure of such legislature, expressly requires any amendment of the constitution to be in 'the manner and form' required by legislation whether imperial or colonial in force at the time. It will be noted that the legislation in question contained an express negative provision with a prohibition against the course of action in the event restrained by injunction. Sir Owen Dixon, whose remarkable judgment will be considered later, has stressed the decision's 'significance as a modern reconciliation of the supremacy of the law and the supremacy of Parliament. For it is a demarcation of the limits of the operation of the two principles. The law existing for the time being is supreme when it prescribes the conditions which must be fulfilled to make a law. But on the question what may be done by a law so made, Parliament is supreme over the law.'[1]

The last case in the trilogy is *Harris* v. *Minister of the Interior*.[2] The Appellate Division was asked to consider the validity of the Separate Representation of Voters Act, 1951, an Act passed by a majority vote in the House of Assembly and in the Senate,

---

[1] Dixon, *The Law and the Constitution* (1935), 50 L.Q.R. 590, at p. 604.
[2] 1952 (2) S.A. 429; [1952] 1 T.L.R. 1245.

each House sitting separately. The court annulled the Act on the ground that it contravened sections 35 and 152 of the South Africa Act, 1909, the entrenched sections, which provide that certain sections of the Act, including section 152 itself, or certain laws made thereunder (the Act of 1951 being admittedly such a law), can only be repealed or altered by a two-thirds majority of both Houses sitting together. It was argued for the Minister that the Act of 1951 was authorized under section 2(2) of the Statute of Westminster, 1931, which provides that thenceforward no law made by 'the Parliament of a Dominion' shall be void or inoperative on the ground that it is repugnant to the provisions of any existing Act of the United Kingdom Parliament (*i.e.*, the South Africa Act, 1909), and also that the powers of the Parliament of a Dominion include the power to repeal or amend any such Act in so far as the same is part of the law of the Dominion. But the court held that a law made by 'the Parliament of a Dominion' meant, in relation to the Union of South Africa, a law made by the Union Parliament functioning either bicamerally or unicamerally in accordance with the requirements of the South Africa Act. The sovereignty of the Union Parliament is divided between Parliament as ordinarily constituted (*i.e.*, sitting bicamerally) and as constituted under the entrenched sections. It should be noted that the decision in no way denies the sovereignty of the Union of South Africa as a state in international law. It concerns only the nature of, and the relations between, the internal organs of sovereignty in the Union. Nor does it call in question the sovereignty of the Union Parliament in internal affairs. It imposes no fetter or restriction on area of power—somewhere within the four corners of the South Africa Act there is power to legislate upon every topic which a civilized state in the mid-twentieth century might wish to touch upon.[1] The decision merely meant that for some purposes the

---

[1] So in *Collins* v. *Minister of the Interior*, 1957 (1) S.A. 552 the Appellate Division pronounced valid the South Africa Act Amendment Act, 1956, which removed the Cape Coloured voters from the common roll. This Act had been passed in the manner required by the 'entrenched sections'—namely, a two-thirds majority at a joint sitting. But this was only a nominal compliance with the spirit of the decision in the *Vote Case*, for this majority had been obtained by enlarging the membership of the Senate. The precaution had also been taken of enlarging the member-

component parts of the Union Parliament must combine together in some ways, and for other purposes in other ways. A measure which did not result from the appropriate combination required by the law in the particular case was simply not an authentic expression of the will of the sovereign.

SOME OBJECTIONS CONSIDERED

It may perhaps by now be accepted that a court, when its jurisdiction has been properly invoked, has the power to determine whether everything has been done which the law prescribes as necessary for the production of a valid statute. To deny that the courts have this power would indeed be to adopt the doctrine of the separation of powers in an extreme form.[1] For the doctrine of the Rule of Law requires that the courts should determine legal questions, and if their jurisdiction is invoked they must answer the question whether the document is a *statute* duly *enacted* by a *Parliament*. (It is the obverse of this proposition that the body which decides these questions should be a *court*. This was the point of the *High Court of Parliament Case*).[2] In England the constitution has always been a matter of private law: questions of public law are decided in the ordinary courts according to the ordinary rules of the Common Law.

But it is sometimes argued that even if this jurisdiction exists it is excluded for either or both of two reasons, which may be put thus: (*a*) 'the Parliamentary Roll is conclusive and no court can look behind it;' (*b*) 'such an inquiry would be an interference with the privileges of Parliament.'

As to (*a*), reliance is placed on the words of Lord Campbell in *Edinburgh & Dalkeith Railway Co.* v. *Wauchope*:[3] 'I think it

---

ship of the Appellate Division, which by a majority of ten to one upheld all this legislation. Each step in the scheme, taken by itself, was perfectly legal, even though the scheme as a whole created a two-thirds majority by introducing into the legislature persons nominated for the sole purpose of securing that majority.

[1] Beinart, (1954) S.A.L.R. 134, at p. 162.

[2] *Minister of the Interior* v. *Harris*, 1952 (4) S.A. 769. In this case the (unreconstructed) Appellate Division had declared invalid a statute which made every order of that court invalidating an Act of Parliament subject to review in a parliamentary court to be known as the High Court of Parliament. Every Senator and member of the House of Assembly was to be a member of the court.

[3] (1842), 8 Cl. & F. 710, at p. 724. (Italics supplied.)

right to say a word or two upon the point that has been raised
with regard to an Act of Parliament being held inoperative by
court of justice because *the forms prescribed by the two Houses* to be
observed in the passing of a Bill have not been exactly followed
. . . I cannot but express my surprise that such a notion should
have prevailed. There is no foundation for it. All that a court
of justice can do is to look to the Parliamentary Roll; if from
that it should appear that a Bill has passed both Houses and
received the royal assent, no court of justice can inquire into
the mode in which it was introduced into Parliament, nor into
what was done previous to its introduction, or what passed in
Parliament during its progress in its various stages through
both Houses.'

It will be submitted that these remarks have been misinter-
preted. First of all let us be accurate. The 'Parliamentary Roll',
whatever exactly it may have been, disappeared in England
over one hundred years ago, though even good authors sometimes write as if it still exists.[1] Since 1849 there has been no
'Roll', simply two prints of the Bill on durable vellum by
H.M.S.O., which are signed by the Clerk of the Parliaments
and regarded as the final official copies. One is preserved in the
Public Record Office and one in the library of the House of
Lords. Some more may be added for the benefit of those who
think that Bills are 'presented' to the Queen for her 'signature'.
The truth is that in England nothing is presented to or signed
by the monarch: with us an Act is still something done by the
Queen-in-Parliament.[2] The royal assent is signified orally in
the House of Lords with the Commons standing at the Bar, not
as strangers but as forming in conjunction with the Lords the
High Court of Parliament in the presence of the monarch.
Further, the royal assent has not been given in person for over
a century. Indeed, ever since the faraway day when someone
plucked up the courage to hint to Henry VIII that it would
hardly be seemly for him to assent in person to 'the Bill of

---

[1] See, *e.g.*, Jennings, *The Law and the Constitution*, p. 138. Yet the Act 'must be
looked on just as if it were' enrolled: *Claydon* v. *Green* (1868), L.R. 3 C.P. 511, *per*
Willes J., at p. 522.

[2] Hence it is wrong to think of the vellum prints as being 'original copies' of the Act.

Attainder of Mistress Catherine Howard, late Queen of England, and divers other persons her complices',[1] it has been usual for the assent to be signified by Commissioners appointed under the Great Seal. (The only document which is in any way 'presented' to the monarch is the 'humble submission' in which the Lord Chancellor advises the Queen to sign the Warrant for the issue of Letters Patent under the Great Seal. A list of Bills to which it is proposed to obtain the royal assent is prepared by the Clerk of the Parliaments and enclosed with the 'submission'. It is very doubtful whether a Bill which is not in the Commission can subsequently be passed through its Parliamentary stages). On the appointed day the business of the House of Lords is interrupted by a ceremony which is a characteristic mixture of splendour and informality. The Lords Commissioners, in scarlet robes and cocked hats, are seated on a narrow bench placed between the steps of the throne and the woolsack. Black Rod is told to inform the Commons that their immediate attendance is required to hear a Commission read. The Commons assert their privileges by shutting the door of their chamber in his face, but eventually appear at the Bar with the Speaker. After the Commission has been read by the Reading Clerk, the Clerk of the Crown in Chancery and the Clerk of the Parliaments stand up, one on either side of the table, and face the Commissioners. The Clerk of the Crown in Chancery[2] reads out the title of the first Bill on the list; both bow deeply to the Commissioners; the Clerk of the Parliaments[3] then turns slightly towards the Bar of the House[4] and cries out 'La Reine

---

[1] Since the Statute Law Revision Act, 1948, this has been effectively disguised with the short title of the Royal Assent by Commission Act, 1541.

[2] At present Sir George Coldstream, K.C.B., Q.C.(Rugby and Oriel).

[3] At present Sir Victor Goodman, K.C.B., O.B.E., M.C. (Eton and the Coldstream Guards).

[4] Mr. A. P. Herbert, M.P., once got into serious trouble with Speaker FitzRoy for interpreting this movement as a bow. 'For the Clerk of the Parliaments to bow to the Commons without at the same time bowing to the Lords would imply a distinction between the two Houses in respect of their relations to His Majesty which would be completely without warrant': 346 H.C. Deb. 1700. Mr. Herbert had misunderstood the 'graceful innovation' of the then Clerk, for 'his predecessor, when pronouncing the words, used merely to turn his head and the upper part of his body towards the Commons, whereas the present Clerk of the Parliaments turns round on his feet before he pronounces the words.'

le veult'. This procedure is repeated for each Bill on the list. Throughout it all the Commissioners remain silent and motionless, until after the assent has been given to the last Bill, when, with much doffing of cocked hats, they take their departure.

Now the measure which results from this remarkable process, whether recorded on a roll or on vellum, has undoubtedly always possessed a peculiar sanctity. Whether this is to be ascribed simply to the doctrine of parliamentary sovereignty, or as Sir Ivor Jennings would prefer, to the more recondite rule that the record of a superior court cannot be impeached, is doubtful.[1] Such authority as there is would indeed appear to favour the latter view. But here it is enough to point out that what Lord Campbell said in the *Wauchope Case* was 'if it should appear that a Bill has passed both Houses and received the royal assent', and if it should not so appear, if in short there should be an error of law on the face of the record, the cases from 1455 to 1951 show that the courts can investigate its authenticity.[2] No doubt the case for such an inquiry is strongest when the document purporting to be an Act of Parliament 'carried its death-wound in itself', as was said in the *Prince's Case*, just as it is weakest when the document contains a recital (albeit false) that all necessary formalities have been complied with.[3] How far extrinsic evidence would be admissable to prove the invalidity of an Act *ex facie* authentic, is a difficult question to which no definite answer can be given. It is perhaps enough to recall that although the courts are rightly cautious about admitting such evidence, it may serve to validate a document apparently irregular as well as the contrary.[4] In any event the language of Lord Campbell shows that he never had in mind

[1] *The Law and the Constitution*, p. 139.
[2] Y.B. 33 Hen. VI, fo. 17; Y.B. 4 Hen. VII, fo. 18; *The Prince's Case* (1606), 8 Co. Rep. 481; *Gallant* v. *The King*, [1949] 2 D.L.R. 425; *The Vote Case*, 1952 (2) S.A. 429. Dr. Beinart in (1954) S.A.L.R. 134 discusses various other parliamentary precedents (*e.g.*, 6 & 7 Vict., c. lxxxvi) where owing to some mischance a Bill has received the royal assent before one House has considered the amendments made by the other.
[3] This was the suggestion of Centlivres C.J. in *The Vote Case*.
[4] There are several reported cases in which the courts have admitted evidence to show that a measure not on the Parliamentary Roll, or cast in some unusual form, such as a charter, was in truth an Act of Parliament.

the question whether the component parts of Parliament had combined together for action in the manner and form required by law, but rather was considering whether (say) the non-observance by either House of its own Standing Orders would afford a ground for judicial investigation. It may be conceded at once that no court could or should inquire whether a Bill had received the appropriate number of readings required by Standing Orders, for that is entirely a matter of internal pro-cedure.[1] But it is quite another thing to deny that a court has jurisdiction to inquire whether each component part of the legislature has recorded its assent separately: for in this case the constitutional rights of the subject are involved.

This leads us on to (*b*), the question whether such an inquiry would necessarily lead to a breach of parliamentary privilege. Ever since the memorable judgment of Holt C.J., in *Ashby* v. *White*[2] it has been settled that privilege is part of the common law and cannot affect rights to be exercised outside or inde-pendently of the House. Regularity of internal proceedings is one thing, the constitutional rights of the subject are another, and it is the latter which are in issue in such a case. No doubt a judge would hesitate before granting an injunction in such a case but we must not confuse the factors which may be relevant in deciding whether to exercise a discretionary jurisdiction with the factors which may be relevant in deciding whether such a jurisdiction exists. So in *Harper* v. *Home Secretary*[3] Rox-burgh J. granted an injunction to restrain the Home Secretary from submitting to Her Majesty in Council a draft Order made under the House of Commons (Redistribution of Seats) Act, 1949. His order was indeed set aside in the Court of Appeal, but on the ground that he should not have exercised his juris-diction as he did—not on the ground that he has no such dis-cretion to exercise. So too there seems to be jurisdiction to enjoin a person from acting in breach of a statutory or common law obligation not to oppose an application to Parliament for a

---

[1] It is said that on V.E. day one Bill received *four* readings in the Commons. If true, this could not be made a ground of complaint.
[2] (1703), 14 St. Tr. 695.   [3] [1955] Ch. 238.

Private Act, though in fact the jurisdiction has never been exercised.[1] The reason for the reluctance to exercise the jurisdiction in the latter case is plain. A statute is binding even though obtained by fraud or mistake, so it logically follows that the court should not try to prevent anyone from influencing the legislature in his favour. This reason does not exist in a case where the constitutional rights of the subject are said to have been infringed by the failure of the component parts of the sovereign body to combine together for action in the requisite way.

THE NEW THEORY AND THE IMPERIAL PARLIAMENT

Nevertheless some have found it difficult to imagine that the principles expounded in these cases can be applicable to the United Kingdom Parliament. At the outset it may be noted that this difficulty was not apparent in 1931 to Sir Owen Dixon, who explained the matter in a passage remarkable for its sustained elegance of exposition. 'An Act of the British Parliament which contained a provision that no Bill repealing any part of the Act including the part so restraining its own repeal should be presented for the royal assent unless the Bill were first approved by the electors would have the force of law, unless the Sovereign actually did assent to a Bill for its repeal. In strictness it would be an unlawful proceeding to present such a Bill for the royal assent before it had been approved by the electors. If, before the Bill had received the assent of the Crown, it was found possible, as appears to have been done in this appeal,[2] to raise for judicial decision the question whether it was lawful to present the Bill for that assent, the courts would be bound to pronounce it unlawful to do so. Moreover, if it happened that notwithstanding the statutory inhibition, the Bill did receive the royal assent although it was not submitted to the electors, the courts might be called upon to consider whether the supreme legislative

---

[1] *Bilston Corporation* v. *Wolverhampton Corporation*, [1942] Ch. 391.
[3] In *Hughes & Vale Pty., Ltd.* v. *Gair* (1954), 90 C.L.R. 203 Sir Owen expressed doubts on this point.

power in respect of the matter had in truth been exercised in the manner required for its authentic expression and by the elements in which it had come to reside.'[1] It will be observed that Sir Owen contemplated interference not only by way of injunction before the royal assent had been signified but also by way of declaration afterwards.[2]

The objections rest on various grounds. The first seems to be simply an automatic reaction of baffled astonishment that the traditional doctrine of parliamentary sovereignty should be questioned at all, or in this particular way. So in a persuasive article Dr. H. W. R. Wade has argued that there is a sacrosanct rule of the common law that the courts will enforce statutes and that this rule cannot itself be altered by statute.[3] He admits that 'there must be something peculiar about a rule of Common Law which can stand against a statute,' and explains it by saying that the rule is 'above and beyond the reach of statute' because 'it is itself the authority of a statute'—in short, 'It is a political fact.' But, with unfeigned respect to Dr. Wade, this seems to miss the point that the argument turns upon whether the measure which the courts are called upon to enforce is a *statute*. The issue, to repeat, is one of manner and form, and not of area of power. Dr. Wade seems to admit that the rules which identify the sovereign are legal rules, for he says that Parliament without the peers 'enjoys no recognition as a sovereign body'. But to him the existing rules are so sacrosanct that they cannot be changed: he is even driven to regarding legislation passed under the Parliament Acts, 1911 to 1949, as delegated legislation, for he realizes that if he once conceded that the structure of the component parts of Parliament could be changed for one purpose then he would be obliged to admit that it could be changed for other purposes. To say this is not to deny the truth of Dr. Wade's statement that the relationship between Parliament and the courts rests ultimately on a political fact. Supporters of the new doctrine can, with Dr. Wade, cite as proof of this

---

[1] *Att. Gen for N.S.W.* v. *Trethowan* (1931), 44 C.L.R. 394, at p. 426.
[2] For a case in which the court was prepared to exercise its jurisdiction by way of declaration, see *McDonald* v. *Cain*, [1953] V.L.R. 411.
[3] *The Legal Basis of Sovereignty*, [1955] Camb. L.J. 172.

Maitland's well-known *jeu d'esprit*, in which he demonstrated to his lecture-class that the House of Saxe-Coburg-Gotha had no legal title to the throne of England.[1] The statement is perfectly true—provided that the legal system referred to is that of James II. The point is that the courts acquiesced in the Glorious Revolution. To use the language of Kelsen, there was a shift of *grundnorm* in 1688. Yet Maitland, in whose half-sentences there is often more truth than in the whole of another man's books, also, as we have seen, thought it might be a grave question whether a Bill which received the royal assent before one house had considered the amendments to it made by the other was in truth a valid statute.[2]

A second objection rests upon the fact that the legislatures whose powers were in issue in the cases cited owed their origin to imperial statutes, and were therefore in some (never very clearly stated) way inferior to the Parliament of the United Kingdom. There seems to be some confusion here. If we consider the *Trethowan Case*, it is perfectly true that the New South Wales Parliament was set up by an imperial statute, and was also subject to the provisions of the Colonial Laws Validity Act, 1865, which disabled it from passing legislation repugnant to imperial statutes extending to New South Wales. But it appears to have been overlooked that subject to this restriction, and to the express requirement of section 5 that laws respecting the constitution, powers, and procedure of the legislature should be in the manner and form required by the existing law, whether imperial or colonial, the legislature was expressly given full powers to legislate for the peace, order, and good government of the colony. It has long been settled that these are words which confer the widest amplitude of power. Now surely this is exactly the position of the United Kingdom Parliament—the law gives it power to legislate for the peace, order, and good government of the area subject to its jurisdiction, and as these rules are

---

[1] *Constitutional History*, pp. 284–85. In *Hall* v. *Hall* (1944), 88 S.J. 383 the defendants unsuccessfully pleaded at Hereford County Court that the Court of Probate Act, 1857, had never received the royal assent as the Stuart line alone were entitled to the throne.

[2] *Ibid.*, p. 381.

logically prior to it, it must do so in the manner and form which they prescribe.[1] It cannot make any difference whether the rules which identify the sovereign came entirely from the Common Law (as they did before 1911 in the United Kingdom), or entirely from statute (as they do in Ireland, New South Wales, and South Africa), or partly from the Common Law and partly from statute (as they do in the United Kingdom since 1911).[2] It is hard to see why those who argue thus should attach so much importance to the formal source of the complex set of rules identifying the location and composition of the sovereign. In the time of Dicey it was common enough for lawyers to exaggerate the sanctity of the Common Law and regard with contempt the claims of the statute-book, but it is surprising that this attitude should have survived into the mid-twentieth century. The point here is the simple one that until these rules (whatever their source) have been changed in accordance with the manner which they themselves prescribe they must be obeyed. Thus the Parliament Act, 1911, which changed the rules, had itself to be passed under the existing procedure. Asquith was a master of constitutional law and practice whose Lord Chancellor, Loreburn, was another Balliol man of unusual sagacity. It never entered their minds that it would be possible to avoid the tedious process of obtaining the consent of the peers to their own degradation by the simple device of summoning a joint meeting of both Houses at which such Unionist peers and M.P.s who cared to attend would be shouted down by the Liberal hosts. Yet if the constitution were completely flexible such a course of action would appear possible.

A third objection is based upon the terms of section 21(2) of the Crown Proceedings Act, 1947, which provides that no injunction shall issue against a servant or agent of the Crown if the effect would be to grant relief which would not be available

---

[1] *Cf.*, Friedmann (1950), 24 Aust. L.J., at p. 204.

[2] This was well put in *The Vote Case* by Van den Heever, J.A.: 'In this connexion the fact that our constitution is a creature of the British Parliament seems to me a fortuitous circumstance which is quite irrelevant; so too is the fact that we have a written constitution. I would have been of the same opinion if it had been framed by a constituent assembly of the people, made by Solon, or extracted from the code of Hammurabi.'

in proceedings brought against the Crown. This difficult section still awaits authoritative judicial interpretation, but it is at least plain that it does not in terms rule out the prospect of relief by way of injunction against such officials as the Clerk of the Parliaments and the Clerk of the Crown in Chancery.

Finally there are some who believe that all this is so much academic speculation—that, in short, it could never happen here. They may perhaps be reminded that the only occasion since the seventeenth century on which Englishmen came to the verge of civil war was when the sovereignty of Parliament over the loyal Protestants of north-east Ulster was put in issue, and remembering this, dare to speculate a little on the possibilities opened up by section 1(2) of the Ireland Act, 1949. It is in these terms: 'It is hereby declared that Northern Ireland remains part of His Majesty's dominions and of the United Kingdom and it is hereby affirmed that in no event will Northern Ireland or any part thereof cease to be part of His Majesty's dominions and of the United Kingdom without the consent of the Parliament of Northern Ireland.' Now the Government of the Republic of Ireland has not many bargaining counters to use in its assiduous but hitherto unsuccessful efforts to obtain the repeal of this section. Still it has some. In 1940 and 1941 there were eminent persons in London who were willing to pay a very high price to regain control of certain defence bases on the south-western Irish coasts with which they had voluntarily parted only a few years before. The thread was lost in the labyrinth which enfolds all those who enter into negotiations with Mr. de Valera. But such a moment may come again—and great nations in time of stress are sometimes not too scrupulous about consulting the views of minorities before acting in protection of essential interests. If it should come, and if the Ireland Act were about to be repealed, might it not be argued that the Act had so re-defined the composition of or the procedure to be followed by the United Kingdom Parliament in respect of this particular subject-matter, that a measure which had not obtained the consent of the Northern Ireland Parliament was not in truth a valid statute?[1] For it may be accepted that those who sit at Stormont would never consent to such a measure[2]—even though Ireland has been said to be a country in which the impossible always happens and the inevitable never occurs. It could not be said that such an argument would be successful; but at least no counsel need feel ashamed of putting it forward, even in the Chancery Division. It would surely be an advantage to have these grave issues decided in the calm and rational atmosphere of the courts rather than in a political arena disturbed by threats of civil commotion from 'the home of lost causes, and forsaken beliefs, and unpopular names, and impossible loyalties.'

SOVEREIGNTY AND THE RULE OF LAW

For the new doctrine of parliamentary sovereignty is more than a striking affirmation of the supremacy of the law in times of stress.[3] It is also an important development in the history of political thought. Until now it has been thought that the dangers arising from an abuse of sovereignty could be guarded against only by some such device as a Bill of Rights: to the might of Leviathan were opposed isolated strong-points labelled 'fundamental rights', and the task of defence was entrusted to the judiciary. But it was never undertaken with much enthusiasm: it was not that the defenders were regarded as expendable, but they could not help noticing that their efforts met with as much criticism as praise. The Common Law has found it almost impossible to transmute into satisfactory judicial decisions the important but curiously evasive principles of natural justice. Those who have written on the topic seem to be mainly specu-

---

[1] 'That', says the Lord Chief Justice of Northern Ireland of the section 'could be repealed tomorrow, but *quaere* if the subsection had continued "And no person shall at any time present any Bill or take any other step in either of the Houses of Parliament for the purpose of repealing this subsection or altering it or its effect in any way" ': Lord MacDermott, *Protection from Power under English Law*, p. 46, n.3.

[2] It would no doubt be argued that the restriction in question was therefore not a genuine procedural one at all, but in essence a restriction on area of power disguised as one on manner and form.

[3] See Dean Griswold's comment on the *Vote Case* in (1952), 65 Harv. L. Rev. 1360.

lative jurists trained in Germany or North America; there is something about their writings which is peculiarly irritating to an English lawyer; he cannot explain very clearly why this should be, but so it is.[1] What he knows and likes and admires is the strict logic and high technique which Maitland found in the Common Law. When he is good at this he is better than any other lawyer in the world. The great advantage of the new doctrine is that it enables these tremendous issues to be decided according to the ordinary law in the ordinary courts.[2] By re-defining the doctrine of sovereignty from within its own four corners the Common Law has shown its instinctive wisdom.

[1] It is not only the common lawyer who feels uneasy: 'Judicial review is the last doctrine the Labour Party should champion': *New Statesman and Nation*, 1 January 1955. But Professor McWhinney of Toronto has recently assured us that the dons feel happier than they did about the ability of the judiciary in these matters: (1959), 37 Can. Bar Rev. 22.

[2] Lord Evershed, M.R., has recently remarked on the significance of the fact that when the courts were asked to consider questions arising out of the great post-war nationalization statutes there was no appeal by either side to political dogmas: the arguments were based on the familiar technical principles of statutory interpretation.

CHAPTER IX

The Rule of Law as a Supra-National Concept

by Norman S. Marsh

FOR two or three generations the concept of the Rule of Law was regarded by English lawyers as a factual summary of the basic principles of English constitutional law. By a still wider public, including the lawyers, it was thought to express a system of desirable values largely attained in the United Kingdom and, by implication if not openly so said, imperfectly achieved in other countries. A reaction followed, which might be described in terms of the 'rolled-up plea', familiar to defamation lawyers, in reverse: in so far as the Rule of Law purported to be a statement of fact it was untrue and in so far as it expressed a value-judgment it was unsound. More recently there has been a revival of interest in the Rule of Law, although less as a peculiar feature of English constitutional law than as the common basis of legal ideals and practice which unites or might unite what Article 38 (i) (c) of the Statute of the International Court of Justice calls 'civilized nations'; the Rule of Law in this latest reincarnation has in fact much in common with 'the general principles of law recognized by civilized nations' which *inter alia* Article 38 directs the Court to apply.[1]

---

[1] Thus it is significant that among the papers prepared for the Chicago Colloquium on the Rule of Law in September 1957 (see p. 230, *infra*) was one by Professor R. B. Schlesinger entitled 'Research on the General Principles of Law recognized by Civilized Nations, Outline of a New Project'. Professor Schlesinger in an elaborately documented paper argues that 'the breadth of the concept Rule of Law should not obscure the fact that its comparative study is only part of an even larger task: the concrete determination and formulation of the general principles of law recognized by civilized nations'. He shows that the legal importance of these general principles does not arise solely by reason of Article 38 of the Statute of the International Court of Justice but that under another name (*e.g.* 'principles of natural law and equity' in Article 1 (2) of the Egyptian Civil Code of 1949), or in a particular application (*e.g.*, 'the enjoyment of human rights and funda-

It is with this most recent phase in the history of the Rule of Law as a concept that this essay is primarily concerned. In the first section the authorities and sources both national and international will be considered; in the second section an attempt will be made to construct a workable concept of the Rule of Law which might have significance both for the United Kingdom and for other countries within and outside the reach of the Common Law.

I. NATIONAL AND INTERNATIONAL SOURCES OF THE RULE OF LAW

The Rule of Law since Dicey

The earliest phase of interest in the Rule of Law is associated with Dicey's *Law of the Constitution*[1] which was first published in 1885. The attack on the Rule of Law, as Dicey had understood it, was led by Sir Ivor Jennings in *The Law and the Constitution*,[2] which first appeared in 1933, although Dicey in the foreword to the eighth edition published in 1914 and in a later article[3] had to some extent already modified his position. The present phase has yet to find its Dicey or Jennings. The evidence for its existence is scattered over a wide field and on the whole, as far as works of English origin and context are concerned, has been directed to particular aspects of what Dicey understood to be included in the Rule of Law rather than to any

mental freedoms' as in the Peace Treaties of 1947 with Italy, Bulgaria, Rumania, and Hungary) these principles directly concern both municipal and international law. Professor Schlesinger's contribution is not printed in the *Annales de la Faculté de Droit d'Istanbul*, 8th Year, Vol. 9 (hereinafter referred to as *Annales*) but was one of a series of papers in a section of the Colloquium dealing with *The Rule of Law in Receptionist countries, with particular reference to India*. The series is being published by the Faculty of Law of Istanbul in 1960.

[1] Latest (10th) edition (E. C. S. Wade), 1959.

[2] Latest (5th) edition, 1959.

[3] 'The Development of Administrative Law in England' (1915), 31 L.Q.R. 148. It is reprinted as Appendix 2 (p. 493) to the 10th ed. of Dicey's *Law of the Constitution*. On one aspect of the Rule of Law, namely the contrast which it offered to the French system of Administrative Law, Dicey had already in 1901 admitted that he had done less than justice to contemporary France. See (1901), 17 L.Q.R. 302. Professor Robson in *Justice and Administrative Law*, first published in 1928 (latest (3rd) edition, 1951) had criticized that aspect of Dicey's conception of the Rule of Law which rests on the assumption that government officials are, and ought always to be, amenable to legal process in the ordinary courts.

comprehensive formulation. For example, we find in the Franks Committee Report (1957)[1], in a tentative search for possible lines of distinction between adjudication by tribunals and by a Minister, the following definition of the Rule of Law: 'The rule of law stands for the view that decisions should be made by the application of known principles or laws. In general, such decisions will be predictable, and the citizen will know where he is. On the other hand, there is what is arbitrary. A decision may be made without principle, without any rules. It is therefore unpredictable, the antithesis of a decision taken in accordance with the rule of law.'[2] This conception, however, of the Rule of Law deals with only one of the characteristics which Dicey attributed to it, and although the Committee pay formal respect to its importance they are forced to admit that of itself it affords little guidance in the allocation of adjudications between tribunals and Ministers.

Two years earlier, in a widely read pamphlet, a group of Conservative lawyers had published a study under the title of 'Rule of Law',[3] but apart from a statement that the 'two principles which for long formed the foundation of the British Constitution (were) the Sovereignty of Parliament and the Rule of Law',[4] there was little attempt to provide a comprehensive definition of the latter term in a contemporary context. Dicey's threefold definition of the Rule of Law was quoted and supplemented by a much qualified admission of a doctrine of 'a political balance of power between the executive, legislative and judicial functions.'[5] The main emphasis of the study was, however, laid on the importance of improving methods of reaching administrative decisions and the spirit, although not the detail, of its recommendations is to be seen in the findings of the Franks Committee and in the ensuing Tribunals and Inquiries Act of 1958.

Ten years before the Conservative pamphlet Sir Carleton Allen had published 'Law and Orders'[6] in which he had in-

---

[1] *Report of the Committee on Administrative Tribunals and Inquiries*, Cmnd. 218.
[2] *Op. cit.*, p. 6.   [3] Conservative Political Centre, 1955.   [4] *Op. cit.*, p. 10.   [5] *Ibid.*
[6] 1st ed., 1945; 2nd ed., 1956. The ensuing quotations are from p. 22 of the 2nd ed.

voked the Rule of Law as 'the best makeweight' to correct the 'imbalance' of 'our constitutional ship' caused by the magnitude of delegated powers granted to the Executive by the Legislature. But although in this work Sir Carleton Allen is concerned with the details of delegated legislation, with defects in the system and with practical proposals for reform, his reference to the Rule of Law remains tantalizingly brief and his definition more informative as to what it is not than as to its substantive content. It 'is not a mere catchword or incantation'; nor is it 'a Law of Nature, constant and invariable at all times and in all circumstances'. It is not for ever to be associated with Dicey or still less with Lord Hewart.[1] This 'sound and proved principle of the Rule of Law does, however, enshrine a principle which history has shown to be of the utmost moment to our national development and no aspect of that evolution is more remarkable than the capacity which we have shown to adapt principles and institutions to the flux of circumstance, while preserving their essential character.' What lies behind this eloquent but somewhat elusive description is perhaps suggested by the quotation on the title page of 'Law and Orders' from the Petition of the House of Commons on July 7, 1610. In that Petition we read: 'Amongst many other points of happiness and freedom which your Majesty's subjects of this Kingdom have enjoyed under your royal progenitors . . . there is none which they have accounted more dear and precious than this, to be guided and governed by certain rule of law'. As will be pointed out later in this essay,[2] the certainty of the law is one of the elements in the concept of the Rule of Law but it is only one element and, taken by itself, affords little guidance in dealing with the problems of administrative discretion or with the extent to which a dictatorial régime can claim to observe the Rule of Law.

As far back as 1926[3] Sir William Holdsworth had impliedly taken a rather wider view of the Rule of Law, by using the phrase as the title to an essay dealing with the theory of sover-

---

[1] See *The New Despotism*, 1929.   [2] See p. 248, *infra*.
[3] *Some Lessons from our Legal History*, p. 109.

eignty and the recognition of unincorporate groups. He was principally concerned to refute the criticisms of those who set up against the theory of sovereignty the natural rights of the individual and of those who like Duguit repudiate both the sovereign state and the individual endowed with natural rights. 'The great achievements of the doctrine of sovereignty were the mastering the lawlessness of the medieval state, and the provision, in the modern territorial state of an organism which, by keeping the peace, had made political and social progress possible . . . those who go about to deny or minimize this sovereignty . . . have forgotten that in the smaller matters of government, which concern the daily intercourse of man and man, it is the fact of the state's sovereignty which causes the machinery to run smoothly; and that in a time of crisis they may have reason to be thankful for its existence.'[1] On the other hand he was prepared to admit, in the application of the theory of sovereignty to concrete facts, that the theory must not be pressed too far; the rights of individuals and of subordinate groups in the state should be accorded some recognition, always subject, however, to the supremacy of the King in Parliament. It is at first sight difficult to see the connexion between this somewhat indeterminate theory of sovereignty and the Rule of Law. From his later writing[2] it would appear that Sir William Holdsworth conceived of the Rule of Law as the restraining factor which in England had prevented the theory of sovereignty, as expressed in the supremacy of the King in Parliament, from destroying the liberties of the subject. The essential feature of the Rule of Law is that 'the judicial power of the State is, to a large extent, separate from the Executive and the Legislature' and this principle is a 'true juridical principle', and not merely a 'principle of political action' as Sir Ivor Jennings had maintained. He went so far as to say that 'in so far as the jurisdiction of the courts is ousted, and officials or official bodies of persons are given a purely administrative discretion the rule of law is

---

[1] *Ibid.*, pp. 137–138.
[2] Review of the 9th ed. (by E. C. S. Wade) of Dicey's *Law of the Constitution* (1939), 55 L.Q.R. 585.

abrogated'. On the other hand he was prepared to admit that 'it is not abrogated if these officials or official bodies are given a judicial or quasi judicial discretion, although the machinery through which the rule is applied is not that of the Courts'.[1] The main difficulty of this approach lies in the central importance attaching to the word 'juridical' which is presumably intended to be a descriptive term, applicable to given situations without the invocation of political values. In fact Sir William Holdsworth himself deprives his definition of the Rule of Law of legal precision by the qualifying phrase 'to a large extent', without informing us on what principle that extent is to be determined; and, as we have seen, the Franks Committee found the antithesis between what is arbitrary and what is according to the Rule of Law of little assistance in explaining or justifying the actual distribution of decisions between judicial or quasi judicial on the one hand and, on the other, purely administrative processes.[2]

Sir William Holdsworth's difficulty was appreciated by an American observer of English government in a book published in 1949.[3] 'Our concept', says Professor Schwartz—and it later becomes clear that although he thinks primarily of the United States, he also has in mind the British Constitution—'is a normative as much as it is a descriptive term; it expresses an ideal as much as a juristic fact—and *ought* as much as an *is*'.[4] In the United States this idealistic element in the Rule of Law is given a legal form in the principles incorporated in the Constitution. In the United Kingdom this element, in spite of the theoretical supremacy of the legislature, is equally present. Parliament tacitly admits with regard to certain doctrines 'Autolimitations . . . of its own sovereignty. If they were abrogated, the rule of law would cease to be part of the British Constitution.'[5]

---

[1] The foregoing quotations are from Sir William Holdsworth's review (1939), 55 L.Q.R. 587–588.

[2] See p. 225, *supra*.

[3] Bernard Schwartz, *Law and the Executive in Britain*.

[4] *Ibid.*, p. 11.   [5] *Ibid.*, p. 16.

A Supra-National Concept of the Rule of Law

For reasons which are not entirely clear, Professor Schwartz confined his interpretation of the Rule of Law to the Common Law world. 'Law as a bridle upon governmental power is peculiarly the Anglo-American contribution to political science, and any theory in terms of the Rule of Law must of necessity be based upon Common Law constitutional practice'.[1] If Professor Schwartz were right in limiting the effective operation of the Rule of Law to the Common Law world, it would be necessary to admit that the use of the phrase in at least two international instruments is largely meaningless. Thus, the Universal Declaration of Human Rights of 1948[2] declares that:

> 'It is essential, if man is not to be compelled to have re-course, as a last resort, to rebellion against tyranny and op-pression, that human rights should be protected by the rule of law.'

And in a rather vaguer usage the European Convention for the Protection of Human Rights and Fundamental Freedoms of 1950[3] speaks of:

> 'The Governments of European countries which are like-minded and have a common heritage of political traditions, ideals, freedom and the rule of law.'

It is true that the English phrase 'Rule of Law' has no exact translation in French or German and that the usual translations carry different implications from the English expression, at least as it was understood by Dicey.[4] Thus, 'le principe de la légalité', 'la suprématie de la règle de droit' or 'le règne souverain de la loi' in French-speaking, and 'der Rechtsstaat' in German-speaking, countries are imperfect translations of the Rule of Law and 'each tends to divert the attention to a differ-

---

[1] *Ibid.*   [2] Cmnd. 7662, Preamble, 3rd para.
[3] Cmnd. 8969, Preamble, last para.
[4] See General Report by Professor C. J. Hamson on the Chicago Colloquium on the Rule of Law, September, 1957, *Annales*, p. 4.

ent aspect of the legal system.'[1] In the United States the expression 'Rule of Law', although not unknown to lawyers, is
seldom used, its place being taken by such phrases as 'government under law',[2] 'government of laws and not of men'[3] and
even, in a broad sense, by 'due process of law'.[4] Furthermore
there is the concept of 'socialist legality' in Communist countries, which is sometimes alternatively translated as the 'Rule
of Law', although it seems to be generally agreed in Communist and non-Communist countries alike that the terms are
not interchangeable.[5] Nevertheless, it does not follow that England and other countries may not share a substratum of legal
values and practice which, for want of a better term, we may
call the Rule of Law. In this event it would be, however, important to emphasize that the phrase is being used in a comparatively new sense and that it must be largely divorced from
its historical context and from the emotional reactions, both
positive and negative, to which that history gives rise.

The Rule of Law in Western Countries

Two major attempts have been made on an international
basis to clarify the Rule of Law in this broader sense. With one
of them the present writer has been rather closely associated and
a more detailed account of the work which it has involved and
the conclusions which it suggests is given in the second part of
this essay.[6] The other has its origin in the legal aspect of a
Unesco plan to promote intellectual contact between Communist and non-Communist countries. The first part of this
plan was realized in a Colloquium held at Chicago in Septem-

---

[1] *Ibid.*

[2] See *Government under Law*, ed. Sutherland, Harvard University Press, 1956,
which consists of papers read and discussion at a Conference to celebrate the bi-
centennial of John Marshall.

[3] Bill of Rights of the Constitution of Massachusetts (1780), Article XXX.

[4] See Kauper on 'Rule of Law in the United States', *Annales*, pp. 90 and 97.

[5] Thus, as will be seen below, the International Association of Legal Science
found it convenient to divide its investigations into the Rule of Law into two
parts: the first, held at Chicago in 1957, devoted to: 'The Rule of Law as Understood in the West', the second, held at Warsaw in 1958, to the Communist conception of 'socialist legality'.

[6] See p. 240, *infra*.

ber 1957 under the general title of 'The Rule of Law as understood in the West' and gave an opportunity for the reading of
papers and discussion on the Rule of Law in a number of
non-Communist systems, with particular emphasis on England,
France, the German Federal Republic, and the U.S.A. Lawyers
from Poland and the U.S.S.R. were also invited and took part
in the discussion. The following account leans heavily on the
general report prepared by Professor C. J. Hamson, the rap-
porteur of the Colloquium, and on the digest of the discussions
made by Mr. J. A. Jolowicz, its Secretary.[1]

One of the most important preliminary issues which was
discussed in the Chicago Colloquium was the question of how
the inquiry was to be conducted. It was suggested[2] that the
Rule of Law might be ascertained by extracting from the different legal systems under examination those institutions and procedures which are common to all; the values inherent in these
common institutions and procedures would be the basic principles of the Rule of Law. For example, it might be found by
this method that the judicial control of legislation by reference
to a written constitution, as in the German Federal Republic or
in the U.S.A., is not an essential part of the Rule of Law but
that the judicial control (using 'judicial' in a broad sense to
cover both the 'ordinary' as well as 'administrative' courts) of
administrative acts is one of its fundamental features. On the
other hand it was pointed out that this method, which has the
superficial appearance of being scientific and free from any *a
priori* assumptions of value, conceals an unavoidable and, by
this method alone, unanswerable problem of choice: namely, in
what degree of detail is it justifiable to treat a particular institution or procedure when determining whether it is common
to a number of countries. If the idea of an 'independent'
judiciary appears to be common to most systems, can we disregard the varieties of institutional device—appointment by the
Executive, by or with the advice of a special body such as a

---

[1] *Annales*, pp. 1 and 24. I have also had the advantage of consulting an unofficial
transcript of the discussions prepared by Mr. V. Kabes.

[2] Particularly by Professor Rozmaryn of Poland whose views are set out in
Revue Internationale de Droit Comparé (1958), Vol. 10, p. 70.

Public Service Commission or by popular election—whereby the judges are selected? Another objection to what might be called the 'highest common factor' approach is that it assumes, against the evidence provided by even the most superficial comparative study of law and government, that the presence or absence of particular institutions and procedures can be related, irrespective of their country of origin, to the presence or absence of particular values. For example, a country such as Sweden which has developed to a remarkable degree a rule that all governmental documents are in principle open to public inspection may find in this rule the greatest safeguard against administrative abuses and be less inclined to develop a comprehensive system of legal remedies against the state in respect of the acts or omissions of its officials.[1]

The Chicago Colloquium did not aim at reaching final conclusions on the character of the Rule of Law as understood in the West and still less at passing judgment on different legal systems in so far as they reach or fail to reach a standard implied in a particular conception of the Rule of Law. Those who submitted papers on the understanding, and in this sense actual achievement, of the Rule of Law in their country, were given only a broad framework of reference. It was suggested, for example, that consideration might be given to the extent to which the recognition of basic human rights formed an essential part of the Rule of Law and, if this question were answered affirmatively, what might be the content of such rights; similarly attention was drawn to the differing practice of Western states regarding the review by a constitutional court of legislation; and particular emphasis was laid on the new problems which might arise in the modern Welfare State, in particular in relation to non-discriminatory administration of benefits conferred by the state and to the degree to which the administration of the Welfare State could be controlled through the or-

---

[1] See Nils Herlitz, *Public Law*, Spring 1958, p. 50. Similarly in countries with parliamentary traditions comparable to those of the United Kingdom the possibility of asking questions of Ministers in Parliament concerning the conduct of their departments may be an important method of exercising control over the administration. See Goodhart, *Annales*, p. 34.

dinary judicial machinery. This flexible approach undoubtedly gave the contributors to the Colloquium a much freer hand and added to the detail and value of the descriptions of their different legal systems. On the other hand an outside observer reading the record of the Colloquium might well be confused by the simultaneous discussion of what might be called a supra-national concept of the Rule of Law and of the institutions and procedures of particular countries whereby that concept (or some national variation on it) is given practical effect.

In spite of the deliberate intention of the Chicago Colloquium to avoid a dogmatic formulation of the Rule of Law there appears to have been a broad measure of agreement that, however difficult it might be to define, the concept had reality. There was rather less agreement about the actual content of the Rule of Law. There was general reluctance to identify it with Natural Law but there was a widespread feeling that there was much in common between the Rule of Law and Natural Law. 'A good case can be made', said one of the participants in the Colloquium[1], 'that the Rule of Law concept and the concept of natural rights are at least paternal twins; I would not foreclose the possibility that they may be identical twins'. Those participants who came from countries with a written constitution containing a list of fundamental rights, which, under the sanction of review by the courts, the Legislature has to respect, regarded such rights as at least part of the Rule of Law. Those from countries where the sovereignty of the Legislature is undisputed tended to admit, as did Dr. A. L. Goodhart[2] in speaking of the United Kingdom, that the Rule of Law included within it certain principles which are 'binding' on the Legislature, although not perhaps in an Austinian sense; or, like M. Letourneur of the French *Conseil d'État* and Professor Drago,[3] they emphasized the supremacy of the Legislature but at the same time recognized respect for individual rights as part of the Rule of Law because such rights are in fact incorporated

---

[1] Jones, 'The Rule of Law and the Welfare State', *Annales*, p. 249.

[2] *Annales*, p. 271 *et seq.*

[3] *Ibid.*, p. 188. An English translation was published in *American Journal of Comparative Law* (1958), Vol. 7, p. 147.

in a legislative enactment, namely, the French Constitution.[1]
However, there was no detailed consideration as to which fun-
damental rights are to be considered as an essential part of the
Rule of Law on a supra-national plane.

It was generally agreed at Chicago that, even if the recognition of fundamental rights formed an element in the Rule of
Law, it was only one element. The other two were concerned
with the institutions and with the procedures whereby these
rights were given effect. Discussion of characteristic institutions
was selective; no attempt was made to draw up a comprehensive minimum list of constitutions essential to the Rule of Law.
It was, however, recognized that judicial control of the Executive, as distinguished from judicial control of the Legislature,
was a central feature of the Rule of Law, although it was pointed out, by Professor Herlitz of Sweden,[2] for example, that the
Executive can itself build up traditions and procedures which
may protect individual rights in certain cases more efficiently
and more cheaply than the ordinary courts. The same selective
approach was adopted with regard to procedures. Particular
attention was directed to the conception of 'a fair hearing',
both with regard to the circumstances in which it is demanded
by the Rule of Law and to the minimum conditions of its existence. It was not thought possible to define all the circumstances
in which the Rule of Law required a fair hearing, but it was
felt, firstly, that where a criminal penalty was in issue such a

---

[1] The authors were dealing with the Constitution of 1946, but their argument
would presumably be applicable to the Constitution of 1958, the preamble of
which states that 'the French people solemnly proclaim their attachment to the
Rights of Man and the principles of National Sovereignty as defined by the
Declaration of 1789, confirmed and completed by the Preamble to the Constitution of 1946'. A proposal by the Consultative Constitutional Committee that the
Constitution should contain an article guaranteeing to French Nationals and to
persons within the French Community the enjoyment of the rights and liberties
recognized in the Preamble to the Constitution was not accepted. However, in
Article 2, equality before the law is guaranteed 'without distinction of origin,
race or religion' and in the same article the 'principle' of the Republic is stated
to be 'government of the people, by the people, for the people'. In Article 77 all
citizens of the French community are stated to be 'equal in law, whatever their
origin, race or religion' and the States of the Community 'administer themselves
and conduct their own affairs democratically and freely'.

[2] *Annales*, p. 150.

hearing was essential and, secondly, that there were cases not involving a criminal penalty where something in the nature of a hearing was necessary. This raised the question of the meaning of a fair hearing. An independent judge was regarded as an indispensable requisite. Independence in this sense was thought to mean primarily independence from the Executive and of any personal interest in the outcome in one way or the other of the issue to be tried. There was, however, no conclusion as to the methods by which such independence might be achieved, except that different methods might be appropriate in different legal environments. Also implied in a fair hearing was the right to be heard and, although it was admitted that practice falls short of Western ideals in this respect, to be represented by counsel.

A sub-theme of the Chicago Colloquium was the applicability of the Rule of Law in the Welfare State. It was felt, on the whole, with some dissentients that, although the advent of the Welfare State had greatly added to the difficulties of ensuring observance of the Rule of Law, there was no inherent contradiction between the Welfare State and the Rule of Law. It was suggested,[1] for example, that part of the difference between the Rule of Law against the background of Dicey's idealized picture of a Whig-dominated 19th-century England and the Rule of Law in a contemporary setting of National Insurance claims, planning permits, rent tribunals, and the like lay in the matter of scale and number. 'Dicey accurately saw it as a great strength of the Rule of Law in England that most questions of individual right came for decision to a small and homogeneous group of dedicated men, the judges of the "ordinary law". A hundred times as many deciding officers are needed to settle the issues presented by claimants of the new and more widely held rights of the Welfare State.'[2]

Socialist Legality and the Rule of Law

As a sequel to the Chicago Colloquium, and under the same auspices, there was held in 1958 in Warsaw a Conference on the

---

[1] Jones in the article cited in n. (1), p. 233, *supra, Annales*, p. 254 *et seq.*
[2] *Ibid.*, p. 257.

Rule of Law as understood in Communist countries. A most interesting report on the Conference has been given by one of the participants, Dr. A. K. R. Kiralfy,[1] and no attempt need be made here to summarize his account of the proceedings. It would indeed be an achievement of the greatest importance to present a comparison between the Rule of Law as understood in Communist and non-Communist countries, and it is hoped that this will become possible through the further exchanges which are planned to follow the meetings in Chicago and Warsaw. At this stage only a provisional opinion, sketched in very broad terms, is possible. Some mention must, however, be made of the probable attitude of a substantial proportion of the world's population living under Communist legal systems, if the attempt to construct a supra-national conception of the Rule of Law is to keep in touch with the realities of international life. Moreover this is all the more necessary in that the formulation of such a concept at New Delhi, in rather more concrete terms than was attempted or intended at Chicago, was exclusively the work of lawyers from non-Communist countries.

Although it may well be true that, in the words of Dr. Kiralfy, 'we in the West use a liberal Victorian connotation when we speak of the rule of law', it does not follow that it is this conception of the Rule of Law which should be the starting point of a comparison between so-called 'Western' and Communist interpretations of the Rule of Law. Such an approach invites a sterile controversy on the truth, for example, of the provocative definition[2] of the Rule of Law (*Provovoe gosudarstvo* or 'Legal State'; cf. *Rechtsstaat*) given in the Soviet 'Juridical Dictionary'.[3] It is more profitable to relate Dr. Kiralfy's account of the views expressed at Warsaw to the tentative outline of the supra-national Rule of Law which emerged at the

---

[1] *International and Comparative Law Quarterly* (1959), Vol. 8, p. 465. The proceedings are being published under the auspices of the Polish National Committee of the International Association of Legal Science.

[2] See n. (1), p. 261, *infra*.

[3] *Yuridichesky slovar* (2nd ed., Moscow, 1956), II, p. 196. The editor was P. I. Kudryavtsev, then Vice-Minister of Justice of the U.S.S.R.

Chicago Colloquium. It is clear that what, in Communist countries, is called 'socialist legality' is not merely a technical ideal of law carried out at all levels of its operation with the maximum of efficiency.[1] If human rights lie at the basis of the non-Communist conception of the Rule of Law so, Dr. Kiralfy points out, in Communist countries 'a few elemental matters of human dignity', such as a ban on cruel punishments and freedom of private opinion, including religion, seem now to be conceded. On the other hand, freedom of speech and of association are regarded as conditional upon conformity with 'the interests of the workers', and the latter are determined by a system of government in which the only legal party is the effective interpreter of those interests. It may well be that the formula 'the interests of the workers' more effectively draws attention, as Communists would maintain, to economic realities than the traditional insistence of non-Communist democracies on what Sir Isaiah Berlin[2] has called 'negative freedom', that is to say the individual's right to do what he wishes with the minimum possible degree of restraint by others. But, says Dr. Kiralfy, interests may be secured in more than one way; the justification of public welfare may be used to cloak the tyranny of those who know better than the public what is good for them, a danger from which no country is exempt but which is checked in non-Communist democracies by insistence on political freedom expressed in electoral machinery and the possibility of a change of government. As far, therefore, as any basis of values underlying the Rule of Law is concerned, it seems clear that there is a considerable gap between the Western idea of the Rule of

---

[1] *Cf.*, the definition of 'socialist legality' given in 1954 by Nedbailo (*Uchenye Zapiski* (Scientific Papers), Vol. XXVII, Juridical Series, Lvov University, No. 2, p. 12): 'Socialist legality is the method of action of a Socialist State which it adopts in order to lead society to build up Communism. It consists of a strict and persistent execution of law and all other legal acts, resulting in the establishment of a firm legal régime in the country. This régime is characterized by the clearness and definite nature of the rights and duties of State organs, organizations, officials and citizens, by the protection of their rights, by the lawfulness of the actions of the Socialist State, by the stability of legal relations and by the atmosphere of confidence of each and every one in his rights and duties.'

[2] *Two Concepts of Liberty*, Clarendon Press, Oxford, 1958, pp. 7 *et seq.* and 16 *et seq.*

Law, as it found expression, for example, at Chicago, and its nearest equivalent in Communist ideology.

In that aspect of the Rule of Law which is concerned with the execution of the law, Communist legal theory is perhaps somewhat closer to non-Communist principles, even if any suggestion by Western observers that there has in the U.S.S.R. been a return to 'bourgeois legality' is resented. Thus, it is now generally recognized and indeed emphasized that the law must be strictly observed by all. Nor is there at every point a formal difference in legal institutions and procedures in Communist and non-Communist countries. There is, for example, in criminal trials much greater emphasis on the importance of a properly argued defence as a means of ascertaining the facts to which the law is to be applied.[1] Importance, says Dr. Kiralfy, is also attached to the conception of judicial independence, in the sense that a judge should not be influenced by outside interference in the assessment of facts; in the interpretation of the law,[2] however, the judge is admittedly influenced by the Party training and by the conception, which he presumably shares, of the fundamental purposes of a Communist society, although it may be said that a judge in a Western country consciously or unconsciously takes account of the basic assumptions of his own society. In the legal machinery of control over the administration, there are, however, important differences between Communist and non-Communist countries. The difference does not lie primarily in the non-liability, except in a limited number of cases, of the state in the U.S.S.R. for illegal acts committed by its officials;[3] a general liability of the state in tort is a fairly recent innovation in England[4] and is still imperfectly

---

[1] See, for example, Taras, *O niektorych gwarancjach praw askarzonego w polskim procesie karnym* (On Some Guarantees of the Rights of the Accused in Polish Criminal Trials), *Annales Universitatis Mariae Curie-Sklodowska*, Vol. III, 6, Section 6, published by the University of Lublin, 1956, pp. 187–294, reviewed by George Dobry in *Journal of the International Commission of Jurists*, Vol. 1, No. 1 (1957), p. 139.

[2] On the limited significance of the abolition of the use of analogy in Soviet criminal law, see n. (1), p. 249, *infra*.

[3] Gsovski, *Soviet Civil Law*, Vol. I, p. 534. See also Loeber, *Journal of the International Commission of Jurists* (1957), Vol. I, No. 1, p. 59.

[4] Crown Proceedings Act, 1947.

recognized in many Common Law jurisdictions[1]. It lies more in the fact that responsibility for the observance of legality is vested primarily in the Procuracy, which in many cases alone can initiate action to compel administrative authorities to carry out the duties imposed upon them by law or to refrain from illegal acts. Moreover, a civil claim against an official by a private person can only be decided jointly with the appropriate criminal proceedings, the taking of which depends on the decision of the Procuracy.[2] Yet it would be wrong to find the essential difference between Communist and Western conceptions of the Rule of Law in the control which the Procuracy enjoys over the means by which the administrative apparatus is kept within legal bounds. In a non-Communist country, such as Sweden, which would certainly subscribe to the Western conception of the Rule of Law, the control of the administrative apparatus rests to a very small extent on any right of an aggrieved individual to restrain through the machinery of the ordinary courts officials from performing illegal acts or to compel them to carry out their duties; the control lies rather in the supervisory and, if necessary, prosecuting authority of the Attorney-General and the Civil and Military *Ombudsmän*, elected by the *Riksdag*. What are characteristic of the Soviet system are the ultimate political assumptions of the Procuracy, appointed, it is true, by the supreme legislative body, but the work of which 'can only be fulfilled on condition that (it) is carried out under the constant control and direction of the Party organizations'.[3] It is at this point that any attempt to deal comparatively with the Rule of Law from two separate aspects, one concerned with its substantive content and the other with its procedural implications, founders. But it is perfectly possible to see in the new emphasis which has been put in the U.S.S.R. since 1955 on the rôle of the Procuracy as the upholder of 'legality' at least the beginnings of a development which might

---

[1] For example, in India. See n. (6), p. 263, *infra*.
[2] See Gsovski, *Soviet Civil Law*, Vol. I, p. 528.
[3] A. N. Mishutin, Deputy Procurator-General of the U.S.S.R. and Y. A. Kalenov, State Councillor of Justice, 2nd Class, in *Sovetskoe gosudarstvoi pravo*, 1955, No. 3, pp. 40–41.

bring the Soviet legal world closer to recognition, in practice if not in theory, of the values of the Rule of Law as understood in non-Communist countries; in which event Maine's famous aphorism that 'substantive law has at first the look of being gradually secreted in the interstices of procedure'[1] would have found a new field of application.

II. OUTLINES OF A SUPRA-NATIONAL CONCEPT
Values Underlying the Rule of Law

The project of the International Commission of Jurists, culminating in a Congress at New Delhi in January 1959,[2] to clarify and formulate a supra-national concept of the Rule of Law was made on the basis of an assumption which must first be clearly stated. Dicey purported in *The Law of the Constitution* to be stating 'two or three guiding principles which pervade the modern constitution of England',[3] but Sir Ivor Jennings has pointed out that, although he 'honestly tried to analyse, . . . like most, he saw the Constitution through his own spectacles'.[4] The Commission's project could not even pretend that it was seeking to isolate the principles common to all constitutions, if such exist. It assumed rather that the Rule of Law, with which it was concerned, must serve the ends of a free society. By a free society it understood one in which the free spirit of every member can find the fullest expression. It was not asserted that such a free society has ever been, or is likely to be, completely realized in any country, but it was implied that such an ideal corresponds with the aspirations, however inarticulate, of many individuals in countries of differing traditions and

---

[1] *Early Law and Customs*, p. 389.

[2] The Congress consisted of 185 judges, practising lawyers and teachers of law from 53 countries. The work of the Congress was carried out in four committees, which were concerned with the Rule of Law in relation to the Legislature, the Executive, the Criminal Process, and the Judiciary and Legal Profession respectively. The basis of discussion was a Working Paper which had been prepared by the author of this essay, with the assistance of the staff of the International Commission of Jurists, on the basis of answers to a questionnaire sent to representative lawyers in 26 countries. See *Journal of the International Commission of Jurists* (1959), Vol. II, No. 1. A full report on the Congress by the present writer has been published: *The Rule of Law in a Free Society*, International Commission of Jurists, Geneva, 1960.   [3] 10th ed., 1959, p. v.

[4] *The Law and the Constitution*, 5th ed. (1959), p. 316.

economic and social background; it was therefore conceived to be a useful inquiry to consider how far, and in forms appropriate to the conditions of varying countries, the principles underlying a free society require formulation in legal rules, institutions and procedures.

A legal rule, for this purpose, was conceived to be one which the great majority of members of a society accept as binding upon them in virtue of their membership of that society. Dicey in his third principle[1] of the Rule of Law contrasted countries with constitutional guarantees of individual rights and those in which such rights depend on a self-denying ordinance of the Legislature and the assumed bias of the judges in favour of individual liberty. Such a contrast was not denied in the Commission's project, but it was considered to be irrelevant to the kind of Rule of Law with which it was concerned. Thus, the First Committee of the Congress at New Delhi (which dealt with Legislature and the Rule of Law) on the one hand considered that 'in many societies, particularly those which have not yet established traditions of democratic legislative behaviour, it is essential that certain limitations on legislative power . . . should be incorporated in a written constitution, and the safeguards therein contained should be protected by an independent judicial tribunal'; on the other hand, it admitted that 'in other societies, established standards of legislative behaviour may serve to ensure that the same limitations are observed'.[2]

It is the abiding merit of Dicey's third principle of the Rule of Law that it draws attention to the importance of 'the general principles of the constitution' (which a modern writer might call 'civil liberties'), even if he does not satisfactorily solve the clash between such principles and the principle, on

---

[1] 'We may say that the constitution is pervaded by the rule of law on the ground that the general principles of the constitution (as, for example, the right to personal liberty, or the right of public meeting) are with us the result of judicial decisions determining the rights of private persons in particular cases brought before the courts; whereas under many foreign constitutions the security (such as it is) given to the rights of individuals results, or appears to result, from the general principles of the constitution', *The Law of the Constitution*, 10th ed., p. 195.

[2] Clause II (1) of the Conclusions of the First Committee of the Congress of New Delhi, *Journal of the International Commission of Jurists* (1959), Vol. II, No. 1, p. 8.

which he is equally insistent, of the sovereignty of Parliament. He does not in this context define what he means by 'the general principles of the constitution', except by way of example of the right to personal liberty and the right of public meetings; but it is clear from the general structure of *The Law of the Constitution* that he has in mind what may be called the negative political liberies of a *laissez-faire* society. The free society, which lies at the basis of the Rule of Law discussed at New Delhi, was felt to involve more than freedom of speech, assembly or association, which, particularly in an Asian setting, might be illusory for those without the material means or education to make use of them. This raised the question of the place which such rights as are set out in Articles 22 to 27[1] of the Universal Declaration of Human Rights of 1948 ought to play in the concept of the Rule of Law. The characteristic of such rights is that they are positive in form, in so far as they require action by the State rather than abstention from activity in certain protected spheres which are left to the free activity of the individual.

There was perhaps at this point some confusion in the discussions at New Delhi. Few would dispute that a free society must aim at economic and social justice; this is not however the same thing as saying that such aspirations can be reduced to propositions of law of general application in the diverse societies of the world. The Rule of Law is not identical with a free society, although it is an important instrument of such a society. As an instrument it must be capable of translating into practical effect such purposes of a free society, as at their present stage of development are capable of the kind of formulation which the nature of law demands. The extent to which formulation is possible varies widely as between a highly developed Welfare State and a primitive economy. It may well be a proper application of the Rule of Law in a modern Welfare State for

---

[1] Article 22 (the right to social security); Article 23 (the right to work); Article 24 (the right to rest and leisure); Article 25 (the right to an adequate standard of living; the right of mothers and children to special care and assistance); Article 26 (the right to education); Article 27 (the right to participate in cultural life; the right of protection of scientific, literary and artistic productions).

the judges to take into account in the interpretation of a Housing or National Insurance Act the underlying social rights of the individual which it is the purpose of such legislation to secure, even if it is, in so doing, necessary to modify an earlier more unrestricted scope allowed to the individual's economic freedom of action. But the law and lawyers as such have no inherent and original authority to instruct the State as to the positive action which it should take. On the other hand there are undoubted principles of a free society, generally recognized as such and capable of legal formulation, which indirectly may secure the enforcement of policies appropriate to a free society but lacking the precise formulation characteristic of legal principles. For example, the court may, by insisting that, whatever benefits the State may bestow, they shall be equally distributed, in fact secure the adoption of a particular benefit for all.[1] At New Delhi an attempt was made to differentiate between the binding principles of the Rule of Law and the ultimate aims of a free society[2] in the language used to describe the position of the Legislature in a free society under the Rule of Law. Thus, whereas certain duties (indicated by the imperative 'must') were laid on the Legislature, other aspects of legislative activity were dealt with in a purely descriptive way or in merely exhortatory language.[3]

If the sphere of the Rule of Law is thus differentiated from that of the Legislature, the concession made by the lawyer is granted on terms and subject to limitations. It is here that it is important to emphasize the connexion between the Rule of Law and the free society of which it is an instrument. The Rule of Law, in this sense, assumes what Sir Ivor Jennings has called the 'intangibles which nevertheless produce an impression on

---

[1] Thus in effect in the United States the Supreme Court has been seeking to enforce a positive and general right to education, although the form which such action takes may involve only the prohibition of any educational policy which denies to any within the jurisdiction of a State the 'equal protection of the laws' (Fourteenth Amendment). See Greenawalt, *Journal of the International Commission of Jurists* (1959), Vol. II, No. 1, p. 135.

[2] *Cf.*, the 'Directive Principles of Social Policy' in the *Constitution of Ireland* and the 'Directive Principles of State Policy' in the *Constitution of India*.

[3] See n. (2), p. 261, *infra*.

the mind of any observant person who crosses the boundary from a dictatorial State into a free country'. Although Sir Ivor Jennings goes on to say that such ideas 'cannot easily be forced into a formal concept dignified by such a name as the rule of law' it must be emphasized that the Rule of Law, as here understood, does involve what he calls 'the existence of the democratic system'.[1] The Rule of Law as a supra-national concept is not conceived as a convenient formula equally applicable to the legal system of a totalitarian dictatorship and a liberal democracy. If we wish to say that there is no law which can prevent Parliament from prolonging its life indefinitely or permanently abolishing freedom of speech, we are using the word 'law' in a different sense from that in which it is used in the concept of the Rule of Law described in this essay.

The individual liberties of a democratic system involve in the first place the right of the members of each society[2] to choose the government under which they live. In the second place come freedom of speech, freedom of assembly and freedom of association. Such rights are not absolute; their exceptions are justified by the necessity of reconciling the claims of different individuals to those rights, and the criterion whereby this reconciliation can be effected is the concern of the law to ensure that the status and dignity of all individuals is to the greatest possible extent observed. Of these liberties the most important under modern conditions is freedom of speech[3] and it is also the best

---

[1] The quotations are from *The Law and the Constitution*, 5th ed., pp. 61–62.

[2] 'Society' is here used in an abstract sense, not as a guide to the actual delineation of the different units which may be held to constitute separate societies. It is true that the general assembly of the United Nations has passed a resolution (637 (VII) A of December 16, 1952) beginning: 'Whereas the right of self-determination is a prerequisite to the full enjoyment of all fundamental human rights'; but as Mr. Chakravarti (*Human Rights in the United Nations*) has cogently argued (pp. 104–119) the so-called right of self-determination is not an individual right but a 'collective right', for which no precise criteria are available to determine what is meant by the collectivity in question.

[3] Freedom of association is meaningless without freedom of speech and freedom of assembly has, with the advent of modern methods of mass communication, lost much of the importance which it enjoyed at the time of *Beatty* v. *Gillbanks* (1882), 9 Q.B.D. 308 to which Dicey, bringing out the first edition of *The Law and the Constitution* only three years after the decision, naturally paid much attention. On the lesser importance of freedom of assembly in European countries today see (1959), 75 L.Q.R. 547.

illustration of the inter-action between the substantive values on which the Rule of Law, in the sense here considered, rests and the legal procedures and institutions by which such values are given practical effect. Thus, on the one hand, freedom of speech is everywhere limited by appeal to such conceptions as Mr. Justice Holmes's 'clear and present danger',[1] 'attack (on) the free, democratic basic order' in the Constitution of the German Federal Republic[2] or the formidable list of qualifications contained in article 10 (2) of the European Convention for the Protection of Human Rights and Fundamental Freedoms.[3] The reality of freedom of speech will depend on the way in which such exceptions are interpreted, that is to say on the extent to which the application of such exceptions rests on a fundamental regard for the status and dignity of the human person, which is the ultimate and, from the point of view of formal logic, unprovable assumption. On the other hand the institutions and procedures—an independent judiciary, a fair trial, for example—by which such an interpretation is effected, will be the determining factor in the character of the latter. In short the Rule of Law is neither a matter exclusively of 'rights' or of 'remedies', each being complementary to the other.

The Equivocal Position of Equality

Even those lawyers inclined to see the Rule of Law solely as a matter of institutions and procedures, and to deny that it

---

[1] *Schenck* v. *United States* (1919), 249 U.S. 47. See also the later variations of Vinson C.J. ('a clear and probable danger'—*Dennis* v. *United States* (1951), 351 U.S. 494) and of Harlan J. who has distinguished between 'advocacy of forcible overthrow as an abstract doctrine and advocacy of action to that end': *Yates* v. *United States* (1957), 354 U.S. 298.

[2] Article 18.

[3] 'The exercise of these freedoms (*i.e.*, freedom of expression, including 'the freedom to hold opinions and to receive and impart information and ideas without interference by public authority and regardless of frontiers'), since it carries with it duties and responsibilities may be subject to such formalities, conditions and restrictions or penalties as are prescribed by law and are necessary in a democratic society in the interests of national security, territorial integrity or public safety, for the prevention of disorder or crime, for the protection of health or morals, for the protection of the reputation or rights of others, for preventing the disclosure of information received in confidence, or for maintaining the authority and impartiality of the judiciary.'

is concerned with substantive values, would probably require at this point in the argument some consideration of equality. The extent to which equality as a concept implies, even if negatively, some substantive values depends on the interpretation which is given to this much disputed word. In a restricted sense it implies only that the law must be equally applied to those whom the law regards as equal. It is here only a consequence of the character of law itself as a system of generally binding rules. It is not concerned, for example, with whether one class of the community is subject to different penalties or is tried by a different procedure for the same offence from those applicable to another class of the community, as long as the appropriate penalty or procedure is *equally*[1] applied to each class. In a wider sense it may imply that the law should treat human beings as equals—*i.e.*, should in its content be the same for all human beings—in respect of those qualities with regard to which it is right so to treat them. The difficulty of determining what is right in this context springs from the obvious inequality of men in terms of their natural endowment, still more from their inequality in society as far as social standing, education and economic power are concerned.

The reference is to the concept of equality in constitutions do not on the basis of the actual language used always make clear whether equality in the first or second sense described above is intended. Phrases such as 'equality before the law' or 'equal protection of the laws'[2] are in themselves equivocal. The fact that at some other point the constitution in question imposes some restriction on discrimination on named grounds does not necessarily mean that a reference to 'equality before the law' or to 'equal protection of the laws' may not be interpreted in a substantive sense in a way overlapping a provision against a

---

[1] *Cf.*, *Oxford English Dictionary* which gives as the first meaning of 'equally': 'to an equal degree or extent; as much in one case as the other'.

[2] *Cf.*, Fourteenth Amendment of the U.S. Constitution, Section 1: '. . . no State shall . . . deny to any person within its jurisdiction the equal protection of the laws'; Article 3 (1) of the Basic Law of the German Federal Republic: 'all men shall be equal before the law'; the Indian Constitution (Article 14) uses both phrases.

specific type of discrimination.[1] When the courts use such phrases to restrict legislative power, the principles on which they work are extremely difficult to disentangle. Their task is somewhat easier when they are dealing with a specific ground which is declared not to provide a proper basis for discrimination in the law, such as race or religion, but such grounds cannot be exhaustive; the differences between human beings of which the law might take account are infinite; there are many grounds so obviously providing no sufficient reason for discrimination that no constitution or international instrument would think it worthwhile to mention them. The European Convention on Human Rights admits this difficulty by forbidding discrimination in respect of the rights recognized by the Convention not merely on a number of specified grounds (sex, race, colour, language, religion, political or other opinion, national or social origin, association with a national minority, property, birth) but also by reference to analogy ('on such grounds as . . .' and in a final reference to 'or other status'). The same approach is to be found in the Conclusions of the Committee on the Legislative and the Rule of Law at New Delhi which considered that "the Legislature must not discriminate in its laws in respect of individuals, classes of persons, or minority groups on the ground of race, religion, sex *or other such reasons not affording a proper basis for making a distinction between human beings, classes, or minorities*.[2]

On a supra-national plane equality as an element in the concept of the Rule of Law does not take us much further than the free society, based on regard for the individual, which was the starting point of our inquiry. This is not to say that it is not a formulation of the basic assumptions of the Rule of Law which may not have the greatest practical importance. In a case[3] before the Indian Supreme Court, Bose J. has said: 'What I am

---

[1] For example, in addition to Article 14 referred to in the preceding footnote, the Indian Constitution contains prohibitions against discrimination in specified contexts on the grounds only of various combinations of religion, race, caste, sex, place of birth, language, descent, and residence (see Articles 15, 16, 17, 29 (2)).

[2] Clause III (3) (*a*) of the Conclusions of the First Committee, printed in the *Journal of the International Commission of Jurists*, Vol. II, No. 1 (1959), p. 9. (Italics added.)

[3] *State of West Bengal* v. *Anwar Ali*, A.I.R. (1952) S.C. 75.

concerned to see is whether the collective conscience of a sovereign democratic republic can regard the impugned law contrasted with the ordinary law of the land as the sort of substantially equal treatment which men of resolute minds and unbiased view can regard as right and proper in a democracy of the kind we have proclaimed ourselves to be.' That such language must ultimately appeal to a moral judgment does not necessarily detract from its effectiveness.

The Supremacy and Certainty of the Law

The Rule of Law in its most direct and literal application means that all action taken by the authorities of the State, as much as by individuals, must be based on and traceable back to an ultimate source of legal authority. It is this aspect of the Rule of Law which Dicey, in the first meaning which he attributed to the expression, contrasted 'with every system of government based on the exercise by persons in authority of . . . arbitrary . . . powers of constraint'.[1] Dicey in fact spoke in this context not only of 'arbitrary' but also of 'wide . . . or discretionary' powers. As Sir Ivor Jennings has pointed out[2] the principle of the supremacy of the law is not necessarily contravened merely because wide or discretionary powers are conferred on the Executive, as long as they are in fact conferred by law. On the other hand Dicey anticipated the criticism of Sir Ivor Jennings that 'if the rule of law means only that powers must be derived from the law, all civilized States possess it' by drawing a distinction between the condition of most European countries in 1908 (when he made his final changes in the text) and the 'lawlessness' of continental Europe, compared with

---

[1] *The Law of the Constitution*, 10th ed., p. 188. The contrast here cited is preceded by the statement that in its first meaning the Rule of Law implies that 'no man is punishable or can lawfully be made to suffer in body or goods except for a distinct breach of the law *established in the ordinary legal manner before the ordinary courts of the land*'. The first part of this passage forms a natural antithesis to the sentence cited above but the second part, here italicized, strictly belongs in Dicey's scheme of thought to the second meaning which he ascribed to the Rule of Law. This is considered under the heading of *Institutions and Procedures of the Rule of Law* (p. 251 *infra*).

[2] *The Law and the Constitution*, 5th ed., p. 306.

England, in the eighteenth century. And in the condition of the world since 1933 it may appear less of a platitude to say that a dictator cannot claim to govern under the Rule of Law if he cannot show a legal right to exercise authority.[1]

Even if we concede the recognition by all civilized States today that powers must be derived from the law, not stopping to ask what 'civilized' in this context may mean, we are not committed to the proposition that such powers are in fact always derived from the law. The supremacy of the law in the field of delegated legislation, for example, in practice depends on the form of the parent law, the institutions and procedures by which the delegated legislation is made, the machinery of control over such legislation once made, and above all on the integrity of the persons involved in the process. But whatever the Rule of Law as a supra-national concept may have to say on these matters,[2] it is true that we cannot deduce it from the bare statement that the law should be supreme.

The supremacy of the law is closely associated, but not to be confused, with the certainty of the law. Thus, the maxims *nullum crimen sine lege* and *nulla poena sine lege*[3] in one sense merely apply to the penal sphere the principle of the supremacy of the law; in a second sense, which is often not clearly differentiated from the first meaning, they suggest that no action can be

---

[1] Dictators can seldom show a clean legal title to power. The oft-quoted Enabling Act of March 16, 1933, was preceded by a reign of terror instigated by National Socialist Storm Troopers and S.S., which Göring, as Prussian Minister of the Interior, not only condoned but even encouraged. See Bullock, *Hitler*, p. 236; Clark, *The Fall of the German Republic*, p. 477.

[2] See p. 251, *infra*.

[3] See Mannheim, *Criminal Justice and Social Reconstruction*, pp. 207–214. Dr. Mannheim discusses the maxims from the point of view of the second meaning here suggested. He says they are sometimes expressed in the form of a prohibition of the use of analogy in the interpretation of criminal statutes. He points out, however, that the use of analogy, although permitted by a National Socialist law of June 28, 1939, and by Article 16 of the Soviet Penal Code (now superseded by s. 3 of the Basic Principles of Criminal Legislation of the U.S.S.R. and Union Republics—see *Law in Eastern Europe*, No. 3, ed., Szirmai, Leyden, 1959, p. 9 *sub nomine* 'Return to the *nulla poena* rule') is not an essential characteristic of totalitarian legal systems or completely alien to democratic countries, citing Denmark as an example of the latter. His conclusion (p. 213) is that 'the fate of civil liberty depends on the men who have to administer civil liberty much more than on this (*i.e.*, prohibition of analogy) or any other legal formula'.

treated as a crime, or lead to the infliction of a punishment, if at the time when such action was taken the relevant law was non-existent. The maxims are here being used to prohibit the retroactive application of the Law. The first Committee (which dealt with the Legislature and the Law) at New Delhi in requiring in absolute terms that 'the Legislature must abstain from retroactive legislation' perhaps thought of retroactive legislation as the negation of the supremacy of the law.[1] The objection to retroactive legislation would seem rather to be that the position of those to be affected by it is, before it is passed, rendered uncertain.

It was with the importance of certainty in human relations in mind that the Greeks spoke of *nomos* as the principle of political association which assigns to each citizen his position in society and defines its nature and extent,[2] and it is not difficult to illustrate the hardships which uncertainty imposes not only in the criminal sphere[3] but also in other fields of human activity.[4] On the other hand it was also a Greek, Aristotle, who pointed out that the rigid certainty of law is not applicable to all circumstances,[5] and his plea would be echoed by the modern

[1] Conclusion III (3) (e), *Journal of the International Commission of Jurists*, Vol. II No. 1 (1959), p. 9. On the other hand the Third Committee (which dealt with the Criminal Process and the Rule of Law) was more cautious: 'It is always important that the definition and interpretation of the law should be as certain as possible, and this is of particular importance in the case of criminal law, where the citizen's life and liberty may be at stake. Certainty cannot exist in the criminal law, where the law or the penalty for its breach, is retrospective' (Conclusion I of the Third Committee, *ibid.*, p. 13).

[2] Barker, *The Politics of Aristotle*, p. lxx.

[3] An extreme case would be the Conspiracy and Corruption Act of August 10, 1958, in Iraq. It was made retroactive to September 1, 1939, and thus made criminal political activities under the previous régime which might when undertaken have been permissible or even commendable.

[4] For example, a merchant who has built up a trade connexion on the basis of a licence granted by the government is suddenly and unexpectedly deprived without compensation of his livelihood by the withdrawal of the licence. See Schwartz, *An Introduction to American Administrative Law*, 1958, p. 167, where he criticizes those cases where judicial review is not available because the person affected has only a 'privilege'. As he points out, the hardship to the individual in the disturbance of his settled way of life may be as great as when there is interference with his personal or 'property rights'. (*Cf., Nakkuda Ali* v. *Jayaratne*, [1951] A.C. 66.)

[5] 'It is because law cannot cover the whole of the ground, and there are subjects which cannot be included in its scope that difficulties arise . . .'; translation in Barker, *op. cit.*, Bk. III, Chap. xvi, 1287a, s. 11 (p. 148).

administrator called upon to deal with the ever changing circumstances of economic and social life and with the delicate adjustments of political and diplomatic relations. As Aristotle turned from the certainty of law to the question whether 'the rule of the best law is preferable to that of the best man,'[1] so we are forced to cease chasing the myth of an absolutely certain law and to concentrate in a pragmatic spirit on the methods by which law is administered. This does not mean, however, that we can afford to neglect the basic concern of the Rule of Law with the status and dignity of the individual, for our whole concern with procedures and institutions springs from the belief that, although never perfectly realizable, their ultimate aim is to isolate and make use of the moral judgment of the truly independent individual.

Institutions and Procedures of the Rule of Law

Dicey in the second meaning which he gave to the Rule of Law said that it implied 'not only that with us no man is above the law, but (what is a different thing) that here every man, whatever be his rank or condition, is subject to the ordinary law of the realm and amenable to the jurisdiction of the ordinary tribunals.'[2] In so far as this proposition suggested that officials in England are not, and ought not to be, in respect of any of their activities outside the jurisdiction of the 'ordinary' courts as opposed to that of other sorts of tribunals, it has been subjected to well merited criticism[3]; and the corollary that the administrative courts and administrative law of Continental Europe were in principle opposed to the Rule of Law has been similarly criticized,[4] and indeed Dicey himself later modified his attitude.[5] However, Dicey's proposition does at least emphasize that aspect of the Rule of Law, which is concerned with

---

[1] Barker, *loc. cit.* [2] *Law of the Constitution*, 10th ed., p. 193.

[3] See Robson, *op. cit.*, n. (3), p. 224, *supra*; Jennings, *Law and the Constitution*, 5th ed., p. 232 *et seq.* and pp. 311–313.

[4] See *e.g.*, in an extensive literature now available in English: Street, *Government Liability: a Comparative Study* (1953); Hamson, *Executive Discretion and Judicial Control* (1954); Schwartz, *French Administrative Law and the Common Law World* (1954).

[5] See (1901), 17 L.Q.R. 302.

the institutions and procedures by which the law is put into effect. It is possible that the characteristics which Dicey, rightly or wrongly, attributed to the 'ordinary' courts and denied to other tribunals are themselves a necessary part of the Rule of Law even in a supra-national context.

If the substantive law in a free society under the Rule of Law must be based on and explicitly or, frequently, tacitly assume the dignity of the individual, it follows that the interpretation and administration of the law must be entrusted to men and women in a position to understand and to act in accordance with the implications of such a conception of human dignity. The legal institutions and procedures characteristic of the Rule of Law seek simply to make this possible. But there is no fixed relationship in any society between the specifically legal machinery and the more intangible factors of social tradition which may, as powerfully as a writ of *Habeas Corpus* or an order of *certiorari*, serve to ensure that human rights are respected. More particularly, as is here in point, the institutions and procedures of the Rule of Law conceived as a supra-national concept, can only be determined by laborious comparative study not merely of the institutions and procedures themselves but also of the various settings—both legal and extra-legal—in which they operate.[1] It is clear that whatever may have been accomplished at Chicago, Warsaw or New Delhi, such a task has only just begun; it is moreover one which, with the rapidly changing conditions of many, particularly Asian and African countries, continuously requires revision and reassessment.

(a) JUDICIAL INSTITUTIONS AND PROCEDURES: THE JUDICIAL PROCESS

In spite of these evident difficulties of the comparative assessment of legal institutions and procedures, it is clearly felt in the discussions at New Delhi that, on the basis of experience rather than as a matter of dogmatic assertion, a society under the Rule of Law requires in the first place certain institutions and procedures, which we may call the judicial process. A jud-

[1] See n. (3), p. 261, *infra*.

icial institution was here taken to mean one in which the judge or judges (under whatever name and whether sitting in so-called 'ordinary courts', 'administrative courts', or 'administrative tribunals') is or are in a position to exercise an independent judgment. But such independence is not licence to act in an arbitrary manner. The Rule of Law is not the Rule of the Judges. The judge in this broad sense is bound by the law, and the fundamental assumptions of a free society underlying it, which he must interpret to the best of his abilities in the light of his own conscience.[1]

Some attempt was made at New Delhi to go beyond this rather elementary conclusion, which is already embodied in Article 6 of the European Convention for the Protection of Human Rights and Fundamental Freedoms in the requirement that 'in the determination of his civil rights and obligations or of any criminal charge against him, everyone is entitled to a fair and public hearing within a reasonable time by *an independent and impartial tribunal established by law*'.[2] Thus, the problem of securing the conditions in which the independent judge may function was given some attention, although in a tentative formulation. A difficulty frequently raised in this connexion is that methods which are open to obvious abuse do sometimes at least not prevent the appointment and effective functioning of an independent judiciary. On the other hand machinery designed to safeguard the independence of the judiciary, although it may not be successful, does not inherently make it more likely that judges will be subservient.[3] The cautious conclusion reached at New Delhi was that there are dangers in an exclusive power of appointment resting with the Executive, Legislative or Judiciary; that the election of judges by popular vote (as in most States of the U.S.A. and in Switzerland) has special difficulties

---

[1] The reference to the judge's abilities and conscience, although included in the Working Paper, was omitted in the Conclusions of the Committee on the Judiciary and the Legal Profession at the New Delhi Congress, presumably for fear that it might suggest an arbitrary and incalculable element in the judicial function. It is submitted, however, that trust in the moral judgment of the individual, isolated as far as possible from distracting pressures and influences, lies at the basis of the Rule of Law as outlined in this essay.

[2] Italics supplied.   [3] See n. (4), p. 262, *infra*.

and only works well where firm tradition as circumscribed by prior agreement the list of candidates and limited controversy, and that where on the whole there is general satisfaction with the calibre and independence of the judges it will be found that either in law or in practice there is some degree of co-operation (or at least consultation) between the Judiciary and the authority actually making the appointment.[1]

Closely associated with the concept of the judicial institution is that of the legal profession. It is indeed commonly said that a 'free' legal profession is characteristic of the Rule of Law, but just as the judiciary is not independent in the sense that it is able to exercise arbitrary power, so the legal profession is not free, if by freedom is meant liberty to pursue its own ends or those of its clients without regard to the law or its underlying assumption. But like the judge the lawyer must be free from interference within his proper field of competence. What in this connexion is proper is suggested by the Conclusions of the Committee on the Judiciary and the Legal Profession at New Delhi that: (1), 'Subject to his professional obligation to accept assignments in appropriate circumstances, the lawyer should be free to accept any case which is offered to him;' (2), 'It is the duty of the lawyer, which he should be able to discharge without fear of consequences, to press upon the court any argument of law or fact which he may think proper for the due presen-

---

[1] The system in force in India appears on the whole to have worked well. Judges of the Supreme Court are appointed by the President of India (acting on the advice of the Prime Minister, although the opinion of the President carries great weight) and except in the case of the Chief Justice, the Chief Justice of India must always be consulted. The practice so far has been to appoint the most senior member of the Supreme Court as Chief Justice, although it is not required by the Constitution. In the High Courts the appointment is also by the President, after consulting the Chief Justice of the High Court concerned, the Governor of the State and the Chief Justice of India. There is undoubtedly the potentiality of 'political' appointments but it is understood that no appointment has yet been made without the concurrence of the Chief Justice of India, his veto being always accepted. At lower levels District Judges are appointed by the Governor of the State after consultation with the Public Services Commission of the State concerned and the High Court. At the lowest level on the criminal side (Magistrates Courts) separation between the Executive and the Judiciary is not yet complete but the danger of political decisions is minimized by the fact that their decisions are subject to appeal to the District Judge (acting as the Sessions Judge), to the High Court and finally to the Supreme Court.

tation of the case by him'. The freedom of the lawyer in this sense can be strengthened in practice by the degree of corporate organization which he enjoys and by the professional standards which such organization can develop. But in this field much comparative work remains to be done. There are at present wide variations in different countries as to the way in which the legal profession is organized: a high degree of autonomy with centrally organized bodies and an indirect or ultimate supervision by the courts or by the judges of the courts;[1] a measure of control by some other organ (as, for example, by a Ministry of Justice[2]); local organizations centred on a particular court,[3] with sometimes national organizations on a voluntary basis exercising great *de facto* influence;[4] or indeed the absence of an obligatory organization for those pursuing the legal profession.[5] No detailed criteria applicable to all countries for the organization of the legal profession were or could be suggested at New Delhi. While the desirability, or at least permissibility, of general supervision by the Judiciary of the legal profession was admitted it was also recognized that in certain circumstances the Bar may need protection from the Bench itself and that this requires a certain minimum of autonomous organization for the former.

On the procedures involved in the judicial process, as distinct from the scope of their application (which is considered below) there is a wide measure of international agreement. In s.6 of the European Convention for the Protection of Human Rights and Fundamental Freedoms, which has been cited in part above,[6] a 'fair and'—subject to some exceptions—'public

[1] See n. (5), p. 263, *infra*.

[2] In the German Federal Republic admission to and dismissal from the legal profession is the ultimate responsibility of the Ministry of Justice of the appropriate *Land*.

[3] In France the local autonomy of the different Orders of Advocates (one of which is centred on each Court of Appeal) is emphasized. See Siré, 'The Bar in France,' *Journal of the International Commission of Jurists*, Vol. I, No. 2 (1958), p. 261.

[4] As in the United States by the American Bar Association.

[5] In Sweden, although the great majority of those engaged in legal advisory work and advocacy do have legal training, any one in principle is entitled to assist a party in a case and to act as an advocate in a Swedish court. The legal profession thus enjoys no monopoly.

[6] See p. 253, *supra*.

hearing' is required in the determination of the individual's civil rights and obligations and of any criminal charge against him. In relation to personal liberty, a detained person must be promptly informed of the charge on which he is held and promptly brought before a 'judge or officer authorized by law to exercise judicial power' and tried within a reasonable time or released pending trial.[1] Wrongful arrest or detention in contravention of the Convention must give an enforceable right to compensation.[2] In criminal trials the accused is entitled to know the charge against him, to have adequate time and facilities to prepare his defence, to be able to defend himself or to employ counsel of his choosing, being provided if he is without means with free counsel 'if the interests of justice so require', to examine the witnesses against him and to be able to summon witnesses on his own behalf.[3]

At New Delhi a modest advance was made in giving more explicit form to these principles in criminal and more particularly in civil matters. For example, in civil matters it was agreed that even where review of the acts of the Executive affecting the person, property or rights of the individual comes not before ordinary courts or regular administrative courts (as in France or Germany) but before, in the English sense, 'administrative tribunals', the following requirements must be satisfied: the right to be heard, if possible in public; to have advance knowledge of the rules governing the hearing; the right to adequate representation (including save for sufficient reason to the contrary, the right to legal representation); the right to know the opposing case; the right to receive a reasoned judgment, with the ultimate right of review by the ordinary courts. The European Convention (Article 13) speaks only of 'an effective remedy before a national authority' for violations of the rights and freedoms recognized by the Convention 'notwithstanding that the violation has been committed by persons acting in an official capacity'. The Congress at New Delhi more specifically required that 'a citizen who suffers injury as a result of illegal acts of the Executive should have an effective remedy against the

[1] Article 5 (3).   [2] Article 5 (5).   [3] Article 6 (3).

State or against the individual wrongdoer, with assurance of satisfaction of the judgment in the latter case, or both'.[1]

In criminal matters particular emphasis was laid at New Delhi on the importance of the right to legal advice from the earliest time of arrest, a right which is not available or not observed in practice in many countries. Release on bail (subject to stated exceptions)[2] was declared to be a right and not merely an alternative to trial within a reasonable time, as in the European Convention. Attention was also paid to the methods used by the authorities to obtain evidence which must not include anything calculated to impair his (the prisoner's) will or to violate his dignity as a human being; and evidence illegally obtained must not be used against the accused.[3] In all criminal cases there should be a right of appeal to at least one higher tribunal, a view which corresponds with the fundamental position of the individual in the concept of the Rule of Law for, on the one hand, this concept presupposes faith in the rational and fair judgement of the individual and, on the other, it admits that it is in the nature of the human condition to make mistakes.

Not merely in criminal but also in civil cases it was recognized that legal aid for those unable to pay for it is a necessary corollary of substantial rather than formal equality before the law, although there was some difference of emphasis (by State provision or by voluntary action of the legal profession) as to the way in which such legal aid should be ensured.[4]

---

[1] See n. (6), p. 263, *infra*.

[2] Conclusion IV (2) of the Committee on the Criminal Process and the Rule of Law (see *Journal of the International Commission of Jurists*, Vol. II, No. 1 (1959), p. 14) listed the following: the exceptionally serious nature of the charge; likelihood of escape of the accused outside the jurisdiction; likelihood of the accused interfering with the evidence; likelihood of the accused committing further criminal offences.

[3] Not only, it would seem, evidence obtained by involuntary confessions. This, as far as English law is concerned, would appear to go beyond *Ibrahim* v. *R.*, [1914] A.C. 599 and to be contrary to *Elias* v. *Pasmore*, [1934] 2 K.B. 164 and *Kuruma* v. *The Queen*, [1955] A.C. 197. But see the criticisms of Cowen and Carter, *Essays on the Law of Evidence*, pp. 72–105.

[4] See *Journal of the International Commission of Jurists*, Vol. II, No. 2 (1960), containing a provisional report on a Colloquium of the United Kingdom National Committee on Comparative Law held in Oxford in September, 1959, on 'Comparative Aspects of Legal Aid'.

(b) THE SCOPE OF APPLICATION OF THE JUDICIAL PROCESS

It is comparatively easy to reach a wide measure of international agreement on what are the constituents of the judicial process; it is much more difficult to decide in what circumstances and to what extent the judicial process should be applied. That it is applicable to issues in which the life or liberty of the individual is concerned would probably be fairly readily agreed. Preventive detention (which is here understood to involve imprisonment without trial by decision of the Executive) was only incidentally discussed at New Delhi, but the fact that it was not covered in the final conclusions of the Congress suggest that it was felt to be inconsistent with the Rule of Law. On the other hand, preventive detention has been imposed in Great Britain in wartime, has been introduced in peacetime in various dependent territories of the Commonwealth (such as Kenya and Nyasaland)[1] and exists in the territory of independent Commonwealth members such as Ghana and India. There would however probably be a considerable international consensus for the view that preventive detention, when imposed, must (1) be effected under direct and not delegated legislative authority, (2) be operative for a limited period, and (3) provide machinery analogous to the judicial process for the hearing of appeals by detainees.[2]

It was clearly indicated at New Delhi that, whereas judicial review of legislative decisions was not an inherent part of the machinery of the Rule of Law, it was essential 'to ensure that the extent, purpose, and procedure appropriate to delegated legislation are observed . . . that it should be subject to ultimate review by a judicial body'. The succeeding conclusion that

---

[1] See Holland 'Personal Liberty in the Commonwealth,' *Current Legal Problems*, 1958, p. 151.

[2] The Indian Preventive Detention Act, No. 4 of 1950 (s. 8) sets up Advisory Boards, each consisting of three persons who are, or have been or are qualified to be appointed as judges of a High Court, with a judge or former judge as chairman. By s. 11 (2) the Government concerned has to revoke the detention order if the Advisory Board reports that there is insufficient cause for the detention of the detainee.

'in general, the acts of the Executive which directly and injuriously affect the person or property or rights of the individual should be subject to review by the Courts'[1] was rather less informative. Unless a qualifying reservation is to be found in the words 'in general', the statement appears to go beyond the practice of most countries and certainly beyond that of Great Britain; it does not make allowance, for example, for the generally unchallengeable power of the Executive to expel an alien[2] or to withhold a passport from a citizen.[3] If the conclusion is to be explained by giving to the conception of 'rights' a restricted meaning,[4] the argument is in danger of becoming merely circular: the judicial process should be employed in the determination of 'rights'; 'rights' are those interests to which the judicial process is applicable.

It is, however, broadly true to say that in most countries of the Western democratic pattern it is mainly in matters which directly or indirectly affect the State's foreign relations that what in French administrative practice are called *actes de gouvernement* remain outside the ultimate jurisdiction of the courts.[5] In the procedural field the State sometimes claims privilege for information, otherwise relevant to law suits, which

---

[1] 'Courts' is explained to mean not merely the ordinary courts and administrative courts (as in France or Germany) but also administrative tribunals and agencies (on the British or American pattern) provided the latter are subject to ultimate review by the ordinary courts and involve the characteristics of a judicial hearing mentioned on p. 222 *et seq.*, *supra*.

[2] But this power may be limited by international agreement. See the decision of the Federal Administrative Court of Germany (October 25, 1956, N.r.BVerwG.I.C. 58.56, published in *Deutsches Verwaltungsblatt* (1957), p. 57; note by Mr. H. Golsong in B.Y.I.L., Vol. XXXIII (1957), 317), which held that the power of the police under German Law to expel an alien had been limited by German ratification of the European Convention for the Protection of Human Rights and Fundamental Freedoms, whereby under s. 8 special protection is given to 'family life' and 'home'.

[3] But see as regards the United States *Kent* v. *Dulles* (1958), 357 U.S. 116, in which the Supreme Court said: 'the right to travel is part of the "liberty" of which a citizen cannot be deprived without due process of law under the Fifth Amendment'.

[4] As distinguished from 'privileges'. See n. (4), p. 250, *supra*.

[5] For a comparative treatment see Rumpf, *Regierungsakte im Rechtsstaat*, Bonn, 1955 reviewed in *Journal of the International Commission of Jurists*, Vol. I, No. 2 (1958), p. 336. The *Conseil d'État* in France has progressively narrowed the field of *actes de gouvernement*; see Waline, *Droit Administratif*, 8th ed., 1959, p. 190 *et seq.*

involves not only State security or diplomatic relations but also the proper functioning of the public service as judged by the department concerned. Such a claim is made, but has been widely criticized, in Great Britain;[1] the rights of the State are in this respect more restricted in France[2] and in the U.S.A.[3] But as regards the proper scope of the judicial process much comparative investigation is still to be done, most usefully by comparison of particular types of governmental activity in approximately similar political, economic, and social environments and the different degrees to which they are or might be subject to the judicial process.[4]

III. CONCLUSION

The Rule of Law on a supra-national plane may on examination thus appear to lack at its edges the sharpness of definition which we expect of legal concepts. But this does not mean that there is no agreement on the basic values which it represents and on many, although not all, of the methods and procedures by which it is sought to put those values into effect. Such a consensus among representative lawyers from a large number of countries was demonstrated at New Delhi. Their agreement does not of itself make law, either on the municipal or on the international plane, but it may serve to create a climate of opinion in which international law, slowly extending into the sphere of domestic jurisdiction,[5] may eventually reach a more practical recognition of human rights.[6]

---

[1] See Hamson, 'Government Privilege and the Rule of Law', *The Listener*, October 18, 1956, p. 612; Bell, *Public Law* (1957), p. 28; *Auten* v. *Rayner*, [1958] 1 W.L.R. 1300 and leading article in *The Times*, November 5, 1958.

[2] The Conseil d'État may draw inferences against the State if it fails to produce the documents, on being ordered to do so. See Hamson, *Executive Discretion and Judicial Control*, p. 36.

[3] *United States* v. *Reynolds* (1953), 345 U.S. 1, shows that while the court will not generally insist on seeing the allegedly privileged document 'judicial control over the evidence cannot be abdicated to the caprice of executive officers' (*per* Vinson C.J.). See further Schwartz, *Introduction to American Administrative Law*, 1958, p. 237.

[4] See n. (7), p. 264, *infra*.

[5] See 'Domestic Jurisdiction and International Concern', *Journal of the International Commission of Jurists*, Vol. I, No. 1 (1957), p. 3.

[6] *Cf.*, Goodhart (1958), 106 University of Pennsylvania Law Review 943, at p. 945: 'The rule of law is the machinery by which effect can be given to such basic rights as are recognized in any particular legal system.'

[1] 'Anti-scientific conception, established in bourgeois legal literature, picturing the bourgeois state as if in it there is no room for arbitrary executive power and where allegedly law and legality reign.

'It is characteristic of the theory of the Rule of Law—as is true of the praise accorded to bourgeois democracy as 'pure' and as being of a supra-class nature—to assert the priority of law over the State, to regard law as something independent of the State and standing above it (the ideal State under the Rule of Law). In all phases of the existence of the bourgeois State the doctrines of the Rule of Law were anti-scientific doctrines which, deliberately or not, identified the ideal State under the Rule of Law with the existing real bourgeois—'democratic' States in order to mask their class nature (and) to strengthen the rule of the bourgeoisie.

'In the age of imperialism and proletarian revolution—due to the turning of the imperialist bourgeoisie democracy to reaction—the doctrines of the Rule of Law are relegated to an inferior plane in favour of the contemporary doctrines of the ideologists of the imperialist State. Such doctrines substantiate this reactionary trend, the destruction of bourgeois legality, the removal of the last remnants of the democratic achievements of the masses. Nevertheless the bourgeoisie of many countries utilize even in this age, by way of demagogic appeal, the doctrines of the Rule of Law in their class interests, by giving them a particularly reactionary meaning and by trying to inculcate with their help harmful illusions into the masses to mask the imperialist nature of the contemporary bourgeois state and law.

'The doctrines of Rule of Law are pointedly directed at the revolutionary movement of the working class, and, since the establishment of socialist States, at these States (as such).'

[2] Thus Clause I of the Conclusions of the First Committee reads as follows: 'The function of the Legislature in a free society is to create and maintain the conditions which will uphold the dignity of man as an individual. This dignity requires not only the recognition of his civil and political rights but also the establishment of the social, economic, educational and cultural conditions which are essential to the full development of his personality.' Clause III (1) reads: 'Every Legislature in a free society under the Rule of Law should endeavour to give full effect to the principles enunciated in the Universal Declaration of Human Rights'. The Working Paper, specifically recognized that the negative political rights conventionally covered by the Rule of Law, as Dicey had conceived it, might prove illusory without economic and social security; but, in the conclusions which it suggested to the Committee, it dealt only with what were conceived to be the strictly legal propositions involved in the Rule of Law. Clause I was suggested by the author of the Working Paper and present writer as a compromise to meet the strong criticism particularly of Asian participants that a more positive approach to the Rule of Law was required.

[3] It would, for example, be an interesting field of study to compare the differences in terms of practical results between the French and English systems of bringing prosecutions. In England the right to prosecute is in principle the right, although not the duty, of every citizen (subject to the responsibility of the Director of Public Prosecutions to prosecute in certain serious crimes such as murder and to take over other cases when the public interest so requires). In practice, the great majority of prosecutions are instituted by the police (88% of indictable offences), and such are commonly spoken of as 'police prosecutions', although, strictly speaking the police act in their capacity not of officials but of individual citizens. However, the actual conduct of the prosecution in more serious cases is normally entrusted to members of the Bar in those courts where they have exclusive rights of audience and to barristers or solicitors before other courts. The fact that a member of the Bar, subject to its traditions and discipline, may appear for the prosecution in one

case and for the defence in another and the absence of any comprehensive hierarchy of professional prosecutors is widely felt in English legal circles to provide
an important safeguard against the over-zealous exercise of the prosecutor's
position. At the apex of the system there is the Attorney-General who exercises an
ultimate responsibility for the enforcement of the criminal law and is entitled to
take over or to stop (by entering a *nolle prosequi*) any prosecution for offences triable
by indictment (in summary cases he must obtain the leave of the court). But the
Attorney-General, although a member of the Government and of the House of
Commons and chief Law Officer and legal adviser to the Crown and departments
of State, exercises in relation to criminal prosecutions 'his own judgement and his
own discretion' (Lord MacDermott, *Protection from Power under English Law*, p. 33)
and not that of the government of which he is a member. See also Sir Patrick
Devlin, *The Criminal Prosecution in England*, p. 16 *et seq.*

On the other hand it is emphasized by French commentators that in France the
fact that the prosecuting body (*Magistrature debout*) forms part of the judiciary in the
widest sense (*Magistrature*) is an essential safeguard of the fairness of prosecutions
and of the exercise of the prosecutor's discretion in a judicial spirit. It is true that
the Minister of Justice exercises ultimate control over the prosecuting hierarchy,
and issues general instructions by means of circulars to the *Procureurs Generaux*
attached to the different Appeal Courts, who in turn are responsible for the
Procureurs de la République attached to the lower courts. In theory an order not to
prosecute does not relieve a particular prosecutor from his duty to prosecute if the
public interest and the fact warrant it, but the theory is modified in practice by
the internal disciplinary control of the prosecuting body. It is clear, however, that
the prosecutor can be ordered to prosecute by his superiors but, whatever his
written insructions, the prosecutor is always entitled orally to express his own
convictions: *La plume est serve, mais la parole est libre*. Moreover, once the trial court
becomes seized of a case, the discontinuance of proceedings passes under its jurisdiction. Thus, in the prosecuting practice of England and France there are many
points at which extra-legal factors might play an important rôle, but they are not
necessarily the same factors, nor would they always intrude at the same places in
the legal pattern.

⁴ The judges of the High Court and Court of Appeal (and the Lords of Appeal in
Ordinary, Appellate Jurisdiction Act, 1876, s. 6) hold office during good behaviour
(which means that they might be removed without recourse to Parliament by
proceedings commenced by *scire facias* or by a criminal information—a possibility
which does not appear ever to have arisen in practice) subject to removal on an
Address voted by both Houses of Parliament (Act of Settlement, 1701 and Supreme
Court of Judicature Act, 1925); but the Lord Chancellor may dismiss County
Court judges and may remove a magistrate's name from the Commission. This
aspect of judicial independence has rarely arisen in practice; much more real are
the difficulties of ensuring that independent-minded judges are appointed. The
English system distributes responsibility for strictly judicial appointments between
two members of the government of the day, the Prime Minister and the Lord
Chancellor; the Chairmen of certain administrative tribunals have to be selected
by the 'appropriate authority' from a panel of persons appointed by the Lord Chancellor (Tribunals and Inquiries Act, 1948, s. 3 (1)) and in respect of the members of
certain administrative tribunals a Council on Tribunals (appointed by the Lord
Chancellor and the Secretary of State) may make recommendations to the appropriate Minister—*i.e.*, to the one making the appointment or in charge of the government department concerned with the tribunal in question (*ibid.*, s. 4 (1)). Such a
system is clearly capable of abuse; that it is not in fact abused we owe to a fairly recently established tradition and to a vigilant public opinion. In other countries the

difficulty of establishing a tradition of non-political appointments by a political Minister of Justice has frequently led to the transfer of the appointing power to a composite body, representing various interests in the State. Thus in France the Constitution of 1946 set up a Superior Council of the Judiciary with members drawn from the Executive, Legislature, the Judiciary itself and the practising legal profession; the Council is retained under the new Constitution but its function is only advisory and its composition, apart from the President of the Republic and the Minister of Justice, is not fixed by the Constitution itself. The *Conseil d'État*, the *Section du Contentieux* of which performs judicial functions vital to the maintenance of the Rule of Law in France, falls outside the general system for the selection of judges. Entry to the lowest grade is by competitive examination. Subsequent promotion, and, to the limited extent to which this is possible (never more than one quarter of the vacancies), appointment from outside the *Conseil d'État*, is made by the Minister of Justice (or in the case of higher grades by the Council of Ministers on his proposition) out of a list of candidates put forward by the Vice-President of the *Conseil d'État*, who is its effective head. Professor Hamson (*Executive Discretion and Judicial Control*, p. 141) in referring to the freedom of the *Section du Contentieux* from political and executive influence, has said that by the test of actual experience its independence is 'self-evident'.

[5] As in England with its Bar Council, Inns of Court, and Law Society. The Bar Council, which is a mainly elected body, has no direct powers of discipline, but it makes rules as to professional etiquette and can forward a complaint against a barrister to his Inn of Court, which has power to disbar, reprimand or suspend the offender, subject to appeal to the Lord Chancellor and a Committee of Judges of the High Court. See Boulton 'The Legal Profession and the Law: the Bar in England and Wales', *Journal of the International Commission of Jurists*, Vol. I, No. 1 (1957), pp. 113–116. Solicitors as 'officers of the court' are more directly subject to judicial control and their functioning has been closely and frequently regulated by statute (Consolidating Act of 1932 and Supplementary Legislation of 1933, 1934, 1936, 1939, 1941, 1949, 1950, 1956, 1957, and 1959), but the Law Society as the representative body is recognized by statute and entrusted with many duties although the removal of solicitors from the Roll is the function of a Discipline Committee consisting of past or present members of the Council of the Law Society appointed by the Master of the Rolls, with appeals to the Queen's Bench Division and (with leave) to the Court of Appeal and to the House of Lords.

[6] The position reached in Great Britain, that there may be action against the individual and (since the Crown Proceedings Act, 1947) against the State, is by no means universal. By a curious paradox in Republics such as the U.S.A. and India the influence of the old maxim, 'The King can do no wrong', limits the remedy against the State. In the U.S.A., Federal and State legislation has allowed limited categories of claims against the State, and in some cases judicial decisions have attempted, not without confusion, to draw a distinction between acts done in a 'proprietary capacity' for which there may be liability and acts done in a 'governmental capacity'. See Gellhorn and Byse, *Administrative Law*, p. 352. In India a distinction is made between acts for which the East India Company before 1858 would have been liable as belonging to its private trading capacity and acts which would before that date have involved the exercise of delegated sovereign power. In a characteristic Civil Law country, such as France, the individual official is only liable, if at all, when he has committed 'personal' fault. Where the delays of the process before the administrative courts are considerable, this may weaken the effectiveness of the remedy against illegality on the part of officials. For an illustration of the working of the French system in a delicate political issue (seizure of a pamphlet alleging torture in Algeria) see *The Times*, December 28,

1959, in which the dismissal by a civil court of an action for damages against a Prefect of Police on the ground that no sufficiently serious fault had been disclosed, is reported. In *Political Studies*, vol. VII, p. 109, (1959), Professor F. H. Lawson, in an interesting reassessment of Dicey, defends, (at pp. 119–125), the emphasis put by the latter on the existence in English Law of personal liability in tort on the part of the wrong-doing official: 'If Dicey meant to say, as I believe he did, that the purpose of allowing personal actions against public officials was deterrence, not compensation, he was right in saying that *droit administratif*, which looks more to compensation, did not at its highest development conform to what he meant by the Rule of Law'. A rather similar conclusion had been reached by the present writer in the Working Paper for the New Delhi Congress: 'The feeling of the individual member of society that the executive is composed of ordinary citizens who owe a personal duty to one another within the framework of the law lies at the heart of the conception of the Rule of Law in a free society'. See *The Rule of Law in a Free Society*, p. 218.

[7] Mention should also be made of those methods, which cannot be characterized as essential to the Rule of Law but which, at least in some countries, have been found a useful supplement (and sometimes a partial substitute for) the judicial process. For example, the Committee on the Executive and the Rule of Law at New Delhi considered that 'judicial review of delegated legislation may be usefully supplemented by procedure for supervision by the Legislature or by a committee or a commissioner of the Legislature or by other independent authority either before or after such delegated legislation comes into effect'. On the work of Parliamentary Commissioners not merely as regards delegated legislation but in respect of the acts of the Executive in general, with particular reference to Scandinavian countries, see Hurwitz, *Journal of the International Commission of Jurists*, Vol. I, No. 2 (1958), p. 224; *Public Law* (1958), p. 258; the Legal Correspondent of *The Observer*, May 31 and June 7, 1959; Pedersen, *Public Law* (1959, p. 115; Wold (Chief Justice of Norway), *Journal of the International Commission of Jurists*, Vol. II, No. 2 (1960). The Committee also pointed out that 'irrespective of the availability of judicial review to correct illegal action by the Executive after it has occurred, it is generally desirable to institute appropriate antecedent procedures of hearing, inquiry or consultation through which parties whose rights or interests will be affected may have an adequate opportunity to make representation so as to minimize the likelihood of unlawful or unreasonable executive action'. As regards antecedent control of administrative acts see also the discussion at the First International Congress of Comparative Law at Barcelona in 1956 (*Revista del Instituto de Derecho Comparado*, No. 8–9 (1957). The Common Law view has generally been that it is desirable that before an administrative decision is made interested parties should be able to some extent to make representations, whereas Civil Law countries have tended to be satisfied with the possibility of a subsequent review of the administrative act by judicial means. In Austria, however (see Professor Spanner, *op. cit.*, p. 449) 'Every individual administrative act or decision of an administrative authority must as a rule—apart from a few exceptions—be preceded by a preliminary procedure which is designed to provide the basis for the decision or order.'

CHAPTER X

Justiciability

by Geoffrey Marshall

ISSUES are sometimes resolved by judicial processes which might have been resolved by political processes, and justice is often contrasted with politics, not because it is even *prima facie* expected that political decisions will be unjust, but because there are characteristic (though disputed) differences between the ways in which decisions may be reached. There is admittedly a sense in which it is not contradictory to say that a judicial decision may also be a political decision, in that a decision of any kind may be felt to have political consequences. But the same decision cannot simultaneously be reached in a political and in a judicial way. It is primarily this which is hinted at in asserting of an issue that it is 'justiciable'. A judicial way of resolving it is implicitly contrasted with other ways. But what does this contrast amount to, and are there some types of disputes which are inherently suited to one sort of decision rather than the other?

THE NOTION OF 'JUSTICIABILITY'

The notion of 'justiciability' is to be found attached sometimes to disputes and sometimes to rules. There is a necessary connexion between the two usages. All disputes—if they are civilized ones—imply rights or entitlements, and entitlements in turn imply procedures and rules. Some simple disputes may appear to involve only the clarification of a matter of fact rather than an entitlement (*e.g.*, 'Which horse got its nose in front?'), but the justification for calling anything a dispute or an issue rather than an uncertainty or an antagonism, is that the clarification involved is of a particular kind—namely deciding who, under some conceivable set of rules or conditions, is entitled to succeed, pay the penalty, scoop the pool, or reap the credit (if only the credit of being correctly informed). The characteristic feature of a justiciable dispute, however, is not simply that it is one governed by pre-existing rules. Rules may be applied injudiciously or informally. For example:—'A father may . . . in applying the rules of good manners to a reported case of bad behaviour on the part of his son . . . first impose a part of the punishment, with exclamations of anger; then his excitement having subsided, deliver his authoritative judgement; then ask the culprit for an explanation; then perhaps execute the rest of the punishment; or conversely justify his previous acts by mumbling that the boy, though innocent for once had deserved his punishment in view of other undetected misdeeds; and on other occasions he may proceed in quite other ways. The same is true of cases in which rules of tact or such problems of style as "how to address a Bishop", are authoritatively decided.'[1] Such informal applications of pre-existing rules by authoritative persons, though they cannot, if honest, be purely discretionary decisions, are not 'judicial'. A rule may lack a definite and consistent procedure for its application. It may also be of a kind for which such a procedure is, or is felt to be, inappropriate or unacceptable. Uncertainty about the exact formulation or ambit of a rule may encourage such feelings. More than one form of uncertainty is possible. There may be vagueness or extreme generality in a rule agreed in principle, or perhaps, in other cases, precise rules competing for agreement with either vagueness or sharp differences of opinion about their relative authority or the methods to be used in reconciling them. Unfortunately, assertions that rules are not justiciable are as a matter of usage employed ambiguously both to indicate the *absence in fact* of a fixed procedure and to proclaim the *unsuitability* of a rule for application by that procedure. It might, for example, be announced to someone unacquainted with the provisions of the Indian Constitution that the Directive Principles of state policy which it contains are 'not justiciable'. No legal arrangements are laid down for deciding disputes about

[1] Herman Kantorowicz, *The Definition of Law* (1958), p. 75.

their applicability. On the other hand the same statement might be used by way of appraisal of such provisions as that the State shall promote international peace, or that it shall have the obligation to protect youth against moral and material abandonment.[1] The suggestion would be that these are issues not proper, apt, or suitable for submission to the judicial process—whatever arrangements have in fact been made for their settlement. The same ambiguity is present whenever an issue is said (without further explanation) to be a 'political' or 'legal' question. A well-known *dictum* of the Privy Council about the freedom of trade guaranteed under section 92 of the Australian Constitution has it that 'the problem to be solved will often be not so much legal as political, social or economic, yet it must be solved by a court of law'.[2] In distinguishing between the 'judicial' and the 'political' sphere, we are in fact drawn by one usage to refer simply to the status or description of the arbiters of an issue, or to their actual procedure, and yet also to feel that some issues are inherently or properly of one kind or the other whoever decides them and by whatever means. Some instances could be cited from the discussion of the British Restrictive Trade Practices Act. When, in 1956, the Act gave to a division of the High Court responsibility for decisions previously taken by Ministers, Opposition speakers in the Commons urged that determination of the social and economic questions involved was 'not a suitable question for a court of law.' 'In the power which is handed over to the court' (it was argued) 'we are handing over something which is not justiciable.' 'We cannot', another speaker said, 'convert a political matter into a legal matter . . . by asking the opinion of a judge about it.'[3] Yet, as the actual passage of the Act and the unhappy tasks of Supreme Courts testify, there is a plain sense in which the possibility exists. Indeed De Tocqueville suggested that the United States had founded a system of government upon it.

Frequently a context makes clear whether 'justiciability' is

[1] Indian Constitution, Articles 51 and 39.

[2] *Commonwealth of Australia* v. *Bank of New South Wales*, [1950] A.C. 235, at p. 311.

[3] 549 H.C. Deb. c. 2033 (March 6, 1956).

being used in its fact-stating or in its prescriptive sense. The second is plainly in question when the term 'justiciable' is used to characterize disputes which 'by their nature and in their effect upon the parties *ought* to be regarded as predominantly judicial in character'.[1] What courts are in fact compelled by legislation to decide may or may not possess this suitability. But issues, suitable or not, which for good or bad reasons are unambiguously committed by statute to a judicial forum are also described as 'justiciable'. Where it is unclear what has been done by statute, any use of the term is question-begging unless its two senses are clearly separated. In 1942, for example, Sir William Holdsworth, approving the decision of the majority of the House of Lords in *Liversidge* v. *Anderson*[2] argued at some length that the decision of a minister authorized to intern persons whom he had reasonable cause to believe to be of hostile associations or origin was 'not a justiciable but a political or administrative issue'[3] in the sense that it raised questions of policy unsuitable for application or examination by a court, and was the type of decision which fell under the head of administrative and quasi-judicial powers as those terms had been defined by the Committee on Ministers' Powers of 1932. But these persuasive propositions about the nature of the issue would have remained true however clearly Parliament had provided that the reasonableness of the Minister's decision should be examinable in the courts. They could hardly be invoked without circularity to dispose of Lord Atkin's dissenting view that Parliament on a fair construction of its words had in fact, appropriately or not, declared the ministerial decision to be judicially examinable. That the discretion discussed in *Liversidge* v. *Anderson* did not possess the features which have been associated with 'judicial' decision would not, in any event, be decisive as to whether its exercise might appropriately be reviewed by a court of law. It is certainly easier for a judicial body to review decisions which are themselves 'judicial' as that term has been envisaged by the Common Law. But tradition may, in

[1] Lord MacDermott, *Protection from Power Under English Law* (1957), p. 56.
[2] [1942] A.C. 206.   [3] (1942), 58 L.Q.R. 2.

any given case, have been ignored by statute, as it has been in a different way when laymen have been charged with the making of decisions normally (or formerly) thought appropriate to the judiciary.

AGENT, ISSUE, AND PROCEDURE

'Justiciability', when openly used in its appraising sense, refers, then, to the aptness of a question for judicial solution. But what is to be understood by such a solution? Is it a matter of decision by persons of a certain status? decision by certain sorts of rule? or decision in certain conditions and with certain specifiable results—finality, for example? The notorious difficulty or, some might add, pointlessness of this question, if it is to be answered in terms of criteria historically suggested in the courts,[1] lies in the potential lack of agreement between criteria developed for different purposes. Some have been based on the status of persons, some on procedure and some on attempts to define issues or situations. The last of these is particularly volatile, if only because no description of a situation is uniquely correct. 'Clearing a slum', 'Implementing a social policy', 'Extinguishing private rights', 'Resolving a dispute between parties' are, for example, all possible descriptions from different standpoints of what may be the same process. Moreover it is difficult to separate the idea of an issue from the procedure by which it is settled, and difficult to define a deciding agent without reference to an implied mode of action.

In other words, although the concept of deciding anything does admittedly involve the notions of an issue, a procedure, and a person or body of persons who decide, these are interdependent notions. Though any one of them could *prima facie* be used as the basis of an attempt to define 'judicial' decision, some reference to procedure in a broad sense is difficult to keep out of the picture. For example, persons on the face of it possessing judicial status may follow procedures associated with other types of decision and it may be necessary to decide what

---

[1] Professor S. A. de Smith has made a comprehensive classification of these criteria in *Judicial Review of Administrative Action* (1959), chap. II.

the decision is properly to be called. In 1896, the Privy Council considered the nature of a decision as to land claims required by a Tasmanian statute to be taken in the light of 'equity and good conscience only'. The decision was held not to be judicial though taken by the State Supreme Court.[1] In 1908, Holmes J. was of opinion that 'the character of the act' and not 'the character of the agent' was decisive. 'The nature of the final act', he added, 'determines the nature of the previous inquiry. So when the final act is legislative, the decision which induces it cannot be judicial.' The question 'depends, not upon the *character of the body*, but upon the character of the proceedings.'[2] 'Character', however, is itself ambiguous. It may mean what a body or procedure is called, or alternatively what its true nature is (what, in other words, it ought, on closer inspection, to be called). Deciding whether a body described by one name is properly described by it must therefore involve looking at the characteristics it possesses. Some characteristics, such as the Christian names of its members, might always be irrelevant, and others, such as their political allegiance or their mode of appointment might be more relevant. But the way in which the body acts—in other words its procedure—can hardly fail to be relevant and important in a complete description of it for this purpose. So it is almost necessarily true that the nature of judicial action is to be sought in terms of the procedure followed as much as in the nature of the agents who follow it; for a full description of both agents and issues can hardly be complete without some reference to rules and procedures.

DEFINITIONS OF 'JUDICIAL'

A constitutional separation of powers raises the problem of characterizing the judicial function in a direct and fundamental way. In *Prentis* v. *Atlantic Coastline Co.*, Mr. Justice Holmes defined a judicial inquiry as one which 'investigates, declares, and enforces liabilities as they stand on present or past facts and

---

[1] *Moses* v. *Parker*, [1896] A.C. 245.
[2] *Prentis* v. *Atlantic Coastline Co.* (1908), 211 U.S. 210, at pp. 226, 227.

under laws supposed already to exist'.[1] In the same year, in Australia, Griffith C.J. referred to the judicial power as that 'which every sovereign authority must of necessity have, to decide controversies between its subjects, or between itself and its subjects, whether the right relate to life, liberty or property'. It implied 'a tribunal which has power to give a binding and authoritative decision (whether subject to appeal or not)'.[2] But these generalities have needed refinement when confronted with novel types of decision involving degrees of discretion and technical or economic expertise. Moreover, there has evolved in both Britain and the Commonwealth countries, for different reasons, a distinction between different degrees of 'judicialness'. *Rola Company (Aust.) Pty., Ltd.* v. *The Commonwealth*[3] illustrates both points. There a board was charged with deciding whether work came within certain categories upon which females might be employed. A majority of the court held that the body in question was not exercising judicial power. The power to decide contested questions of fact and to make determinations binding upon parties was not, in the view of Latham C.J., necessarily a judicial power. In 1931, in *Shell Co. of Australia* v. *Federal Commissioner of Taxation*, the Privy Council had made similar reservations.[4] Judicial power was not exercised by a body merely because its decision was final, or because it heard witnesses on oath, or because it decided between contending parties, or because its decisions affected the rights of subjects. An administrative body, in other words, might act in all of these ways and remain an administrative body. Rich J. in the *Rola Case* added that it might also be subject to the rules of natural justice since 'judicial power and power in the exercise of which there is a duty to act judicially are two different things'.[5] Rich J., however, thought that the board in question was in fact exercising judicial power since, unlike the majority, he thought that it *was* deciding whether legal rights, already determined by pre-existing law, existed in a particular case.

[1] *Ibid.*, at p. 226.
[2] *Huddart, Parker & Co. (Pty.), Ltd.* v. *Moorehead* (1908), 8 C.L.R. 330, at p. 357.
[3] (1944), 69 C.L.R. 185.　　　　[4] [1931] A.C. 275, at pp. 296–8.
[5] (1944), 69 C.L.R. 185, at p. 203.

This principle—which is similar to that laid down by Holmes —seems one of which little can now be made. What will lead us to call a procedure 'the determination of whether pre-existing legal rights exist in a given case' rather than 'the creation of new legal rights'? It is not absurd to say that judicial decision is constantly creating new rights and that the exercise of discretionary powers under an enabling law is determining pre-existing legal rights drawn in wide terms. The legal right to whatever is fairly decided under prescribed conditions by an administrative body might be thought at least as pre-existent as that derived from an unexpected decision of the Court of Appeal.

'ACTING JUDICIALLY' AND 'AFFECTING LEGAL RIGHTS'

On the face of it, 'exercising judicial power', 'acting judicially', and 'dispensing justice' might seem to be the same thing, but the requirements of Commonwealth constitutions have led to a body of case law in which they are not. Perhaps because of the serious consequences of holding otherwise, bodies of a fairly formal kind which are admittedly under a duty to act judicially have been said not to exercise judicial power. Thus there is a sense of the term 'justice' in which it is synonymous only with 'the judicial power' or 'the powers of a court' and not necessarily with what subjects get when they are dealt with judicially. This vocabulary, which, outside the context of the separation of powers doctrine, seems an inconvenient one, has not been confined to the Antipodes. In *Fisher* v. *Irish Land Commissioner*[1] a distinction similar to that in the Australian cases was drawn. In considering whether land should be taken from private use for public purposes, the members of the land commission, it was said, were 'bound to act judicially, just as a great number of administrative tribunals are bound so to act; but it does not follow from this that they are administering justice or exercising judicial power.' The commission was to 'exercise as fairly as possible a discretion belonging to the sphere of economics and politics (in the original sense of that word) not to the

[1] [1948] I.R. 3.

judicial sphere'. 'Emphatically it was not being commissioned to dispense *justice* . . . it was not being asked to determine any conflict of *legal rights.*'[1] 'Dispensing justice' and 'acting judicially' do not seem to be distinguished in quite this way in English decisions, (although in cases decided before the Report of the Committee of Ministers' Powers a distinction was made between acting 'with the uniform procedure of a court of law' and acting 'judicially' or dispensing 'substantial justice').[2] In the Report of 1932, 'judicial' action was defined so as to exclude bodies applying an administrative policy. It was equated with dispensing *justice* in the sense used in the *Rola Case* and in Holmes's definition—namely applying the law of the land defining pre-existing legal rights to individual cases. Both 'quasi-judicial' and 'administrative' decisions were set off as not being applications of the 'law of the land'.

The phrases 'applying pre-existing law', 'dispensing justice', and 'determining legal rights' are, however, wide enough to cover any application of principles which takes place under legislative authority. Whilst adequate, therefore, to stating what is characteristic of the judicial rôle as distinct from the *legislative* rôle, they are not equally well adapted for distinguishing judicial decisions from discretionary decisions made by administrative bodies procedurally confined by at least some of the requirements of natural justice. An administrator to whom a law gives a wide discretion *is* applying the law, *is* determining legal rights and *is* applying a pre-existing rule to a given situation. These phrases cannot in themselves adequately set off judicial decision from policy decisions made under an empowering rule.

An object lesson in the ambivalence and uncertainty of the 'pre-existing right' formula is provided by the decision of the New Zealand Court of Appeal in *New Zealand Dairy Board* v. *Okitu Co-operative Dairy Co., Ltd.*[3] In that case the court had to decide whether a body whose zoning order had given an ex-

---

[1] *Ibid.*, at p. 13.

[2] *Local Government Board* v. *Arlidge*, [1915] A.C. 120, at p. 132; *R.* v. *Local Government Board for Ireland*, [1902] 2 I.R. 349, at p. 373. See also the Privy Council cases mentioned below at p. 275, n. 2.

[3] [1953] N.Z.L.R. 366.

clusive trading right to the Kia Ora Company had failed, whilst hearing representations from a competitor company, to act judicially in a matter affecting the legal rights of subjects. The court divided on the question. Hutchison J., in a dissenting judgment, thought that a duty to act judicially could not be drawn out of the statute empowering the board to act. On the one hand, he said, it had been argued that the width of regulations conferring these powers indicated that the board was to use its own knowledge of the industry to reach its decisions, and on the other that the width of discretion to affect the position of subjects indicated a duty to act judicially. But the regulations which envisaged the undertaking of inquiries before a decision of the Board were colourless on the point. They contained nothing to indicate that, if undertaken, they were to be judicial and it was not the business of the court to *add to or take away from the rules laid down for the Board by Parliament*.[1] He obviously felt these rules to be clear.

A majority of the court, however, thought that the Legislature's intention to provide a judicial form of procedure could be inferred from the *nature of the issue to be decided*. Finlay J. observed that there was no doubt that the question was one affecting property and the liberty of a man to do what he chose with his own. The zoning order was a prohibition against everyone except the party in whose favour it was made, and any breach of it was subject to penalties. The conclusion was inescapable, therefore, that the *right*[2] of the ousted company to carry on its manufacturing undertaking was in question. Under the exercise of the Board's powers some party must gain and some must lose. It could not have escaped the authors of the empowering regulations that there would be resistance and therefore a contest between parties. In such circumstances involving conflicting interests and conflicting *rights* the intention must necessarily have been that the Board should obey the principles of natural justice.[3] Cooke J. agreed. Though he conceded that the empowering regulations should not be approached with any pre-

---

[1] *Ibid.*, at pp. 411–414.   [2] Italics added here and in following paragraphs.
[3] [1953] N.Z.L.R. 366, at pp. 401–405.

sumption one way or the other, he was equally prepared to find that the legislative intention could be discovered by examining the nature of the issue to be decided by the Board. In *Errington's*[1] case, he noted, reference was made to ministerial functions as being of a character to deprive the appellants of important *rights* which they held as citizens, namely the rights of owners to have their buildings left intact. There was no difference in principle between the curtailment of property rights and curtailment of the right to trade. There had been a current of authority in the Privy Council in which the duty to act judicially had been drawn out of the context and language of an Act of Parliament.[2] The decision in *Nakkuda Ali* v. *Jayaratne*[3] in which the withdrawal of a textile trading licence in Ceylon had been held to be an administrative action could be distinguished. In Ceylon there had been no unrestricted right to trade in textiles. The trade could be carried on only by those privileged to hold a licence, and the withdrawal of such a licence was an executive action to withdraw a privilege and not, as in the present case, action affecting a Common Law right or liberty of a company to trade with whomever it chose. In a number of cases it had been held on the particular provisions of statutes that no judicial duty existed,[4] but this was not incompatible with the view that such a duty might arise in widely different circumstances which it was impossible to define.[5]

'RIGHTS' AND 'PRIVILEGES'

In the *New Zealand Dairy Board* case, the issue as to the nature of the question decided by the administrative body was not complicated by the fairly explicit statutory provisions considered by

---

[1] *Errington* v. *Minister of Health*, [1935] 1 K.B. 249.

[2] *Smith* v. *The Queen* (1878), 3 App. Cas. 614; *De Verteuil* v. *Knaggs*, [1918] A.C. 557; *Wilson* v. *Esquimault and Nanaimo Railway Co.*, [1922] 1 A.C. 202. In each of these cases 'substantial justice' or 'the judicial nature of the inquiry' was distinguished from 'ordinary judicial procedure' and 'proceedings in a court of justice'.

[3] [1951] A.C. 66.

[4] Cooke J. here instanced *Robinson* v. *Minister of Town and Country Planning*, [1947] K.B. 702.

[5] The last sentence is a quotation from *R.* v. *Manchester Legal Aid Committee, ex parte Brand & Co.*, [1952] 2 Q.B. 413, in which it was held that there was a duty to act judicially though no *lis inter partes* existed.

the English courts in such cases as *Franklin* v. *Minister of Town and Country Planning*.[1] Nor did the court lean upon any general considerations about the responsibility of administrators to Parliament. Much clearly turned upon the distinction between questions affecting the rights of citizens, and questions concerning administrative regulation of privileges conceded by the state. Yet in one sense the distinction is empty. If a right of the citizen is an activity in which he is protected by the law, it will be impossible to decide the extent to which it *is* a right until it is clear in what way liberty to pursue the activity in question may be withdrawn and whether withdrawal must be made by a discretionary or by a judicial process. A right, on the other hand may also imply that which *ought* to be protected by law; but the right/privilege distinction can only be meaningful in this sense for a legislator and not for a judge; and only then if it is possible to give a clear answer to the question: what activities have hitherto been considered (apart from the procedure for their restriction under current consideration) as fields proper for free individual choice not subject to discretionary interference by administrative officials?

Both the classification of a decision as involving 'privileges' rather than rights, and the use of a term such as 'disciplinary decision', suffer from the defect that the force of these terms as describing the result of a decision-process is not logically incompatible with a classification such as 'judicial' based upon procedural characteristics. It is not contradictory to say that a decision which is judicial (as to its procedure) is disciplinary (as to its effect on persons); nor that privileges can be conferred on the basis of judicial procedure. Yet, in certain cases, characterization of decisions as involving 'privileges' in some not very specific sense has been allotted as a reason for refusing to regard the procedure in question as apt for the safeguards of a judicial process. For good reasons, critics have stigmatized some judicial reasoning in this sphere as 'conceptual'. Clearly, conceptual reasoning in the course of judicial interpretation is bad if (as in the right/privilege dichotomy) the classification itself has not

[1] [1948] A.C. 87.

been carried out on criteria independent of the very question arising for decision. It is bad, also, if (as in the case of 'licensing') the concept is uncertain in its extension, or if the criteria are disputed or unsettled. The judicial/administrative distinction suffers from the latter two, rather than the first of these difficulties. There are at least some other independent criteria, even if disputed ones, for deciding whether to call a procedure 'administrative' apart from its accessibility to review. It is not certain that the stricture 'conceptualist' is equally deserved by critics who have tried to supply general definitions of these terms. The inadequacy of certain concepts used in the judicial process is not a reason for a cessation of thinking in terms of concepts by critics and legislators, since there are no other terms to think in. It is perhaps doing less than justice to dub Laski and Holdsworth and their colleagues on the Donoughmore Committee arch-conceptualists for their efforts to guide legislative action. It is not necessary to draw from the well-known definitions of 'judicial', 'quasi-judicial' and 'administrative' functions in the Committee's Report the conclusion that concepts should be applied uncritically; or that there is a simple gulf fixed between the judicial and the non-judicial; or that these definitions could be mechanically applied in interpretation; or that judges exercise no creative rôle. Laski was surely far from thinking that at least.

To sum up: there are two interlocking questions involved in the notion of 'justiciability' when it functions as an appraising term: (1) How far is it possible to make the concept of 'judicial' methods precise? and (2) How far is it possible to specify situations or disputes which are inherently suitable to such methods?

To the first question one answer seems clear: namely that it is not possible to construct from judicial materials a single set of reasonably unambiguous criteria for calling a procedure 'judicial'. Moreover, many of the tests historically enunciated by the courts are now insufficiently precise to discriminate within a large *penumbra* of doubtful cases, and too great an element of chance enters into the question of classification where there is no specific guidance by the Legislature.

To the second question, there seems an equally plain answer. No dispute or issue is inherently justiciable or suited to judicial solution. The supposition that it might be involves the assumption that a dispute can be clearly contrasted with its methods of settlement and described independently. But once an issue or contest of interests is defined it is impossible to avoid mentioning or implying at least some indication of what constitutes winning or losing (*e.g.*, that the contest is not to the death or one for physical combat) and therefore indicating some limitations upon procedure. Yet once the description of the issue is filled out the contrast between the issue itself and its mode of settlement crumbles. These difficulties are crucial but they ought not perhaps to be allowed to suggest that there is nothing further to be said in reply to either question. As to judicial methods it is clear that certain (admittedly imprecise) characteristics—for example, objectivity of decision, independence of administrative or popular pressure, and finality of conclusions— have been regarded as necessary ingredients of judicial processes as distinct from discretionary or legislative ones; and there must have been some motives operating upon legislators who have provided for what they intended to be procedures of the first rather than of the second kind. Perhaps, then, the notions and occasions in question may best be made more precise by attempting to specify negatively, and in as neutral a way as possible, circumstances and motives which have led to the deliberate *avoidance* of non-discretionary procedures and to the description of procedures and issues as involving 'policy' rather than 'justice'.

POLICY ISSUES: IMPLICATIONS OF THE FRANKS COMMITTEE EVIDENCE

One reason for not permitting a decision to be made by administrative discretion has been that the sphere of activity involved is one in which official interest or interference is simply novel. Sense could be made on these lines of the insufficiently analysed distinction between 'rights' and 'privileges conceded by the state', if the discussion were openly carried out in terms of novelty (which may wear off). There are recent examples where the effect upon livelihood of penal provisions in a new field (for example state supervision of private school facilities) has accounted for the handing over to independently appointed tribunals of decisions, extremely factual in kind, which in other fields might be decided under the influence of administrative policy. If regulatory interference is long-standing, terms such as 'livelihood' and 'penalization' tend to lose their suggestive force. The regulation of land, public transport, and private education offer interesting possibilities of comparison here. The idea of 'penalization' of the property-owner played a considerable part in the decision in 1863 of *Cooper* v. *Wandsworth Board of Works*,[1] whilst the 'penalization' of unsuccessful applicants for *certiorari* in more recent times has evoked less sympathy. But a sudden change of legislative policy may well result in something which is thought of as a right rather than a privilege being subjected to a discretionary decision. Because of this, and because of the fact that discretionary decisions always apply *some* pre-existing rule to the facts of a situation, neither the Holmes definition nor the elaborations made of it are in themselves very satisfactory concepts for either courts or legislators to dwell on. Nor was Parliament in Britain urged much further along by the recommendation of the Committee on Ministers' Powers in 1932 that issues which ultimately turned upon administrative policy should be kept for ministers and not made subject to independent adjudication.[2] For anything can be made to turn upon administrative policy and the question for the legislator is precisely what shall be made to do so. The examples given by the Committee did, however, reflect a view about some types of issue then considered as suitable for discretionary decision and ministerial responsibility.

A contemporary view is provided by the official evidence given to the Franks Committee[3] on the nature of policy issues. Two rather different ideas lie behind the notion of 'policy'. In

---

[1] (1863), 14 C.B., N.S. 180.   [2] Cmnd. 4060, at p. 93.

[3] *Report of the Committee on Administrative Tribunals and Enquiries* (1957), Cmnd. 218.

the first place the word suggests generality of principle and is *opposed* to 'administration'. But, rather differently, it is used almost *synonymously* with 'administration' or 'discretion' to contrast with 'adjudication', as a method of decision. In the second sense there is no *a priori* reason why a 'policy' or 'discretionary' matter should be a matter of general principle. But the attraction of the first sense inclines many arguments towards the suggestion that it should. There is also the association of 'policy' with 'politics' and political responsibility, and with the further suggestion that matters for which there is political or parliamentary responsibility must be general in their nature. But this is precisely what needs to be discussed. There are senses in which things which are general may be non-political and things which are political may be non-general and detailed. The things ('detail', 'uninterestingness', 'individuality') with which 'generality' is contrasted are not, anyway, always clear.[1]

Much of the official evidence to the Franks Committee involved the witnesses in discussion of whether all issues decided by Departments could properly be called issues of policy. A possible criterion for 'policy' might be that questions for which ministers are answerable to the Legislature should be so described. But the category of things which are defended or defensible in Parliament at the present time is one which embraces everything for which an opportunity of discussion can be found under the rules of order. Even if the category be narrowed to those issues for which ministers currently accept responsibility at question time, the fact remains that many issues with which the Legislature might deal do not in fact receive its attention, and this fact may be relevant to the question whether a particular issue might be removed from the sphere of policy decision altogether. The Committee commented on the evidence of the Ministry of Education that it might be pushing the notion of

---

[1] *Cf.*, H.C. 92–1 (1959), *Report from the Select Committee on Procedure, Minutes of Evidence*, p. 67. The Committee discussed the distinction between 'a matter of detail' and a 'narrow but important point'. The Clerk to the House described debate on a bus strike as 'a comparatively *narrow* point, but . . . an issue of policy and not of detail'. (Italics added.)

policy too far to see it in matters with which Parliament does not deal (*i.e.*, could, may spasmodically, but mostly does not, deal). The question of the merits of a particular site for a school, or the virtues of alternative sites where land is compulsorily acquired were not, for example, matters of parliamentary consideration.[1] Official witnesses, on the other hand, were inclined to suggest a rather different test for policy issues, namely that their characteristic feature was the weighing of hardship to an individual against the public interest. All such issues are clearly not of legislative importance. The two tests for policy here do not give the same answer. In addition, administrators, whose individual decisions are involved with, and affect the activities of, other administrators may have more reason for wishing to extend the span of discretionary decision than those whose field of action is relatively self-contained. A ministry which, in settling particular questions affecting individuals, needs to seek or to be given the views of other departments may have an additional reluctance (now partly overcome)[2] to expose internal processes of this kind to public criticism or inspection. This particular motive for wishing to treat a question as one of policy is not necessarily proportionate to the magnitude or legislative interest of the question at issue. The same is true of the felt need for freedom to alter policy and to decide similar cases differently if external administrative or political pressures should indicate the wisdom of so doing.

Neither the 'public interest' test not the 'legislative responsibility' test then seems able unaided to provide a clear guide to the proper field for policy. The first suggests that only administrators are fit to weigh issues in which the public interest is involved; the second is too vague and is of no assistance in informing the Legislature whether the boundaries of parliamentary responsibility are drawn at the right point, or in other words whether some issues now decided by ministerial discretion should be decided by a procedure independent of de-

---

[1] *Report of the Committee on Administrative Tribunals and Enquiries* (1957), Cmnd. 218, *Minutes of Evidence*, Day 1, p. 18.

[2] *Ministry of Housing and Local Government Circular* 9/58, paras. 13–18.

partmental influence. The implicit or explicit view of most of the unofficial witnesses who appeared before the Franks Committee was, however, that as many issues as possible should be independently adjudicated and that wherever individual interests might be prejudiced by departmental action the policy of the department should be 'crystallized' or 'concretized' in a *corpus* of public statements or regulations which might in principle be applied in an objective way by some person or tribunal independent of the department.[1]

THE CRYSTALLIZATION OF POLICY

In itself, prior articulation of the rules to be applied is only a partial subversion of 'policy' in the sense used by official witnesses. Such publicized rules might still be applied and altered (though more formally and upon notice) by departments themselves. But concretization in the form of regulations plus independent application is a total subversion of 'policy'. Against it the administrators' contentions could be summarized as follows: 1. We do not know what our policy should be until presented with actual situations. 2. We may know our present policy but it is desirable that we should be able to change it. 3. We are responsible to Parliament for what is done in the Departmental field and, whilst the result of an individual independent adjudication might be indifferent to the Minister, a series of decisions taken independently without regard to overall policy may make that policy impossible of fulfilment. 4. Matters of governmental and parliamentary interest should not be decided by independent persons not responsible for the content of their decisions. 5. Policy often cannot be defined in detail in such a way as to be objectively applicable in a judicial manner.

In some part these administrative attitudes hang by their own bootstraps and invite the retorts that: 1. Policy is not known precisely because no effort has been made to formulate it. 2. Feelings about the Rule of Law require that individuals should be able to predict within a reasonable period what the

[1] See particularly *Minutes of Evidence*, Day 21, pp. 974–988, and Day 13, p. 512.

future impact of ministerial policy upon their interests will be. The formulation of general principles does not in any event prevent those principles from being altered upon due notice. There may admittedly be particular types of regulatory action in which administrators believe uncertainty to be of the essence.[1] But it does not follow from the fact that individual decisions must sometimes be unexpected and without notice that no attempts should be made to formulate a policy. 3. The frustration of a policy for which a minister is answerable can be deleterious to him only in the assumption that he is in fact answerable. This principle would necessarily be modified to the extent that decisions of a particular kind were hived off from the administrative and parliamentary sphere and parliamentary questioning correspondingly restricted. Objections 5 and 6 however are of a different kind. They cannot be made to dissolve in quite the same way. Whether some legislative policies can be set out in a sufficiently detailed objective way, whether some decisions are best controlled by elected persons, and whether some rights are best protected by a predominantly political process rather than a predominantly judicial one, are questions upon which strong views of opposite kinds are likely to be held. Many arguments on either side were put in the course of the Commons' debates on the Restrictive Trade Practices Act of 1956, setting up the Restrictive Trade Practices Court.[2] On the one hand the then President of the Board of Trade stated the Government's 'firm intention to remove these issues from the political to the judicial sphere'. The control of restrictive practices had, he argued, led to 'the interminable delays and endless debate which is inevitably associated with the administrative solution'. The Government's proposals were 'a new perhaps even an adventurous constitutional advance'. If they were not adopted the House of Commons would have to be prepared to discuss and determine not principles to be followed but the detailed merits and demerits of such issues as whether there should be a

---

[1] Anti-trust action in the United States provides an example. But administrative discretion has appeared in a different light to American industry.

[2] 549 H.C. Deb. 1927 (March 6, 1956).

percentage quantum scheme in the calico printing industry or whether there should be exclusive dealing between manufacturers and traders in dental goods. But having chosen between the two methods of control it would not, he added, henceforth be proper to make governmental decisions on matters which were now to be made justiciable.

Opposition speakers on the other hand argued that the Government were shuffling off their own responsibilities on to a tribunal. It was the judicial method which it was alleged would present 'an appalling vista of confusion and delay'. The balance of rights between public and private interest ought to come to the House for decision. The Bill was handing over governmental and parliamentary power. It would be possible for all the decisions in a series of cases to be in favour of the individual companies charged with restrictive practices, yet for the cumulative effect to be against the public interest. Each individual decision ought to be taken in the light of general knowledge affecting the whole of the economy. They were submitting 'essentially political matters to the decision of a court'.

In this case the crystallization of policy took the shape of principles admittedly wide in scope. But reasons for feeling that principles cannot be applied 'objectively' but only 'politically' may be maintained even in the face of apparently detailed codification of rules. Despite the objective-looking list of criteria in the 1956 Act, a balance of an inscrutable kind may have to be struck between such elements as persistent local unemployment and the potential public benefit of price reductions.[1] Again on a lesser scale the question of unfitness of property for habitation, though defined in certain statutes in relation to a number of apparently fairly detailed criteria, still may be argued by the administrator to involve policy. What to the judicial mind may seem 'a pure question of fact' entirely apt for a tribunal may present itself alternatively to him as a type of decision involving flexible standards.[2]

---

[1] *Cf., Re The Yarn Spinners' Agreement,* [1959] L.R. 1 R.P. 118.

[2] Compare the comments of Parker J. and the Treasury Solicitor (*Franks Committee, Minutes of Evidence,* Day 8, p. 258) on the 'objectivity of statutory criteria

Attempts at 'crystallization' of policy may sometimes be inappropriate and occasionally the use of a tribunal form of decision may signal deliberate departure from, rather than obedience to, principle. An administrative tribunal is in a position of unstable equilibrium between the judicial and political processes. It faces the potential criticism that if its decisions involve discretion of a policy kind its work might be more properly done by responsible administrators. On the other hand if its decisions are fairly narrowly defined matters, involving the interpretation of statutes and regulations, it may, be criticized as not being judicial enough. Not many out-and-out policy tribunals of the first kind exist in this country and it is arguable that none ought to exist. Elsewhere they have some-times been dubbed 'legislative tribunals', and may in some cases be adapted to serve particular political purposes in industrial fields. The casting of labour negotiations into the form of a tribunal decisions has been commended for example in New Zealand as placing a buffer between Government and interested pressure groups. The appeal against or non-acceptance of a tribunal decision may, it has been suggested, be represented as dishonourable in a way that appeal against departmental decision appears not to be and thus strengthen resistance to certain minority demands.[1] But once Government becomes prepared to modify or override decisions of this type—as it usually does—or to treat them as 'recommendations' rather than 'awards',[2] dishonour withers away. Outside the field of wage arbitration the nearest approach to the 'legislative' or policy tribunal in this country is perhaps to be found in transport matters. The rules applied in public service and goods

for the demolition of unfit houses'. *Q*. No doubt it is a question of policy whether the time has come for an attack to be made on the slums, but the question whether four, five, ten, or twenty houses are fit or unfit for habitation is a pure question of fact is it not? *A*. I would not have called it a very pure one. . . . It could be looked at as a question of opinion—what standard you have got.

[1] K. J. Scott, 12 *New Zealand Journal of Public Administration* (1949), pp. 17—18.

[2] The machinery for the arbitration of railway wages was said by the Minister of Labour in May, 1958, to result in something which was 'more than a recommendation but less than an award'. This provided a justification for ministerial intervention in a dispute.

licensing bear a closer relation to policy[1] and are more discretionary in nature than those applied by tribunals in, for
example, national insurance or industrial injury. It has historically been thought a virtue of administrative adjudication that
apart from its speed, cheapness and procedural informality it
might result in impartial decisions which were nevertheless
'infused with policy'. But this notion seems to have little to
commend it. It is not easy even to see what it means. It might
mean several things—that the same rules should, in comparison
with the ordinary courts be applied in a different spirit; or that
different and more flexible rules could be enjoined upon tribunals; or that tribunals might properly be subject to forms
of ministerial guidance and intervention as to the general lines
of decision or standards to be applied, though not subjected to
intervention on the merits of individual decisions.

But there is a conflict of purpose between policy influence in
the last sense and the notion of independent adjudication. If it
is thought necessary for undefined and flexible policy considerations to influence decisions then it could be argued that the
work ought to be done as part of the routine of a department
headed by a responsible minister and that if independent application of rules is desirable the only policy which ought to infuse
the process is that set out on the face of the statute or regulations which contain them. And what sort of infusion is this,
which is different from the relation between any general rule and
its correct application?

Twenty years ago argument about tribunals was provoked
mostly by the alleged deficiencies of the judicial process. Today
it turns rather upon the alleged deficiencies of the political
process. If it had not been for its restrictive terms of reference
the Franks Committee might itself have been able from the
evidence placed before it to construct some detailed proposals
about the type of issue which the Legislature might allow to be
subject to adjudication and final disposal subject to the rules

---

[1] Section 63 (1) of the Road Traffic Act, 1930, and section 57 of the Transport
Act, 1947, give the Minister of Transport power to issue general directions to road
licensing authorities. Conferences of tribunal chairmen are held at the Ministry to
discuss policy. (Cmnd. 218 (1957), *Minutes of Evidence*, Day 8, p. 229.)

of natural justice, and the type of issue to which policy or complete ministerial discretion is best applied. 'Crystallization' was in fact supported in the brief suggestion that where administration affects private interests preference should be given to a tribunal rather than to a Minister and that every effort should be made to express policy in the form of regulations. The recommendation was not backed by much argument in the Report, though it was debated with several witnesses during the taking of evidence. To follow this advice as a general policy is clearly to restrict the area of ministerial responsibility. To remove issues from this net is not merely to provide a particular method of decision but to confer a status upon persons. Whatever is hived off and stamped with the seal of non-political judgment is not something which is reversible with propriety on political grounds. Whatever goes amiss in reaching decisions in that field cannot easily and immediately be made the subject of political agitation and redress—a result apt to induce a degree of parliamentary nervousness. (Compare the ambivalence of legislative feeling about administrative decisions in nationalized industry and the quasi-political discretion exercised by the Law Officers of the Crown.)

Since the conclusions of the Committee on Ministers' Powers in 1932 have not been supplemented by further consideration or by any legislative codification in the administrative law field, obscurities in statutes about the use of discretion have been judicially resolved with the aid of concepts which could plausibly be attacked as arbitrary. Only Parliament can satisfactorily decide what is in issue, namely the relation to ministerial responsibility of planning a New Town, clearing a slum, routing a trunk road, approving a development plan, siting a school, giving or withholding a permission to carry on a trade or livelihood. The characterization of interests as 'rights' or 'privileges,' of decisions as 'licensing', 'disciplinary' or 'adjudicatory', and of issues as 'justiciable' or 'non-justiciable' is a legislative job.

Index of Names